VISITOR'S GUIL

World Trav‹

G000060353

About the Author:
Barbara Mandell spent several years in Africa, where she became an announcer/producer with the South African Broadcorporation. Back in England she worked for the BBC in both radio and television, mainly writing and voicing withe the 'TV Newsreel'. When Inependent Television News when on the air she became the first woman newscaster in Britain. She has travelled widely in Europe, Africa and America, and now combines this with travel writing.
Barbara Mandell has written several other MPC Visitor's Guides:
The Dordogne, Massif Central, Southern Spain & Costa del Sol, Costa Brava to Costa Blanca, Northern Spain, as well as contributing to MPC's *Off the Beaten Track: France and Off the Beaten Track: Spain.*

VISITOR'S GUIDE
PORTUGAL

Barbara Mandell

MPC
HUNTER
PUBLISHING INC

Published by:
Moorland Publishing Co Ltd,
Moor Farm Road West,
Ashbourne, Derbyshire
DE6 1HD
England

© Barbara Mandell 1991

All rights reserved. No part of this
publication may be reproduced,
stored in a retrieval system, or
transmitted in any form or by any
means, electronic, mechanical,
photocopying, recording or otherwise without the prior permission
of Moorland Publishing Co Ltd.

British Library Cataloguing in
Publication Data.
A catalogue record for this book is
available fromthe British Library.

ISBN 0 86190 461 3

Published in the USA by:
Hunter Publishing Inc,
300 Raritan Center Parkway,
CN 94, Edison, NJ 08818
ISBN 1-55650-496-9

Colour origination by:
P & W Graphics Pte Ltd, Singapore

Printed in the UK by:
Richard Clay Ltd, Bungay, Suffolk

Cover photograph: Rock formations
on the Algarve coast at Praia do Vau
(*International Photobank*)

Illustrations have been supplied as
follows:
Martin Gray: pages 10, 14, 31, 47
(lower), 63, 111 (lower), 115, 122,
134, 135 (top), 190 (top), 191 (top),
195 (top), 198 (lower), 202 (lower):
all the remainder have been supplied by the Portuguese
National Tourist Office, London to
whom the author and publisher
offer their grateful thanks.

MPC Production Team:
Editor and design: John Robey
Cartographer: Alastair Morrison

While every care has been taken to ensure that the information in this
book is as accurate as possible at the time of publication, the publisher
and author accept no responsibility for any loss, injury or inconven-
ience sustained by anyone using this book.

CONTENTS

Key to Symbols Used in Text Margin and on Maps

♠	Church/Ecclesiastical site	大	Recommended walk
♜	Castle/Fortification	⊞	Building of interest
⊼	Archaeological site	♜	Castle/Fortification
♨	Beautiful view/Scenery, Natural phenomenon	🦌	Nature reserve/Animal interest
⌂	Museum/Art gallery	♣	Parkland
✳	Other place of interest	⏀	Birdlife
✻	Garden	⛵	Sailing
		⛁	Cave

Key to Maps

●◢	Town/City	—·—·	National boundary
═══	Motorway	─ ─ ─	Regional boundary
━━	Road	∿	Rivers
▭▭▭	Railway	◠	Lakes

How To Use This Guide

This MPC Visitor's Guide has been designed to be as easy to use as possible. Each chapter covers a region or itinerary in a natural progression which gives all the background information to help you enjoy your visit. MPC's distinctive margin symbols, the important places printed in bold, and a comprehensive index enable the reader to find the most interesting places to visit with ease.

At the end of each chapter an Additional Information section gives specific details such as addresses and opening times, making this guide a complete sightseeing companion.

At the back of the guide the Fact File, arranged in alphabetical order, gives practical information and useful tips to help you plan your holiday — before you go and while you are there.

The maps of each region show the main towns, villages, roads and places of interest, but are not designed as route maps and motorists should always use a good recommended road atlas.

1

INTRODUCTION

Portugal is a small but extremely interesting country, being one of the oldest nations in Europe, having been welded into a kingdom in the early twelfth century when most of the other countries on the Continent were fragmented and fighting to establish a permanent identity. It soon becomes apparent that the Portuguese tolerate the Spanish, but have a soft spot for the British, based to a certain extent on an efficient treaty of alliance which has been in existence for more than six hundred years. Like Britain, Portugal once ruled a vast empire, the result of voyages of exploration by men of the calibre of Bartolomeu Dias who rounded the Cape of Good Hope before Columbus set out across the Atlantic in search of a sea route to India. However, this was gradually eroded by time and circumstances until today the country has reverted to more or less its original dimensions.

Although Portugal only covers about one sixth of the Iberian peninsula it offers as much variety as any other region of comparable size. This long, fairly narrow strip of territory separates most of Spain from the Atlantic seaboard with the Spanish province of Galicia taking care of its northern frontier and the ocean turning sharply round Cape St Vincent and following the coast of the Algarve eastwards, past Spain's Costa de la Luz to meet the Mediterranean at the Straits of Gibraltar.

The country itself is mountainous, especially in the north and east, although its highest range, the Serra da Estrela, inland from Coimbra, runs briefly northeast to southwest, petering out a mere 100km (60 miles) from the ocean with its loftiest peak just failing to reach 2,000m (6,506ft). The high plateaux of the Trás-os-Montes — the province 'beyond the mountains' — with its bare summits and arid scrubland, are separated by narrow valleys, deeply etched over many centuries by tributaries of the River Douro. Flocks of sheep and goats graze rather dolefully on the deserted uplands, but where the ground becomes more fertile there are woods full of oaks and chestnuts which give way in turn to terraces planted with olives, fruit trees and quite extensive vineyards.

The provinces of Minho and Douro, bridging the gap between Trás-os-Montes and the sea, are splendidly wooded with only an occasional rocky peak rising above a luscious blanket of oak trees and sweet chestnuts. These are augmented in places by the dark green of eucalyptus and small groups of pine trees planted like regiments on a barrack square, to provide their owners with an additional source of income when times are hard. It is an area of smallholdings whose patchwork of tiny fields, hardly bigger than pocket handkerchiefs and surrounded by solid dry-stone walls, produce good crops of maize and other animal fodder, thereby cutting down the need for larger meadows and pastures. Where hedges are used in place of stone walls vines are encouraged to clamber up the tree trunks and make use of any other support they can find. This leaves the ground underneath free for vegetables and in the late autumn turns the roadsides into a tapestry of greens and yellows, copper, bronze, crimson, deep red and every shade of brown.

Below the Rio Douro the low-lying coastal region of Beira Litoral is well-watered and ideal for growing rice, particularly in the vicinity of Aveiro with its sizeable lagoon, salt marshes, extensive beaches and low sand dunes securely anchored in place with pines. Further inland there are fields of wheat and maize as well as orchards, olive groves and the inevitable vines. Fishing is a way of life all along the coast whereas the companion provinces of Beira Alta and Beira Baixa become progressively mountainous towards the Spanish border, specialising in raising live-stock, producing a variety of crops and mining on a fairly modest scale. The local rivers have been harnessed to form part of an ambitious hydro-electric scheme to off-set the country's limited supplies of coal.

Alternating cliffs and sandy beaches are a feature of the Estremadura coast, many of whose picturesque little fishing villages are making deter-mined efforts to rebuilt themselves into modern holiday resorts. At the southern tip it winds itself round the mouth of the Tagus which widens out into the so-called Sea of Straw where Lisbon — Lisboa to the Portu-guese — spreads itself over seven hills in the manner of ancient Rome, and is still expanding. The countryside is undulating and largely agricultural, supplying the capital with produce from its thriving market gardens. There is some attractive hilly terrain on either side of the estuary — the tree-covered Serra de Sintra to the north and the somewhat lumpy, flower-encrusted Serra da Arrábida prodding the Atlantic with limestone fingers round Cabo Espichel further south. This lonely, weatherbeaten promontory is a place of pilgrimage, marked by a lighthouse, the Sanctu-ary of Nossa Senhora do Cabo and some derelict outbuildings, but other-wise it is almost unchanged since the days when a passing dinosaur left its footprints to be fossilized in the sand.

The Tagus, following a southwesterly course from the Spanish border down to its straw-coloured Mar de Palha, cuts the province of Ribatejo neatly in half and at the same time subtly changes the character of Portugal itself. On one side the hill farmers concentrate mainly on vines and vegetables while on the other they go in more for wheat and olive groves. The plain between them consists largely of rice paddies and extensive meadows which provide grazing for horses and herds of black fighting bulls. However it is in Alentejo, by far the largest province of all, that wheat really comes into its own. The region is a sprawling expanse of rolling, open country covering something like one third of Portugal from the Tagus to the line of hills dividing it from the Algarve and from the Atlantic eastwards to the Spanish frontier. Much of it is carpeted with fields of grain, contrasting sharply with the seemingly endless vistas of cork oaks whose gnarled trunks and contorted lower branches account for at least half the world's supply of cork. Once every decade or so, when the rough bark reaches the correct density, it is peeled away leaving the trees looking strangely pink and nude until they turn black and start the process all over again. The Alentejo coast has escaped the attention of all but the most solitary-minded holidaymakers, with the result that there are comparatively few small villages tucked away in the bays and inlets between the stern grey cliffs.

Finally there is the Algarve, essentially tourist conscious and blissfully aware of all the attractions it has to offer. These range from the delightfully wooded slopes of the Serra de Monchique to the barren headland of Cape St Vincent, the most southwesterly point in Europe, where savage winds lacerate the tufts of herbs and scrub covering the rock-strewn plateau high above the cliffs. Further east the coast becomes more colourful and kindly. Small white fishing villages appear beside the sandy fringes of the bays before modern developments take over in a welter of highrise blocks and holiday villas drenched in hibiscus, bougainvillaea, roses and geraniums. Flowers, fruit and vegetables grow in profusion throughout the area — everything from avocado pears, figs and oranges to sugar cane, cotton, rice and almonds. There is a legend connected with the thousands of almond trees that has become something of a cliché. It appears that the Scandinavian bride of an ancient Moorish king was so homesick in the palace at Silves that she was in danger of dying from a broken heart. Unable to do anything about the lack of snow he decided to plant forests of almonds instead and the sea of pinky-white blossom every January and February was so enchanting that she made a miraculous recovery. A little far-fetched perhaps, but this so-called 'winter snow' is still one of the most beautiful sights in the Algarve.

Although the Moors occupied much of southern Portugal for the best part of five hundred years they were by no means the first foreigners to invade the country and decide to settle there. The earliest inhabitants were the Iberians who had established residence in about 8,000 BC. They built the occasional dolmen here and there, created several characteristic settlements and left a lot of their personal possessions lying around, to be excavated centuries later and put on display in an assortment of archaeological museums.

Their first major problem seems to have been the arrival of the Celts in 1,000BC or thereabouts. These northern tribes found their way across the Pyrénées, mingled with the locals and generally made themselves very much at home. At more or less the same time the Greeks and the Phoenicians established trading posts at various places along the coast but they do not seem to have made any serious territorial claims nor objected too vehemently when the Carthaginians decided to poach on their preserves.

The situation was quite different when the Romans marched in, determined to acquire the whole Iberian peninsula, by force if necessary. The Lusitanian chieftain, Viriatus, resisted furiously and to good effect before he was assassinated in 139BC, leaving the way clear for the Romans to consolidate their gains. This they did by developing existing towns and cities, building aqueducts and creating a network of roads and bridges, some of which are still in use today. A series of milestones in the Peneda-Gerês National Park near the frontier indicate the line of a major highway that once linked Rome with *Bracara Augusta*, now known simply as Braga. When the Roman empire began to crumble its place was taken by the Visigoths, ousted in their turn by the Moors who crossed over from North Africa in 711AD.

Even in Roman times the Rio Douro had made communications be-

Flocks of sheep along the roadsides are a familiar sight in the hills between the Algarve and Planicies

tween northern and southern Lusitania extremely tedious, so much so that two independent towns grew up facing each other across the estuary. *Portus*, which included the harbour, was on the right bank and *Cale* on the left. In the face of a constant Muslim threat from the rest of the country the Christians took up their positions behind this natural barrier, venturing out now and again to recover a slither of territory which was added to the region they called *Portucale*. Eventually the Spanish king of Castile y Léon launched a determined campaign against the Moors with the help of several French knights, including Henri and Raymond of Burgundy. When the fighting was over they married two of the Spanish princesses, one of whom, Teresa, presented her husband with the county of

Portugal has a long tradition as a sea-faring nation

Portucalense as part of her dowry. Following his death Teresa acted as regent for their son Afonso Henriques but when the king of Galicia invaded their territory the young prince took up arms against his mother and her Spanish relations. He defeated them at the battle of São Mamede in 1128 and eleven years later proclaimed himself King of Portugal.

It was forty years before the newly-independent kingdom of Portugal was recognised by the Vatican, during which time Afonso I had driven the Arabs out of large tracts of his country, recapturing Lisbon in 1147. However it was 1249 before Afonso III recovered Faro and shook the Algarve free from Moorish domination. Afonso was also particularly fortunate in his son Dinis who succeeded him thirty years later. Regarded as one of the greatest Burgundian monarchs he founded universities, strengthened the nation's defences, created at least one religious order, encouraged new methods of agriculture and forestry and decreed that the dialect of the northern region should be the official language of the country. His successors proved to be less farsighted. They became increasingly involved with their Spanish neighbours until eventually, when Beatriz, the heir to the throne, married Juan of Castile it was agreed that if they had no children Juan would become king of Portugal. Although the nobility were quite satisfied with this arrangement the people decided otherwise. On the death of her father Fernando they refused to accept Beatriz as queen, preferring her illegitimate uncle, João of Avis. He was declared king in 1385 and soon afterwards defeated Juan at the battle of Aljubarrota, thereby ensuring the independence of Portugal for nearly two hundred years.

The first treaty of alliance between England and Portugal was signed in London on 16 June 1373. It was ratified by the Treaty of Windsor thirteen years later and given an added dimension when Philippa of Lancaster, the sister of Henry IV, married João shortly afterwards. Their reign marked the beginning of Portugal's transformation from a modest European kingdom into an important seafaring nation whose overseas empire grew by leaps and bounds. It started modestly enough with the capture of Ceuta, on the Moroccan coast, in 1415. This gave Portugal a measure of control over the Straits of Gibraltar and helped to discourage the raids by Barbary pirates on Spanish ports along the Mediterranean.

However, one of the royal princes, Henry the Navigator, was fired with the idea of finding a sea route to India round the southern tip of Africa. He established a nautical school at Sagres, near Cape St Vincent, to improve instruments and existing methods of navigation, as well as the ships themselves, and at the same time developed his ideas for setting up trading posts and colonising newly-discovered territories. His experienced crews claimed Madeira and the Azores and ventured beyond Cape Bojador, but it was only after his death that Diogo Cão reached the mouth of the Congo River and Bartolomeu Dias sailed round the Cape of Good Hope.

Once Columbus had discovered the New World for Spain, the Portuguese having refused to finance his expedition, the two countries agreed to divide whatever lands existed beyond San Salvador. Under the Treaty of Tordesillas Castile was to have everything to the west of a meridian 370 sea leagues beyond the Cape Verde Islands, leaving Portugal with all the rest. The fact that this included Brazil has led some historians to suspect that the Portuguese already knew it was there, but only admitted to finding it the following year. By that time Vasco de Gama had arrived in India via East Africa and the stage was set for commercial agreements to be drawn up with China, Siam and the East Indies.

Vast riches flowed into the coffers of Manuel I. Lisbon was flooded with gold and precious stones, as well as ivory, spices, silks and carpets, but within less than a century they were nothing more than a vivid memory. A lack of expert advisers, the temptation to spend and keep on spending, a slump in the spice market and an apparent aversion to hard work all took their toll. Finally, when the young King Sebastião led an ill-conceived and ill-equipped expedition to Morocco in 1578, and was killed at the battle of Alcácer-Quivir, there was barely enough left in the national coffers to ransom those of his troops who had been taken prisoner. The situation went from bad to worse until Philip II of Spain seized his opportunity and proclaimed himself Filipe I of Portugal.

The first sign of a reprieve came about sixty years later whenPhilip IV was occupied with a revolt in Catalunya. The Duke of Bragança, who had the necessary royal connections, was crowned King João IV and at once set about signing new treaties with England and Holland. In 1662 Catherine of Bragança married Charles II, an arrangement that gave the English a considerable sum of money, Tangier and trading rights with Portugal's overseas possessions in return for a promise to defend all Portuguese territory in the event of an attack.

The eighteenth century got off to a good start with the signing of the Methuen Treaty and a subsequent trade agreement. Even an attempted invasion by Spain with the help of French troops ended in failure. The discovery of diamonds in Brazil briefly restored the fortunes of the monarchy but once again this was frittered away leaving the country almost bankrupt. Then in 1755 a massive earthquake destroyed most of Lisbon and reduced Faro to rubble for the second time in only thirty years. At this stage the power behind the throne was Sebastião de Carvalho e Melo, a minister who had been given the job of pulling the country together, and he immediately assumed responsibility for rebuilding the capital. As a reward for his many and varied successes Carvalho was given the title of Marqês de Pombal but he was also cruel and autocratic, traits which led to his downfall during the reign of Dona Maria I.

In 1807, when Portugal refused to assist Napoleon in his attempts to blockade Britain, a section of the French army under Junot marched on Lisbon. The royal family took refuge in Brazil, Wellington landed and engaged the enemy near Óbidos, winning his first victory of the Peninsular campaign, but the country suffered so badly that it was soon plunged into civil war. After that had been settled a succession of kings and queens followed each other in fairly rapid succession until Carlos I and his son Luís Filipe were assassinated in Lisbon, the younger Manuel II fled to Britain and Portugal became a republic on 5 October 1910.

Deprived of Brazil, which gained its independence in 1822, and restricted in its control over Angola and Mozambique, the new administration found it virtually impossible to restore order at home or rebuild the country's economy. Nor did it help when Portugal sided with the Allies and sent its troops to fight in France during World War I. By 1928 the situation had become critical. As a result Dr Antonio de Oliveira Salazar was persuaded to leave his post as a professor of economics at Coimbra University and become the new Minister of Finance. There could hardly have been a better choice. Within a year he turned an enormous deficit into a surplus and continued to ensure that the budget balanced throughout his time in office. Ostensibly he served as Prime Minister from 1932 until 1968 although to all intents and purposes he ruled as a dictator complete with press censorship, the abolition of political parties and the introduction of secret police.

Portuguese souvenirs, including the well-known cock and typical windmills of the Costa de Prata

Officially Portugal adopted a policy of neutrality during World War II but nevertheless maintained close links with Britain, even going so far as to allow her ships to use the Azores during the Battle of the Atlantic. More recently similar facilities were made available during the Falklands War. In the years between the Portuguese had combat problems of their own. Trouble broke out in Angola in 1961, at the same time as India annexed Goa, and this was followed by uprisings in Mozambique, so that by the time Salazar died in 1970 the army was involved in expensive and highly unpopular anti-guerilla wars in Africa. Eventually an armed forces movement seized power, the former territories were given their independence and nearly a million refugees returned to their homeland. At last, in 1986 Mário Soares was elected President and settled into his icing-sugar pink and white residence in the Belém area of Lisbon, presiding over the Assembly of the Republic which is voted in on a system of proportional representation.

Due in no small measure to the earthquake of 1755 Lisbon is sadly lacking in ancient monuments and those that do exist had to be largely reconstructed afterwards. However, for visitors in search of historic fortresses, splendid castles and ancient churches there are any number to be found throughout the country. Close at hand are the magnificently ornate summer palaces at Sintra, augmented by the remains of a Moorish *alcázar*, a clutch of little medieval chapels and the sparse remnants of a Roman villa.

Further afield there are the ruins of *Citânia de Briteiros*, a partially restored settlement dating back to the Iron Age, and a wild boar carved out of granite below the pillory in Bragança which is thought to be just as old. The Romans are also quite well represented, especially at *Conimbriga* on the original highway from Lisbon to Braga. Here excavations have uncovered the centre of the town with its ruined forum, a hostelry and public baths, a number of villas whose floors are covered with remarkably fine mosaics, along with vestiges of the ramparts and parts of an extensive aqueduct. The Roman remains at Milréu, in the Algarve, are much smaller and less impressive, consisting mainly of foundations interspersed with pools, an occasional motif and fragments of the marble columns that were once part of a temple. The Visigoths left little of interest behind them except for a few small, understated churches, whereas the Moors lost no time in building castles and fortifications to protect their new Iberian empire. These include the red limestone *alcazaba* at Silves, ramparts at Óbidos and elsewhere, hilltop fortresses in Lisbon, Sintra and Sesimbra and a converted mosque in Mértola on the banks of the Guadiana.

With the emergence of Portugal as a nation churches and castles started to appear all over the region. Existing forts were restored or altered whenever necessary and cathedrals were designed to the glory of God but were frequently reinforced with functional towers and battlements to act as strongholds during an emergency. It was not until later that the more extravagant forms of Gothic architecture made an appearance, the most superb example being the fairytale monastery of Batalha.

During the reign of Manuel I a large percentage of the country's new-found wealth was used to finance ambitious building programmes such as the magnificent Jerónimos Monastery in Lisbon, which somehow managed to survive the earthquake. At the same time the interiors became much more decorative with spiral pillars, sculptured tombs and wooden ceilings that were intricately carved and painted. Windows, doorways and balustrades broke out in a rash of oak and laurel leaves, roses, acorns and even artichokes as well as ropes, anchors and other nautical impedimenta inspired by the current voyages of discovery. Among many outstanding examples of these new trends are the Church of Jesus in Setúbal, the Convent of Christ at Tomar and the Monastery of the Holy Cross in Coimbra. Castles also came in for their full share of lavish decorations, memorable among them being the National Palace of Sintra.

Meanwhile other castles were being built for strictly practical reasons — to augment the various strongholds and fortified villages already standing guard along the Spanish frontier. It is almost impossible to drive any distance from Guarda without coming within range of an ancient tower complete with ramparts poised precariously on a rocky peak, or even a modest hillock, surrounded by small granite houses and perhaps an occasional mansion.

The baroque style barely had time to establish a toehold in Portugal when the Lisbon earthquake forced the authorities to embark on a massive programme of reconstruction. There was no time or money for elaborate façades or eccentric innovations, although some attractive gilt carvings did make an appearance in the northern part of the country. The capital itself adopted what has become known as the Pombaline style, after the Marquês de Pombal, who insisted on wide avenues lined with buildings that had to be as functional and down-to-earth as possible. However this did give a fresh impetus to the ceramics industry and soon it became fashionable to decorate everything in sight with coloured tiles. Houses and fountains, patios and park benches all came in for the same treatment which proved so effective that it is still very much in vogue today.

The domestic architecture of Portugal is less flamboyant but no less distinctive. In the north the houses tend to be built of granite with tiled roofs and external staircases leading up to a wide veranda, leaving the ground floor space available for storerooms and sometimes even animals. However the owners of extensive vineyards were more likely to favour whitewashed manors set slightly apart from their outbuildings. In coastal areas, especially round Aviero, the homes of local fishermen were often built of wood and perched up on stilts that raised them above the level of the drifting sand. On the other hand, people living in the Alentejo region, who have to cope with extremes of temperature, usually preferred low, boxlike structures made from clay or mud mixed with straw and left in the sun to harden, a technique they learned from the Moors several hundred years ago. The small doors and windows minimise the heat of summer while large chimneys take care of the smoke and fumes from all the fires in winter. There are no such problems in the Algarve where the buildings range from traditional designs to modern villas, all painted white, and often with the addition of slender, graceful chimneys with little perforated hats, for all the world like tiny, would-be minarets. A reasonable number of up-and-coming holiday resorts have resisted the temptation to festoon their seafronts with highrise tourist warrens made from steel, glass and concrete, but where they do exist the effect is just as bland and devoid of character as similar developments anywhere else.

Regardless of the fact that Portugal has much to offer in the way of historic sites, interesting museums, wild life reserves and splendid golden beaches, many people feel that the country's greatest asset is the Portuguese themselves. They are warm and friendly, proud without being arrogant, courteous, somewhat casual and intensely fatalistic. They are also very ready to help anyone in trouble. A tourist who parks on the side of a country lane to admire the view or take a photograph may well receive offers of assistance from a passing van or a farmer working in his fields. In towns and villages passers-by will go out of their way to direct anyone who seems to have lost their bearings, often accompanying a bewildered stranger to make sure that he or she finds a bank, a post office, a special shop or a particular hotel without wasting any further time searching for it. During a torrential downpour anyone who takes cover near a lonely farmhouse may be invited inside and given something to eat and drink until the worst is over. Nor is language a serious problem. A surprisingly large number of people, especially the younger ones, speak a modicum of French or English but are delighted if the visitor attempts a few words in Portuguese, with or without the help of a dictionary or a book of useful phrases. It is not an easy language to master and, contrary to popular belief, bears very little relation to Spanish apart from the Galician dialect, which also has Celtic undertones.

The population of Portugal is very unevenly distributed across the country with slightly more than one third of the total concentrated in Lisbon and Oporto. Most other towns of any size are situated to the north of the Tagus — or Tejo — with some noteworthy exceptions such as Setúbal, Évora, Beja, Portalegre, Estremoz and Faro. However, quite a few villages are larger than one would expect and even in the sparsely populated Alentejo region there are usually some distant signs of human habitation.

Naturally, most of the farming communities have grown up along the river courses. The most important of these waterways are the Tagus, the Douro and the Guadiana, all of which rise in Spain and find their way to the Atlantic by devious routes. The Tagus makes for Lisbon, while the Douro heads for Oporto and the Guadiana turns due south near Elvas, following the frontier for much of the way down to Vila Real de Santo António, the most easterly town in the Algarve. A good many smaller rivers meander across the countryside. The Mondego and the Zêzere have created wide valleys for themselves on either side of the Serra de Estrela while the Minho separates the Costa Verde from Galicia, the Cávado bypasses Braga on its way to the coast and the Tamega, the Tua and the Sabor are all tributaries of the Rio Douro.

Portugal has always been a nation of seafarers and the fishing fleets still provide a large percentage of the country's food supplies, with a healthy surplus going into the various canning factories along the coast. The catch includes everything from cod to tunny and sardines, augmented by shellfish, octopus, mackerel, red mullet and many more besides. The rivers add their quota of trout and salmon, leaving Setúbal to concentrate on oysters and the Algarve to offer sand eels and cuttlefish.

Fish and seafood generally could almost be described as the staple diet of the country with pork and sausages in second place. Nevertheless each region has its own specialities. Things to try in the north are a vegetable soup called *caldo-verde*, sometimes accompanied by a maize bread referred to as *broas*. Roast kid and tripe also appear on the menu, followed by a sponge cake in port wine known as *pão-de-ló*. Slightly to the south, Peniche is famous for its lobsters, while the Bairrada district makes a feature of suckling pig. Further inland the traditional dishes include partridge and other types of game, as well as chestnuts, which are used in the Beiras to thicken a broth made from tripe. Two unusual blendings are trout and eel served with smoked ham, and roast ham with olives. The Serra de Estrela produces some delicious cream cheese while the surrounding area specialises in a firmer, stronger cheese made from goat's milk.

Lisbon, as befits a sophisticated capital city, offers the full range of international cuisine but it is also possible to find a fairly comprehensive selection of time-honoured recipes in the little family restaurants tucked away in the Bairro Alto district not far from the São Pedro de Alcântara Belvedere and the Igreja São Roque (Church of the Rock). The surrounding Costa de Lisboa produces an even greater variety such as bass, barnacles and mussels at Cascais or Cabo da Roca and scabbard fish in Sesimbra, with tart, cheese and fresh fruit or nuts to follow. Hake's head or *cozido à Portuguesa*, sounds much more daunting than it is and the same applies to dried cod which appears in a dozen different disguises.

Alentejo is the place for stews, made with kid or mutton, as well as smoked sausages, a sweet concocted from eggs and almonds called *pão de rala* and crystallized plums from Elvas. Meanwhile the Algarve runs the gamut from snails, clams and tunny steaks, dried octopus grilled over charcoal and roast sirloin to sweets consisting of almonds and figs, caramels from Tavira and quantities of fresh fruit according to the season.

With so many vines about it is hardly surprising that each area produces its own particular brands of wine. Port needs no introduction but the white *vinho verde* and the Dão reds should definitely not be missed, especially as they are both relatively inexpensive. However the *vinho da*

Markets provide a wide range of food, including loaves of bread . . .

. . . baked in a traditional oven

casa, or house wine, is often quite acceptable and blends well with the traditional dishes of the area concerned. There are some local brandies and liqueurs that are quite palatable, but the clear *bagaceira* has all the properties of firewater and should be treated accordingly. Several of the Portuguese spas not only treat anything from rheumatism to skin complaints and allergies but also bottle vast quantities of water which can be ordered with or without gas. Some of the best comes from Monchique, in the Algarve, where the tap water may be slightly suspect at the height of the season so, if in doubt, it is as well to err on the safe side.

Very few people can resist the temptation to buy souvenirs and although there are any number of the usual run-of-the-mill variety it is possible to find just as many delightful examples of local arts and crafts. Pottery, especially the black variety from Bisalhães, is an obvious choice, along with glazed earthenware that may be functional or simply decorative. Basketwork is just as easy to come by, everything from mats to hats and handbags fashioned from palm in Estômbar. Brass and copper articles are on sale nearly everywhere, the choice ranging from trays, pitchers, bowls and kettles to lamps, coffee pots and candlesticks. Wrought iron is used for shovels and fire tongs while anyone who is looking for a spiked dog collar can settle for one of the type worn by sheepdogs on the Serra da Estrela.

Lace from Vila do Conde or Peniche, hand embroidered articles and heavy fishermen's jerseys are all worth considering and so is the gold filigree work from Gondomar. This is a good deal less weighty than the typical gold jewellery that the women of Viana do Castelo deck themselves out in for special feast days and important religious celebrations. Then there are carpets from Beiriz, bed covers, carved wood, leather, sheep-skin and cork, the last of which is used for containers to keep food either hot or cold. Of less practical use are carved powder horns and cow bells but at least they are easier to transport than the carved and painted yokes worn by oxen that would make quite a talking point if, as suggested, they are utilised as bedheads back at home.

Unlike traditional arts and crafts, very few national costumes are to be seen these days. Women of uncertain age do still appear occasionally in the voluminous pleated skirts and woollen shawls that were once normal everyday wear in Nazaré, but anyone who ties down a small straw hat with a light scarf is usually less concerned with the sartorial effect than preventing it being blown away. It is really only at fairs and festivals that the younger generation prise themselves out of their ubiquitous jeans and shapeless blouses in favour of rainbow-coloured regional outfits that are eyecatching but far less practical.

As in other predominantly Catholic countries many of the more important national festivals are essentially religious celebrations or annual pilgrimages. Holy Week, the Crosses of May, Corpus Christi, the Feast of the Assumption and All Saints Day are among those observed with due pomp and ceremony, as are the two great annual pilgrimages to the shrine of Our Lady of Fátima. In addition nearly every local saint has a special day which may be short and simple, involving little more than a procession to an isolated shrine, or extended to include feasts and folk dancing, fireworks and bullfights. As no bulls have been killed in the ring for well over one hundred years, and the spectacle is presented with all the trappings of the seventeenth century, most visitors prefer the Portuguese *tourada* to the more emotive *corridas* of Spain.

On a somewhat lighter note there is an Almond Gatherers Fair at Loulé, a Lacemakers Procession in Vila do Conde, bullrunning through the streets of Vila Franca de Xira during the Red Waistcoat Festival, and also at Alcochete when the saltworks are blessed as part of the Fiesta of the Green Hat. The grape harvest is another occasion for general rejoicing and so is the St Martin's Day Regional Fair at Golegã when horses receive a special blessing in a ceremony that dates back to the seventeenth century.

The music and dancing that accompanies a large percentage of these events varies from one area to another. The strong rhythms that characterise the celebrations of the northern districts and the coastal areas of Beira Litoral become more muted in Alentejo where the local folk songs tend to be slow and rather mournful, but pick up again in the Algarve to suit the essentially lively attitude of the people. However, the built-in fatalistic streak, common to so many Portuguese, is best expressed by the *fado*, thought by some experts to have evolved from the medieval songs of the troubadours. At all events the *fado* caught on in Lisbon about one hundred and fifty years ago, growing increasingly melancholy and re-signed, with improvised words matched to the strains of a guitar. It was banned for a while on local radio because of its effect on some listeners but was, and still is, especially popular in the old quarters of the city. The melodies were taken up by students in Coimbra where the themes expressed were refined and given greater intellectual and romantic qualities. This appeals to younger listeners but the purists have no time for such lyrics, infinitely preferring unrelieved sadness to sentimentality.

Traditionally Portugal is divided up into nearly a dozen different provinces, dictated to a certain extent by their natural characteristics. However, from the tourist point of view it has proved more satisfactory to reduce these to six distinct regions. They are the Costa Verde in the northwest, the Costa de Prata which runs down the coast to the Costa de Lisboa surrounding the capital, Montanhas and Planicies with only a few of the most obvious holiday attractions but plenty to offer the discerning traveller, and the Algarve which, for the moment at least, is more tourist orientated than any other part of the country.

Itineraries and Excursions

Portugal, like a fine wine, a good book or a piece of classical music, should be savoured in order to appreciate it fully. However not everyone has the time, or even the inclination, to delve very far below the surface. Some holidaymakers are perfectly happy to confine themselves to a sandy beach, a few local attractions or a well-maintained golf course. On the other hand, dedicated travellers tend to explore every nook and cranny in a specially selected area. Somewhere between the two are those sightseers who like to see as much of the country and its main attractions as possible without going into every detail. This can be done quite adequately by joining one of the many organised coach tours, or by working out your own itinerary.

Trains are a good way of getting from one main centre to another, and so are the express coaches, but extensive tours using ordinary public transport can be somewhat time consuming. Visitors with a car and plenty of stamina might just manage to race round Portugal in a fortnight, missing a great deal on the way, but nevertheless getting a general impression of the varied countryside, some of the most outstanding buildings and the contents of a few museums.

The advantage of starting off with the idea of a grand circular tour is that it can be joined quite conveniently by motorists arriving at any of the various frontier posts, and then adapted to requirements, as well as by anyone arriving in Lisbon, Oporto or Faro on a fly-drive holiday.

Lisbon, as the nation's capital, is the most obvious place to start, especially as it is also the centre of the country's communications network. Trains radiate outwards from its three main stations, coaches heading north leave from the terminus in the Avenida Casal Ribeiro, while those covering the south operate from their own centre on the Praça de Espanha. Motorists have several different options, most of which are well signposted.

The majority of visitors need at least two days to find their way round **Lisbon** but it takes much longer to get to know the city. However, if time is short, the best method is to divide it into sections, beginning with the central area round the Avenida da Liberdade. The main things to locate here are the Praça Marquês de Pombal, the Rossio and the Terreiro do Paço, the Parque Eduardo VII with its greenhouses and the Santa Justa Elevador, incorrectly attributed to Gustave Eiffel. The Igreja São Roque is outstanding and has its own sacred art museum. Allow a full morning or afternoon to explore these and other attractions in the area.

It will take roughly the same amount of time to visit the old part of Lisbon to the east of the Terreiro do Paço. The easiest way is to go by taxi or a 37 bus to the Castelo São Jorge, admire the view and then set off down hill to the Museu-Escola de Artes Decorativas in the Rua Augusto Rosa where a guided tour of the museum lasts for about three-quarters of an hour. After looking round the traditional craft workshops next door it is

Portugal gives you the oportunity to dine in a historical setting

a short walk down to the cathedral and the Church of Santo António da Sé just opposite. Alternatively it is very pleasant to wander through the narrow streets and stepped alleyways of the Alfama district beyond the Miradouro de Santa Luzia and reach the cathedral by way of the Rua de São João da Praça. Other attractions nearby are the Museu da Marioneta, the monastery of São Vicente de Fora and the Military Museum.

Trams 15, 16 and 17 and buses 14, 27, 28, 29, 43 and 49 all run to Belém, downriver from the city centre, although it is quicker and not at all expensive to go by taxi. Once there the predominant attraction is the Mosteiro dos Jerónimos with its impressive church and adjacent maritime museum. Within easy walking distance are the medieval Torre de Belém, the comparatively recent Monument to the Discoveries, a Museum of Popular Art and a splendid Coach Museum. The Calçada da Ajuda leads directly to the Ajuda Palace slightly further from the river.

There are so many other places of interest in Lisbon that it would be very difficult if not impossible to visit them all in the space of a single morning or afternoon. One is the superb Museu Nacional de Arte Antiga on the route back from Belém, reached by either the 27 or 49 bus; another is the Calouste-Gulbenkian Museum, north of the Parque Eduardo VII, conveniently close to trams, buses and the Metro, where an average tour can be expected to last for at least two hours. In order to see all the other churches and various museums, ride on a funicular, wander through the botanical gardens, go shopping and visit the zoo it would be essential to spend much more time in the capital.

Several different options are open to anyone planning an excursion to **Sintra**, 28km (17$^1/_2$ miles) west of Lisbon. Trains run frequently from Rossio station in the capital, special coaches make a round trip four afternoons a week during the summer from the Praça da República, while most taxis will agree a set price that varies according to the number of places to be visited in the area. In addition, local buses link Sintra with Cascais on the south coast some 15km (about 10 miles) away, and with Mafra, 23km (14$^1/_2$ miles) to the north.

As far as motorists are concerned the long way round is through Estoril and then up the N6, or alternatively along the coast via Cascais, past Cabo da Roca, Colares and the Quinta de Monserrate. The most direct route is the N249 through Queluz, which can also be reached on the train to Sintra, where a visit to the elegant royal palace with its formal gardens will last for anything up to an hour. In Sintra itself the main attractions are the Palácio Real, accounting for slightly less than an hour, the Palácio de Pena and the remains of the Moorish castle, the last two of which will probably need at least an hour or so between them.

In **Mafra**, 40km (25 miles) north of Lisbon, midway between the N8 and the N247, a visit to the monastery can be expected to take well over an hour, after which the circular route heads northwards to **Óbidos**, one of the most attractive walled villages in Portugal. From here the N8 makes its way through the spa town of Caldas da Rainha to **Alcobaça**, 110km (70 miles) from Lisbon. It will be necessary to allow the better part of an hour for a visit to the Monastery of Santa Maria but considerably less time would be needed to inspect the Museu de la Junta Nacional de Vinho 1km ($^1/_2$ mile) up the N8 on the way to Leira, 32km (20 miles) away.

Just beyond the point where the N8 joins the N1 **Batalha** is, without doubt, one of the star attractions on any tour of Portugal, although it is not well served by either trains or buses. The abbey church is magnificent and should be seen at leisure, especially as there is nothing else of note in the immediate vicinity. **Fátima**, some 18km (11 miles) to the east, is more of a pilgrim centre than a Mecca for tourists, but is nevertheless worth visiting before deciding whether or not to deviate slightly in order to visit **Tomar**. This would entail an additional 23km (14 miles) in either direction in order to spend an hour or two in the town whose main attraction is the ancient Convent of Christ. There are a few trains and buses from Lisbon and a selection of hotels.

Backtracking along the N113, past the turning off to Fátima, **Leiria** is 45km (28 miles) from Tomar and 129km (80 miles) from Lisbon. Apart from its castle, which can be inspected quite easily in half an hour, the town is well placed as a base for touring the caves in the Serra do Aire. On the other hand the circular route presses on northwards along the N1 via Pombal to Coimbra which preceeded Lisbon as the capital of Portugal. Some 15km (9 miles) short of Coimbra it is well worth deviating again to spend an hour or so in the ruins of *Conimbriga*, the ancient Roman city built on the site of a Celtic settlement.

Coimbra, 200km (125 miles) from Lisbon, 118km (74 miles) from Oporto and 70km (44 miles) from Leira, is in rail communication with both Lisbon and Oporto, augmented by express bus services from both these cities as well as a number of other centres such as Faro, Viseu and Guimarães. Local buses and taxis are available in the city, although most places of interest are within walking distance, except, perhaps, for the university and the Santa Clara-a-Nova convent.

The best place to start a sightseeing tour of the delightful old quarter is in the ancient university, with its outstanding library. The nearby Machado de Castro Museum, in the Rua de Borges Carneiro on the way down the hill, provides guided tours lasting about an hour. Slightly further on the Old Cathedral (Sé Velha) is worth seeing, while beyond the Almedina Gate, on the far side of the river, are the drowned remains of the Santa Clara-a-Velha convent and the Portugal in Miniature garden. Other attractions include the Church of Santa Cruz and the botanical gardens, not far from the aqueduct.

One of the loveliest wooded areas in Portugal, the **Buçaco Forest**, is within easy reach of Coimbra, approached by way of a scenic route through Penacova or more directly up the N1 as far as the right-hand turn off to Luso. It would be as well to allow two hours to explore the area on foot but a good deal less by car, even including tea at the Palace Hotel, which is also worth seeing.

The next port of call is **Aveiro** with its vast land-locked lagoon, network of canals and extensive salt flats. It is well served by trains from Lisbon, Coimbra and Oporto but less so by express coaches from the capital. By road it is 56km (35 miles) from Coimbra and about the same distance from the seaside resort of Espinho which makes a pleasant overnight stop before setting off in the morning for Oporto, a bare 16km (10 miles) up the coast.

Oporto, 314km (196 miles) from Lisbon, is the second largest city in Portugal with an international airport, three busy railway stations and two main coach terminals, in the Praça Filipa de Lencastre and the Avenida de Rodrigues de Freitas respectively, which keep the city in touch with the rest of the country. Local buses converge on the Praça de Dom João I. There are plenty of taxis, especially in the Praça da Liberdade, which are not expensive but bump up the fare for a journey across the river to Vila Nova de Gaia. Some of the drivers have a keen eye for a gullible tourist so it is a good idea to check the price in advance or, alternatively, if it seems unreasonable ask for a receipt (*recibo*) with the number of the taxi on it.

The city's main attractions *can* be crammed into a single day but, as in the case of Lisbon, there is plenty to occupy anyone who has enough time to explore at leisure. The most convenient place to start is probably the cathedral on the Terreiro da Sé with its panoramic view over Oporto. This could logically be followed by a visit to the Church of Santa Clara on the opposite side of the Avenida Vimara Peres, the wide thoroughfare leading to the top deck of the double-layer Ponte de Dom Luís I. Thereafter it is a simple matter to recross the Avenida Vimara Peres, explore the old quarter down to the Largo de São Domingos and join a twenty-minute tour of the Palácio da Bolsa. More importantly it provides an excellent opportunity to admire the magnificently ornate Church of São Francisco.

A guided tour of the Ethnology Museum a few blocks away will last about an hour. After this it is not very far to walk past the massive Hospital de Santo António to the Soares dos Reis Museum, the largest and most comprehensive art collection in the city. Slightly further down the Rua de Dom Manuel II, on the far side of the Palácio de Cristal, a pleasant half hour can be spent among the royal relics in the Quinta da Macieirinha Romantic Museum.

Other local attractions include a scattering of small churches, the noisy Bolhão Market and river trips along the Douro. However, enough time should be made to cross the river to Vila Nova de Gaia where several of the port wine lodges lay on tours of their various premises — with samples of course. The district can be reached by bus or taxi from the Estação de São Bento, in addition to which there is usually space for cars in the Parking Aparcamlento off the Rua Serpa Pinto, some 300m uphill from the Avenida Diogo Leite.

Motorists have a choice between the *auto-estrada* and the N14 to **Braga**, which can easily be reached by train from Oporto, although travellers

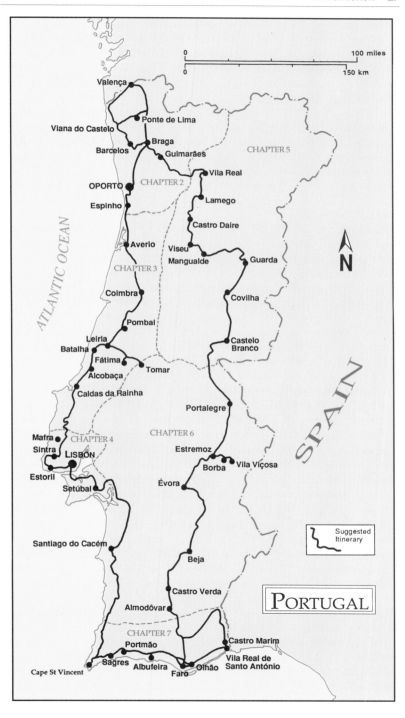

from elsewhere have to change at Nine. There are also plenty of buses from the city but much less convenient coach services from other centres including Lisbon, 368km (230 miles) away. The most outstanding attractions in Braga are the cathedral with its splendid treasury, which will account for well over an hour, and the rather less time-consuming Casa dos Biscainhos Museum.

It would be wise to allow a full morning or afternoon for an excursion to **Bom Jesus do Monte**, about 6km (4 miles) to the east of the town. For this visit one alternative is to park at the foot of the magnificently ornamental stairway, take the funicular to the top and then walk down from the church. A round trip from Bom Jesus to Monte Sameiro, on to the Iron Age settlement of Citânia de Briteiros on the N309, and back via the Church of Santa Maria Madalena to Braga, is a pleasant drive of about 44km (27 miles).

From Braga it is only 19km (12 miles) along the N103 to **Barcelos** with its famous Thursday morning market, and a further 34km (21 miles) to the fishing port of **Viana do Castelo** at the mouth of the Lima River. This is the most northwesterly point on the circular tour and only 53km (33 miles) from Valença do Minho, one of the main border crossings on the frontier with Spain. The main things to see in Viana do Castelo are the Praça da República with its elderly buildings, the Municipal Museum, where the guided tours last for about half an hour, and the hilltop Basilica of Santa Luzia with its extensive view.

Inland from Viana do Castelo there is a pleasant 23km ($14^1/_2$ mile) drive up the river valley to Ponte de Lima with its old Roman bridge. Here the N202 becomes the N203 through Bravães, where there is an eleventh-century church, to Ponte da Barca, a total of 18km (12 miles). At this point the choice is optional, providing an excursion to Lindoso on the frontier, or the southbound N101 back to Braga. Anyone who would like to visit the **Peneda-Gerês National Park** should head east from Braga along the N103, turning off on to the N304 at the Pousada de São Bento for the spa town of Caldas do Gerês, a total distance of 44km ($27^1/_2$ miles).

Meanwhile, **Guimarães**, the first Portuguese capital, is only 22km (14 miles) south of Braga on the N101, and about 50km (32 miles) from Oporto. There are frequent trains and plenty of buses from Oporto but passengers from elsewhere have to change trains or, alternatively, wait quite some time for express coaches from Lisbon or Coimbra. Once in Guimarães a tour of the Paço dos Duques should not take much more than half an hour. About the same amount of time should be allowed for a visit to the Alberto Sampaio Museum, adjoining the Church of Our Lady of the Olive Tree, but rather longer may be needed by those interested in the archaeological exhibits in the Martins Sarmento Museum.

The next stopping place on the way south is **Amarante**, 64km (40 miles) due east of Oporto. It is an attractive base for anyone who would enjoy walking in the hills or taking a return trip on the Tâmega Railway up to Arco de Baúlhe and straight back again. Otherwise it is only 49km (30

miles) from **Vila Real**. Although it is not overblessed with tourist attractions — in fact it would not take much more than an hour to see all the
different sights on offer — Vila Real nevertheless has quite a lot to
recommend it. There are daily trains to Oporto and Chaves, it has coach
connections with several places including Lisbon, Coimbra and Viseu,
and buses to many places in Trás-os-Montes including Bragança. It is on
the main route for motorists from Spain heading south from the frontier
post at San Martin del Pedroso and is almost equidistant from Braga,
Viseu and Oporto, as well as being within reasonable driving distance of
Lisbon, 400km (250 miles) to the southwest. Another advantage is that
Mateus, of rosé fame, is just 3.5km (2 miles) to the east, where conducted
tours of the manor house and gardens take about two hours.

Lamego, 40km (25 miles) south on the N2, has rather more to offer in the
form of a cathedral, the Sanctuary of Nossa Senhora dos Remédios and a
regional museum whose tours are designed to take about three-quarters
of an hour. Other attractions include the Raposeira wine centre which also
lays on guided tours. The nearest railway station is at Peso da Régua but
there are quite a few buses, although not very frequent coach services to
Lisbon, Coimbra, Chaves and Viseu.

The N2 continues on its journey south through Castro Daira, beyond
which there is a turning off to Aveiro, and reaches **Viseu** after 70km (44
miles). This is not an easy place to reach by train but there are a number
of express coaches linking it with other centres such as Lisbon and Oporto
as well as main roads to Coimbra, Aveiro and Guarda, the last of which
carries on through Vila Formoso and into Spain. Foremost among the
various attractions clustered together in the ancient quarter are the cathedral and the Grão Vasco Museum.

The next section of the circuit depends very much on the time of year,
the weather and personal inclination. The most direct route, but by no
means the quickest, is the scenic, convoluted N232 from Mangualde,
18km (12 miles) from Viseu, off the N16, across the Serra da Estrela to
Manteigas, followed by 15km ($9^1/_2$ miles) down the Vale Glaciário do
Zêzere and a further 13km (8 miles) of hairpin bends on the approach to
Covilhã. Alternatively the distance to Guarda along the N16 is 85km (53
miles) with an additional 45km (28 miles) to Covilhã on the N18. Guarda
has constant rail and coach links with Lisbon and other main centres, but
it is necessary for people arriving by train to catch a bus for the last part
of the journey into the town. It has little in the way of tourist attractions
apart from the cathedral, but is well placed for touring the frontier area.

There is really nothing to stop for along the 62km (39 miles) from
Covilha to Castelo Branco, except perhaps at Fundão when the cherry
trees are all in bloom. As the capital of Beira Baixa, **Castelo Branco** is
256km (160 miles) from Lisbon and 155km (97 miles) from Coimbra. It is
in daily contact with Lisbon by train and coach, with less frequent services
to Oporto and Guarda. However it has little in the way of tourist attractions apart from the Tavares Proença Regional Museum and the adjacent

Jardim do Antigo Paço Episcopal gardens. In fact the N18 bypasses the town and presses on in the direction of Portalegre, 82km (51 miles) to the south.

Among the various attractions which **Portalegre** has to offer are the Municipal Museum next to the cathedral, the José Régio Museum, whose hour-long guided tours are a trifle on the lengthy side, and the tapestry workshops near the Bombarda Park. There are plenty of local buses including a regular service to the railway station some 12km ($7^1/_2$ miles) south of the town. Motorists from the north with time to spare might consider turning off the N18 on to the N246 at Alpalhao in order to visit Castelo de Vide, 14km (9 miles) to the east, and the medieval walled village of Marvão, one of the most atmospheric of all the old fortified frontier posts. It is only 10km (6 miles) from the border with Spain, 19km (12 miles) northeast of Portalegre with a daily bus service to the town, and has the added advantage of the Pousada de Santa Maria for visitors who have had enough driving for the day.

Back on the N18, **Estremoz**, 59km (37 miles) south of Portalegre, and 176km (110 miles) from Lisbon on the N4, can be reached by both train and bus, although neither of these services is very convenient. However it is well provided with local buses to and from Évora. The splendid Pousada da Rainha Santa Isabel is situated in the former royal palace, which also contains the Chapel of the Queen Saint. Other attractions include the Rural Museum on the main square, the Church of São Francisco, the Municipal Museum near the palace and a colourful Saturday morning market. The Crucifix Museum is located in the village of Villa-Lôbos, 10km (6 miles) along the N4 to the southeast. Roughly 1km further on, at Borba, the N255 leads to Vila Viçosa, memorable chiefly for its vast Paço Ducal. It would be necessary to allow an hour for a tour of the palace, somewhat less to inspect the castle, and a few minutes for each of the small churches in the vicinity.

It is possible to reach **Évora** from Vila Viçosa by way of the N254 via Redondo, a distance of 54km (34 miles), or direct from Estremoz which is marginally shorter along the N18. Either way this is another gem in Portugal's historic, architectural crown. It is also within easy driving distance of Lisbon, 153km (96 miles) away to the west. There are trains and express coaches from the capital in addition to somewhat less convenient means of public transport from some nearby centres like Beja, Elvas and Vila Viçosa. Taxis are available but seldom necessary because most of the main places of interest are grouped together inside the surrounding walls.

The cathedral with its well-stocked treasury, the Museum of Ancient Art, the Paço dos Duques de Cadaval and the Convento dos Lóios, which contains both the monastery church and the *pousada*, surround the re-mains of the Roman temple in the Largo Conde de Vila-Flor. Although the distances are negligible this will occupy the best part of a morning or an afternoon. Much the same amount of time would be needed to explore the old quarter and visit some of the other places of interest such as the Church of São Francisco with its Casa dos Ossos, the Convent of Calvário and the old university, as well as a clutch of small churches.

From Évora the N18 continues almost without interruption to **Beja**, a distance of 78km (49 miles) further south. There are trains from Lisbon and the Algarve in addition to express coaches linking the town with the capital 194km (121 miles) away. Others are available to Évora and to Mértola on the N122 which is the quickest route to Vila Real de Santo António at the mouth of the Rio Guadiana with its ferry service across to Spain. The main attractions in Beja are the castle, which can be seen in under half an hour, the Convento de Nossa Senhora da Conceição containing the regional museum, which requires slightly more viewing time than the castle, and one or two small churches.

South from Beja the most direct route to Faro, the capital of the Algarve, 186km (116 miles) away, is much easier than it sounds. The N122 accounts for the first 15km ($9^1/_2$ miles) or so, then it transfers on to the N391 as far as Castro Verde where it joins the N2 through Almodovar and Malhão to **Faro**. There are several optional routes for motorists on their way from Faro to Lisbon which naturally vary somewhat in length but nevertheless are all in the region of about 300km (200 miles). There are daily flights to

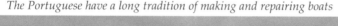

The Portuguese have a long tradition of making and repairing boats

and from Lisbon, trains and express coaches maintain regular schedules, in addition to which there are train and bus services to most places along the coast in either direction. Hire cars are available for visitors who want to explore the Algarve by road as well as taxis for some shorter journeys.

The main things to see in Faro are the cathedral, the adjacent Municipal Museum, both of which are tucked away behind the ancient Arco da Vila, the Ethnology Museum near the Jardim da Alagoa and the Maritime Museum overlooking the harbour. These may prove to be quite time-consuming but there might be enough of the day left to visit the nearby beach at Praia de Faro which can be reached by car, by bus or by ferry.

One day should be sufficient for an excursion eastwards along the coast to Vila Real de Santo António, a distance of 53km (33 miles) using the main highway. Olhão, 8km (5 miles) along the road, may be reached by both train and bus and has its own regular ferry services to the islands of Armona and Culatra which only take about a quarter of an hour. It is a pleasant town in its own right, but has nothing outstanding in the way of tourist attractions. Much the same applies to **Tavira**, 31km (20 miles) from Faro, which is also on the local train and bus routes. Nevertheless it has some attractive little churches and a bridge which dates in part from Roman times. In addition there is a combined bus and ferry service to the island of Tavira for visitors who want to spend some time on the beach.

Vila Real de Santo António, 23km ($14^1/_2$ miles) further west, is the terminal for local trains and buses, has regular ferries across the Guadiana to Ayamonte in Spain and occasional boat trips up the river to Mértola. However there is more to see in the surrounding area than in the town itself. Monte Gordo, 3km (2 miles) away, is a well-equipped and popular seaside resort with every facility including bicycles for hire. Castro Marim, 4km ($2^1/_2$ miles) north of Vila Real de Santo António, is known for its ruined castle and the remains of an ancient fortress and is close to the small, rather soggy Reserva do Sapal. North from here there is a turning off the N122 to Alcoutim, a total distance of some 40km (25 miles) which also has a ruined castle and is surrounded by pleasant walking country. There are a number of different options for the return trip to Faro. One is to strike out across country and connect with the main N2 from the north at Barranco Velho. Alternatively there is a road along the river to Foz de Odeleite and then back to Vila Real de Santo António and Tavira.

From Tavira the N270 provides a pleasant drive of 22km (15 miles) to São Bras de Alportel with the option of carrying on to the village of Loulé with its local arts and crafts, or turning south on the N2 in order to visit the modest Roman ruins at Milreu, 7km (4 miles) down the road. The palace gardens at Estói, 1km ($^1/_2$ mile) from the ruins are also open to the public but it is not possible to visit the palace itself at the moment..

To the west of Faro the N125 calls at São Lourenço with its attractive little church, and then carries on through Almansil beyond which there is a turning off to **Vilamoura**, the sophisticated boating, golfing and holiday playground 22km (15 miles) from the provincial capital. The whole coast in this area is being developed, but so far there is no direct link with **Albufeira**, the largest seaside resort in the Algarve, which has frequent buses to Faro, 38km (24 miles) to the east. A minor road rejoins the highway at Guia with a number of little turnings off on either side before it reaches Lagos. Here there is a wine centre which is open to visitors, a short road down to the beach at Carvoeiro and a marginally larger one up to **Silves**, 7km ($4^1/_2$ miles) further inland. The attractions here are the remains of its Moorish castle, the former cathedral and an unusual wayside cross on the N124 to the east of the town. This road soon makes contact with the N226 from the north 7km ($4^1/_2$ miles) from Portimão.

Portimão, 62km (49 miles) west of Faro is another popular holiday resort, well served by both trains and buses as well as by hire car companies. However, anyone without private transport can walk some 2km down to the beach at Praia da Rocha or travel in one of the *carrinhas* drawn by mules that provide a colourful alternative. The most popular excursion from Portimão is up the N266 to Monchique, tucked away in the mountains about 24km (15 miles) from the coast. It is an attractive hill village, set in pleasant walking country, with some magnificent views from the surrounding peaks, the best known of which is Foia, now conveniently accessible by car. The road up is also the best route back, past the little spa of Caldas de Monchique.

From Portimão there is nothing of particular moment on the way to **Lagos**, another popular holiday playground overlooking a beautiful bay. Its architectural attractions are limited to the Chapel of Santo António, the old slave market and the regional museum near the Praça da República, which could all be seen in slightly less than an hour. However there are boat trips to the nearby caves and grottoes which take somewhat longer. Lagos is 82km (51 miles) from Faro, can be reached by either train or bus and has motorcycles, mopeds and bicycles for hire. The coastal railway stops here but there are plenty of buses to Sagres, the most westerly resort on the southern coast of Portugal.

Sagres, 113km (just over 70 miles) from Faro and 33km (21 miles) from Lagos, has two main things to recommend it. Firstly the ancient fortress on a nearby promontory with an enormous compass and a small chapel, and secondly the windswept heights of Cape St Vincent 6km (4 miles) away. There is a road out to the point but no public transport so anyone without transport must walk. Sightseers can either return to Lagos along the same road or make their way up the coast past Carrapateira, Aljezur 110km (70 miles) from Faro and 249km (156 miles) from Lisbon, where there is an hotel, and Odemira to Sines, an industrial port with nothing of interest to delay the average visitor. However **Santiago do Cacem**, slightly inland off the N120, has the remains of its castle walls, an interesting Municipal Museum in the Praça do Municipio and the remains of the Roman settlement of *Miróbriga* on a hill outside the town. There are trains and express coaches from Lisbon, 146km (91 miles) to the north, and buses down to the Algarve.

From Santiago do Cacém it is an uneventful drive up the N120 through Alcácer do Sal and on to the N5 for the last part of the run to **Setúbal**.

The main attractions in this busy port are the Church of Jesus in the Rua Edmond Bartissol, the adjacent Municipal Museum, where a guided tour lasts for about three-quarters of an hour, the Regional Museum of Archaeology and Ethnology, facing the Avenida Luisa Todi, which may take up to an hour, and the Castle of St Philip, a part of which houses the Pousada de São Filipe. There are any number of trains and express coaches linking Setúbal with Lisbon 55km (34 miles) away, with local services to Palmela and Sesimbra and regular ferries across the river to Tróia, a holiday resort with the sparse ruins of the Roman settlement of *Cetóbriga* a shortish walk away.

Apart from the natural attractions of the Serra da Arrábida, **Sesimbra**, 26km (16 miles) along the coast, is an attractive fishing port with a disappointing castle ruin, whereas **Palmela** has both the Church of Santiago and the Pousada Castelo de Palmela inside the battlements of its large, frequently restored hilltop fortress. Both towns have access to the N10 and to the *auto-estrada* which converge on Lisbon across the spectacular Ponte 25 de Abril.

2

THE COSTA VERDE

The Costa Verde is often described, quite inaccurately, as the unknown corner of Portugal. This is probably because it escapes the attention of millions of holidaymakers who flood into the Algarve, play golf and tennis, swim, dance and gamble and then fly home again under the mistaken impression that they are well acquainted with the country. Travellers, on the other hand, are full of praise for this comparatively unfrequented region with its wealth of natural beauty, historical associations, modern facilities and friendly, uncomplicated people. The Portuguese themselves look at it quite differently. Many who have made their fortunes overseas return home to build retirement villas up in the hills or on the outskirts of an attractive fishing village, slightly off the beaten track in what is, after all, the birthplace of their nation.

As its name implies, the Green Coast is an emerald coloured area consisting of the Minho and Douro provinces, located in the northwestern corner of the country with its lowlying coastline pounded constantly by breakers rolling in from the Atlantic. It shares a common border with Spain to the north and is hemmed in by the Costa de Prata and Montanhas along the south and east. The region is large enough to include long sandy beaches, extensive nature reserves, backwoods filled with trees and flowers, patches of maize and intricately terraced vineyards. It is hilly without being aggressively so, threaded through with streams and rivers and divided up into tiny smallholdings separated by hedges and dry-stone walls.

At the same time the area is not too big to be explored at leisure, a decided advantage in view of the fact that many of the routes, although usually well cambered, can be rather bumpy to say the least of it. Motorists soon discover that they are expected to share the road with flocks of sheep and goats, a few cattle or a farm cart pulled by oxen with large spreading horns and amiable expressions.

Highways link most of the larger towns and all the major coastal resorts while lanes and byways keep a multitude of little villages in touch with each other, ably assisted by buses and, occasionally, by small local trains. Getting about often takes longer than expected because the prettiest routes snake their way up and down the hillsides between forests of oak and chestnuts or meander along a river valley with innumerable side turnings leading to minute whitewashed communities grouped round an antiquated church.

The only drawback to the Costa Verde is that it does rain quite a bit, especially in the winter, keeping the countryside marvellously fresh and green but making it necessary for everyone to own an umbrella. These are usually large, black and eminently serviceable. Children share them on the way to school, farm workers carry them out into the fields and even grandmothers riding donkeys have mastered the art of using them in transit. However the showers are frequently spasmodic with welcome bursts of sunshine in between and it seldom gets oppressively hot or bitterly cold, except high up in the mountains.

The whole region was certainly occupied some three thousand or more years ago and still has the remains of Bronze Age settlements where the Celts fought long and bravely against the encroaching Romans. Although the legions were victorious eventually they never felt completely at home in the area which they described as 'an unpleasant, warlike province'. However the Romans made the best of it, chose *Bracara Augusta* — now abbreviated to Braga — as the capital of the territory they called *Gallaecia*, established a health and holiday centre round the nearby mineral springs at Caldelas and built a number of highways, one of which led all the way to Rome.

Bracara Augusta was captured by the Suevi in 409AD, sacked by the Visigoths in 585, appropriated by the Moors and eventually recovered by Ferdinand I of Castile. In 1139 Afonso Henriques proclaimed himself king of an independent country which he called Portugal and declared that his home town of Guimarães was to be its capital. However the province of Braga did not bat an eyelid when the royal court moved down to Coimbra shortly afterwards, everyone was far too busy with agriculture, fishing, religion and border skirmishes with the neighbouring Spaniards who still felt that they had a right to the territory. Thereafter its fortunes ran parallel with those of the rest of the country. It acquired some very handsome buildings, developed trade links with places as far apart as Russia and Brazil, encouraged the British to drink port wine and dabbled in the nation's internal politics, without ever losing sight of its ancient heritage, liberally sprinkled with myths and legends.

As in the olden days, all the major roads converge in Braga with the exception of the coastal highway linking the Rio Minho with Oporto. Some of them cross Montanhas from the east, others make their way northwards over the Rio Douro while the remainder travel south from the Rio Minho, the time honoured boundary between the Costa Verde and Galicia. The most important of these bypasses Vigo on its way from Santiago de Compostela and arrives at Túi on the Spanish side of the river with **Valença do Minho** on the bank just opposite.

This is the epitome of an uncompromising frontier town with an extremely efficient stronghold that held out successfully against the Spaniards during the War of Restoration and later repulsed the French who attacked it vigorously in the course of the Peninsular War. The old quarter is not particularly large but it gives the impression of being two matching towns, grouped round a double fortress with a bridge in the middle, monumental doorways and a large vaulted passageway. Each section has its own attendant houses, separated by cobbled streets enlivened with small unobtrusive fountains and an occasional statue here and there. Cannons are still mounted on the battlements, but they are totally ignored by Spanish visitors who pop over the bridge whenever they feel like a change of atmosphere or something different for lunch.

The more modern part of Valença do Minho has little to offer its visitors although railway enthusiasts should make a point of seeing 'The XIX Century Train' whose engine was built in England by Beyer Peacock in 1875. It has five carriages, three French, one Swiss and one Portuguese, dating from between 1885 and 1891. For nearly one hundred years these little vintage trains were extremely active all over the region, using a narrow gauge railway system, but now only get up steam on very special occasions. The Pousada da São Teotónio, inside the ramparts, is probably the best place to stay but it has a serious rival in the Pousada de Dom Dinis, down the road at Vila Nova de Cerveira. This is a comparatively new addition to the chain, having taken over an ancient fortress whose ramparts still guard the lower reaches of the river.

Anyone planning to explore the area with a tent or caravan has a choice of two official campsites in the vicinity. The Parque de Campismo e Caravanismo Natural at Vilar de Mouros has all the necessary amenities including a swimming pool while the Parque de Campismo de Caminha/ Orbitur offers some furnished accommodation as well as fishing and bathing quite close by.

Caminha, at the mouth of the Rio Minho, was once a busy port and another link in Portugal's northern defensive line but it has not worn as well as some of its contemporaries. These days it is hardly more than a fishing village specialising in copperwork with just a few reminders of the past. One of these is the Praça do Conselheiro Silva Torres, an attractive medieval square ringed by a number of old buildings. The Pitas Palace is a Gothic hangover from the fifteenth century, while the Torre do Relógio is older by about one hundred years, having been part of the early fortifications. The fire station is worth visiting to see its modest collection of antique fire engines that had to be man-handled over the cobbles each time there was an alarm. The archway under the clocktower leads into the Rua Ricardo João de Sousa and up to the Igreja Matriz. This five-hundred-year-old fortified church has a south doorway guarded by saintly statues, a beautifully carved ceiling and the figure of St Christopher, the patron saint of travellers. He was demoted some years ago on the grounds that he may never have existed, but is so universally popular that this has not damaged his reputation in any way. The Pensão Galo d'Ouro, off the main square, is quite acceptable but small enough to be booked up during the season. In this case the best plan is to backtrack to the Estalagem da Boega,

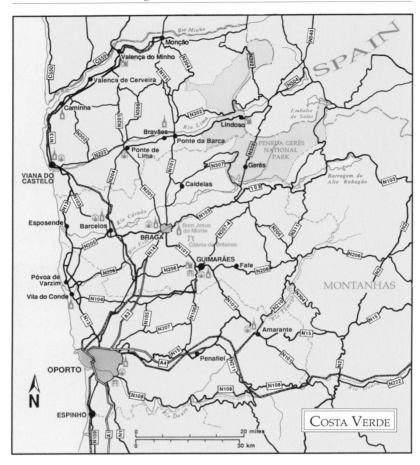

a few kilometres short of Vila Nova de Cerveira, which is larger and offers both tennis and a swimming pool.

The next port of call along the coastal highway to the south is **Moledo do Minho** which has both a beach and a ruined castle, followed by **Vila Praia de Âncora**. This is essentially a fishing village with a pleasing beach, trout in the nearby streams, bass in the ocean and the Hotel Meira, which will supply fishing rods free of charge to any of its guests who would like to accept the offer. Its other amenities include a swimming pool, a games room and a restaurant serving traditional Portuguese dishes. The Rio Âncora is said to have changed its name from the Rio Spaco after the wife of a local nobleman ran off with the Emir of Gaia, was recovered, tied to an anchor and tossed overboard into the river.

A much more fascinating story is associated with the Rio Lima which runs into the Atlantic at **Viana do Castelo**, a short drive down the coast. In 135BC a column of Roman soldiers under their veteran commander

The Fortress at Valença do Minho

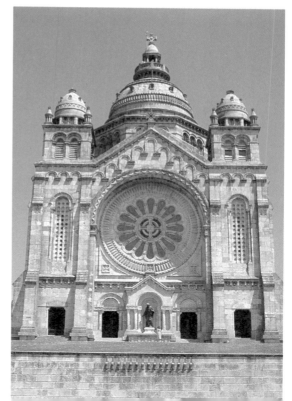

The Basilica of Santa Luzia, Viana do Castelo

Decius Junius Brutus arrived on the south bank of the river and found it so pleasant and peaceful that they decided it must be the *Lethe*, the mythological River of Forgetfulness. Nothing would persuade them to cross it until Brutus rode over alone, turned to face them from the opposite bank and ordered them to join him, addressing each one in turn by name. When they realised that his memory was just as good as ever they all plunged in, no doubt assuring each other that it had only been a very natural mistake.

In its youth Viana do Castelo was a fairly ordinary fishing village backed by the wooded slopes of Monte Santa Luzia. With the discovery of the New World and the sea route to India it grew rapidly into an important trading centre; its fleets ventured far afield, the merchants accumulated fortunes and built themselves large houses and its future seemed to be assured. However wars, uprisings and the loss of Portugal's overseas territories all took their toll and the port went into a decline in the nineteenth century. Nowadays deep sea fishing coupled with industry and tourism are all helping to restore a measure of prosperity, reinforced by some comfortable hotels, furnished apartments, reasonable restaurants, a three-star campsite and the somewhat larger Parque de Campismo do Inatel which only rates two stars but has rather more facilities.

The life of the town still revolves round the Praça da República and its Chafariz fountain, designed by João Lopes the Elder in 1553 and copied more or less faithfully by several other local communities. Water spills over from one basin into another below a sphere topped with the cross of the Order of Christ. João Lopes the Younger was responsible for most of the buildings that surround the cobbled square, the most eye-catching of which is the Misericórdia Hospice. It has a very decorative doorway, a splendid colonnade and granite atlantes who have been holding up the Renaissance balconies for just over four hundred years. The adjacent Church of the Misericord was rebuilt in 1714 and coated inside with tiles recounting well known stories from the Old Testament. The Paços do Concelho has also been updated, although the façade was carefully preserved and still flaunts the coats-of-arms of João III and the municipality. The latter includes a caravel — a medieval Portuguese sailing ship — in memory of the many local seamen who played their part in the voyages of discovery.

A block or so away in the direction of the river the Igreja Matriz started life in the fourteenth century and has retained its Gothic doorway flanked by towers and presided over by biblical characters including St Andrew and St Peter. The nearby Rua de São Pedro is edged with elderly houses, still in possession of their Manueline decorations but now, unfortunately, rather past their prime. The former eighteenth-century palace of the Barbosa Macieis on the Rua Manuel Espregueira, which leads out of the Praça da República, is home to the Municipal Museum. There is plenty to see inside apart from the tiled walls, panelled ceilings and a courtyard devoted mainly to statues and other similar exhibits. From the archaeological point of view it is extremely proud of its 'Lusitanian Warrior', a prehistoric granite relic still holding on grimly to its round shield, although the collection of pottery and ceramics from the eighteenth century is much more colourful. There are some very viewable pictures, items of sacred art, silverware and much beautiful Indo-Portuguese furniture, some of the pieces carved or inlaid with ivory.

It is hardly worth trudging out beyond the docks to inspect the old fortress, built by Philip II in 1592, after he had overrun the country, and captured a bare half century later when the Portuguese rose in revolt and threw out the Spanish garrison. The time would be much better spent visiting the Basilica of Santa Luzia, perched up on the hilltop overlooking the town. It can be reached along a tortuous cobbled road through pine trees interspersed with eucalyptus and mimosa, on foot or by funicular. The church is quite modern, built on Byzantine lines with several domes, three rose windows and a stairway up from the sacristy to the lantern turret where there is a magnificent view over the ocean and the surrounding countryside. Its only neighbours are the Hotel de Santa Luzia, which is predictably expensive, and the sparse remains of a third-century Iberian settlement consisting of a good many foundations but precious little otherwise.

Viana do Castelo insists that it is the folklore capital of Portugal and anyone attending the pilgrimage of Our Lady in Sorrow during the third week in August would probably agree wholeheartedly. On the nearest Friday to the twentieth of the month the statue of Nossa Senhora da Agónia is carried in procession through the decorated streets from her own small church on the Campo d'Agónia, beyond the museum, to the dock area. On arrival she is hoisted on to one of the boats for a brief excursion before returning to the Baroque chapel where she remains isolated for the rest of the year. The festival that coincides with the pilgrimage is memorable for its wealth of traditional costumes, procession of floats and carnival figures, bullfights and bullrunning through the barricaded streets, fireworks, feasting and folk music. Families in the region invest a considerable part of their savings in gold jewellery, a custom they may have inherited from the Arabs, and the women wear every ornament they can lay their hands on when they take part in the various processions. The *romario* is only held once a year but there are also regular events, some designed with tourists in mind, staged throughout the summer with traditional singing and dancing, corn husking, wine and sardines grilled in the open air.

The town is also famous for its many arts and crafts, primarily gold and silver jewellery and *objet d'art*, embroidery, rugs and pottery. Other attractions include tennis and swimming, riding, fishing and sailing with windsurfing as an optional extra. The nearby beaches are backed by sand dunes and can get rather crowded during the season, especially now that the area is becoming increasingly popular with young French and German holidaymakers.

Two nearby villages, one on either side of the Rio Lima, also celebrate in style. **Portuzelo**, on the north bank, organises a three-day folk festival in the first half of August that attracts visitors from far afield as well as contributors who take part in the international competitions. **Vila Franca do Lima**, to the south, is somewhat less ambitious. Its Rose Festival, on the second Sunday in May, centres on a procession of housewives through the streets, each carrying a tray piled high with flowers which are said to weigh anything up to ninety pounds.

One of the most noticeable things about **Barcelos**, a delightful town on both the Rio Cávado and the N103 some 18km (11 miles) short of Braga, is the quantity of tiles used to decorate the houses. Another is the size of the Campo da República, a vast square measuring about 200m by 150m (650ft by 500ft) which is famous for the Thursday morning markets which occupy the entire area. It is possible to buy almost anything from fruit and vegetables to pottery, handmade rugs, lace and tape cassettes, not to mention trees, flowers and even a new ox-cart that still needs painting. It is not the place to look for antiques or other up-market sourvenirs but for colour, noise and everyday variety it is almost unbeatable.

The Igreja do Terço, on the north side of the square, was once part of a Benedictine monastery. It is full of late seventeenth-century tiles recalling episodes from the life of St Benedict, which are illustrated still further on the painted ceiling. Also worth a second glance is the ornately carved and gilded pulpit which was probably installed when the monastery was founded in 1707. The Igreja das Cruzes, also overlooking the square, combines a Baroque cupola with an interior that is smothered in gold, a number of small chapels and a Romanesque doorway. It is decorated with lights for the Festas das Cruzes on 3 May, vaguely calling to mind the sight of Harrods in London at Christmas.

A few blocks away, down by the river, are the ruins of a palace that once belonged to the Ducal Counts of Barcelos. A ceramics museum has been set up inside, leaving the archaeological exhibits to fend for themselves out in the open, as most of them have been doing for centuries. There are bits and pieces of masonry, an archway that does not lead anywhere in particular and, foremost among the crosses, one known as the Cruzeiro do Senhor do Galo. It shows a man being hanged and is said to have been placed there by a wayfarer who escaped death by a miracle in the thirteenth or fourteenth century.

The story goes that a pilgrim from Galicia was suspected of a local murder, arrested and condemned to death. The verdict was announced in the banqueting hall where his judges were about to start eating. Before he could be dragged away the pilgrim pointed to a roast fowl on the table and announced confidently 'As surely as I stand innocent, so will that cock crow when I am hanged'. Everybody fell about laughing but as the rope was put round his neck the cockerel rose to its feet and crowed. The pilgrim was released immediately and Portugal adopted a stylised version of the bird in brilliantly coloured plumage as its national emblem.

Shopping for bargains at the market in Barcelos

An interesting carved window at the Casa Dos Coimbras, Braga

The legend does have its counterpart elsewhere, but not with a Cross of the Gentleman of the Cock to give added weight to it.

Barcelos is particularly well-known for its pottery, quite apart from the cock, which can be seen in the craft centre at the tourist office and bought in any number of shops in the Rua Antonio Barroso, a pedestrian walkway in the town centre. Many of the little ceramic figures owe their existence to Rosa Ramalho who started producing them as a young girl, basing them on religious events, local characters and popular legends. Although she died some time ago the hobby attracted other potters who have turned it into a profitable cottage industry. Among the hotels on offer are the Albergaria Condes De Barcelos and the less expensive Pensão Bagoeira.

The road to Braga is pleasant without being in any way exceptional. The terraced vines on either side enclose small patches of maize and little vegetable gardens while the houses are often encased in roses and hydrangeas. Women sit gossiping on the grass verges with fresh produce piled up at their feet, children and dogs chase each other along the roadside and are shouted at for their pains by young motorcyclists who, unlike their Spanish counterparts, usually wear their helmets instead of carrying them.

Braga would be a fascinating town wherever it was situated but surrounded by orchards, pastures and vineyards it is memorable, not so much for the scenery as for the atmosphere. The modern suburbs tend to bustle, making bricks and textiles, soap and leather goods while craftsmen display examples of their work at the market every Tuesday. The Avenida da Liberdade is lined with shops and supermarkets, within easy reach of all the main hotels and close to the heart of the ancient city.

After it had been recaptured from the Moors Braga became an important ecclesiastical centre whose archbishop, Dom Diego de Sousa, peppered it with sixteenth-century buildings and spent a great deal of time and money on enlarging the cathedral. Nothing very much remains of the original church, founded in 1070, apart from a twelfth-century doorway opening on to the Rua Dom Paio Mendes and a few early treasures in the Museum of Sacred Art.

The eastern end of the cathedral owes its pinnacled silhouette to de Sousa who is said to have commissioned the sculptor Nicolas Chanterene to contribute the lovely statue of Nossa Senhora do Leite under its flamboyant canopy. The interior is just as impressive, successfully blending a number of different styles together, from the fifteenth-century bronze tomb of the Infante Dom Afonso near the south door to a pair of ornate Baroque organs. At the far end of the nave the Chapel of the Holy Sacrament has an altar inspired by Rubens, while another close by is decorated with tiles depicting the life of São Pedro de Rates, the first bishop of Braga.

The Capela dos Reis, leading off the cloister, contains the tombs of Henri of Burgundy and his wife Teresa who founded the cathedral and whose son was the first king of Portugal, as well as the remains of Archbishop

Lourenço Vicente, a survivor of the battle of Aljubarrota in 1385. St Catherine's Chapel, diagonally opposite, has a collection of not very inspiring votive offerings whereas the adjacent chapterhouse is crammed with treasures, some of them desperately in need of expert attention. Among the items on display are illustrated manuscripts, church vestments, an ivory Mozarabic chest from the tenth century and a chalice thought to have been used at the baptism of Afonso Henriques. Gaspar do Bragança's silver-gilt monstrance sprinkled with diamonds usually comes in for more attention than a simple cross that travelled with Pedro Álvares Cabral on his voyage of discovery to Brazil in 1500 and was used during the first mass to be celebrated there.

The former episcopal palace, near the cathedral, has its own collection of books and manuscripts, some dating back to the ninth century, and looks out over the small formal gardens of Santa Bárbara. Other local attractions within easy walking distance are the Moorish-looking House of Screens, or Casa das Gelosias, on the Rua São Marcos, the Baroque Church of Santa Cruz a block or so further on and the nearby Raio palace with its granite casements and eye-catching blue tiles. The Fonte do Idolo, a short flight of steps away, is a Roman relic from the first century AD and dedicated to the god Tongo Nabiacus, one of the more obscure pagan deities who obviously had at least one follower among the ancient citizens of Bracara Augusta.

The Pelican fountain in front of the town hall is a great deal more elaborate, due in part to its bronze cupids who have been keeping the bird company for something like two hundred years. Another of its neighbours is the Casa dos Biscainhos which was a private residence until 1963, when it was sold and transformed into a museum. The exhibits include a little of almost everything to do with the city, starting from a discarded Roman helmet and working their way up through a painting of Braga in the sixteenth century to a collection of porcelain in the old music room. The furniture is pleasant without being very memorable but there are a few nice pieces of glass and some attractive jewellery and decorative fans. The Museu Nogueira da Silva on the Avenida Central tends to be curious rather than informative. It contains a good deal of elaborate furniture, not all of which is genuine, porcelain and silver, odd flights of fancy in the garden and a likeness of Dr Salazar in the hall.

The centre of Braga is a good place to wander round, especially as it can spring one or two modest surprises in the form of a small church or an occasional fountain but, strangely enough, there are hardly any little winding alleys or forgotton corners to explore. Not unnaturally the city's most important celebrations all have an intensely religious flavour. During Holy Week barefoot pilgrims carrying burning torches parade through the decorated streets while Easter Sunday brings out the crowds, many of them in national costumes, to join in the festivities. On the last Sunday in May there is a colourful pilgrimage to the modern sanctuary on Monte Sameiro away to the east, followed by the three-day Festas de São

João beginning on 23 June. This is essentially a time for rejoicing with parades and fireworks to mark the birth of St John the Baptist, processions that include everyone from King David onwards, massed flowers, brilliant illuminations and folklore in all its many guises.

Visitors who want to spend some time in the Braga area, but would rather find somewhere to stay outside the town, would probably discover what they are looking for in the Parque do Bom Jesus do Monte, 6km (4 miles) to the east, off the N103. The Hotel do Elveador has a certain old-fashioned elegance and a beautiful view while its opposite number, the Hotel do Parque, is larger but does not have a restaurant at the moment. They share a densely wooded hillside with the pilgrim church of Bom Jesus, which should certainly not be missed. The site is reached along a road full of hairpin bends through forests of oak and eucalyptus, mimosa and camelias with a small lake that is completely hidden from view. There is also a funicular for anyone on foot who cannot face an additional climb of 116m (381ft).

The church of **Bom Jesus do Monte** with its matching belltowers and attractive, uncluttered façade was built in the early eighteenth century on the site of a medieval sanctuary. It is rather dull inside with nothing to pinpoint other than the shrine of St Clement and a large ivory cross in the sacristy, which is probably just as well because the vast and amazingly ornate stairway more than makes up for it. This Holy Way, as it is called, consists of an interminable series of shallow terraces with zigzag walkways clambering up on either side between little round chapels marking the Stations of the Cross, fountains, statues and solid balustrades. Each chapel has a scene from the Passion with life-size figures that are disturbingly realistic.

The stairs, set out in a fairly conventional manner from a paved area at the bottom, lead up to the double Stairway of the Five Senses which is intricately designed and richly decorated. Above this is the Stairway of the Three Virtues — namely Faith, Hope and Charity — beyond which are immaculate flowerbeds, trees and even more paving stones and statues. Some devout pilgrims still follow this Way of the Cross on their knees, a few sightseers walk up, with frequent pauses to admire their surroundings and the view, while less energetic visitors are inclined to opt for the funicular up to the church and then work their way down to their cars and coaches parked behind one of the small chapels at the bottom.

The area round Braga is particularly rich in sanctuaries and pre-historic settlements. In addition to the fairly modern pilgrim church on the summit of Monte Sameiro, to the south of Bom Jesus do Monte, there is the extremely extrovert Church of St Mary Magdalena on the Serra da Falperra, a trifle to the southeast, and the São Frutuoso de Montelios Chapel off the N201 to the north. This is reputed to have started life in the seventh century, been destroyed by the Moors and then reconstructed by the returning Christians nearly one thousand years ago. Although it is not by any means in mint condition the small building is an interesting

Carved stone details to be seen in Braga

The church of Bom Jesus de Monte

example of Portuguese Byzantine art while the attendant Church of São Francisco was given its Renaissance choir stalls by the cathedral in Braga.

Citânia de Briteiros is by far the most explicit of all the ancient settlements. It was founded in about eight hundred BC and occupied by a large community for at least four hundred years. The foundations of what must have been an impressive Celtic-Iberian town straggle up the hillside, protected by two fortifying walls with clearly defined streets, enclosures for animals on the outskirts and a water system that included a cistern and a public fountain for use by the inhabitants of something like one hundred and fifty little houses. Some of the constructions have not been finally identified, such as a funeral chamber which might in fact have been the public baths and a tunnel leading down from the hilltop to the Rio Ave below.

The site was excavated in 1875 by Dr Martins Sarmento who transferred all the items unearthed in the town, such as stone axes, jewellery and pottery, to the archaeological museum in Guimarães which is named after him. When the initial work was completed two typical little houses were reconstructed on the site to give some idea of how people appear to have lived in prehistoric times. Most of the dwellings would have been circular with stone benches running round the walls, although the grander houses may have had two or more rectangular rooms. They were built of large stones fitted together like jigsaw puzzles with a pole in the middle to support the thatched roof. The nearby settlement of Castro de Sabroso, almost within waving distance, is smaller, older and not so well organised for visitors.

It is barely worth contemplating a visit to **Caldelas**, due north of Bom Jesus, unless it is in order to take the waters, which are said to be beneficial for various skin complaints and upset stomachs. The Romans were the first to discover their medicinal qualities but if they built any baths in the vicinity there is certainly no trace of them nowadays. The hotels are entirely predictable and it is possible to play tennis, swim or go fishing, which all adds up to a relaxing holiday, if hardly a very exciting one. On the other hand it is not all that far along the N103 from Bom Jesus to the Pousada de São Bento at Caniçada. This is quite small, built on the lines of an Alpine chalet up in the mountains overlooking a large dam, with a pleasant terrace and a memorable view. There is a tennis court and a swimming pool in the grounds and opportunities for riding and sailing in the immediate area. It is also only a whisker away from the southern entrance to the **Peneda-Gerês National Park**.

The park was established about twenty years ago, covering some 70,000 hectares (178,000 acres) between the upper reaches of the Rio Minho in the north and the Rio Cávado which rises in the highlands of Trás-os-Montes, skirts round Braga and joins the Atlantic at Esposende. It is a region of wooded mountains and deep valleys, shaped rather like a chunky art nouveau necklace draped round a slender throat that belongs to Spain. The intention was to protect everything in the area, both natural and manmade, ranging from its forests of oak, birch, yews and pines to prehistoric dolmens, Roman milestones, occasional Christian ruins and one or two small deserted villages. There are holly trees and bilberry bushes, ferns and lilies, irises in the valleys and heather on the mountain tops. The wild life consists mainly of deer and wild Luso-Galician ponies, a few wolves and a variety of small game as well as golden eagles, owls, hawks and buzzards, with a sprinkling of vipers and grass snakes for good measure.

Caldas do Gerês, just inside the park, is a slightly old fashioned spa which claims to have been founded in 1699 but only really developed its full potential in the middle of the eighteenth century. It has the requisite number of hotels and pensions, none of any particular moment, although it is ideally placed for anyone who wants to explore the area and take advantage of its many facilities. The lovely artificial lakes, especially those created by the barrages of Caniçada, Salamonde and Paradela, are excellent for fishing and water sports. There are trout streams for enthusiastic anglers and rocky terrain well suited to mountain climbing, horses are available for pony trekking in the backwoods and specially designated areas are set aside for a limited amount of shooting, but only under licence.

Above all the Peneda-Gerês National Park is a walker's paradise — or it will be when the authorities get round to producing reliable maps showing the various unmarked paths and cart tracks, most of which find their way without the help of signposts between the little isolated settlements. Some maps are available from the tourist office in Caldas do Gerês but they are really rather sketchy and should be treated with a certain amount of suspicion. There are some roads, most of them better suited to four-wheel drive vehicles, one of the most acceptable in the southern region being the N308 through Caldas do Gerês to the border. It is here, in the vicinity of the Rio Homem, that it is possible to see the remains of the old Roman road from Braga and some of its original milestones.

It is impossible to get from the southern half of the park into the northern section without returning along the same route, or crossing briefly into Spain and joining up with the N203 which re-enters Portugal via Lindoso, although this is still on the south bank of the Rio Lima which cuts the region neatly in half. It is also as well to remember that both the border posts concerned are only open during the season. However with time to spare it makes an enjoyable outing, with one or two places to visit en route. **Lindoso** has a castle built in the thirteenth century which was modernised and updated at intervals thereafter to discourage any would-be invaders planning an attack from the far side of the river. The village consists of granite houses rising in tiers up the mountainside, surrounded by terraces planted with maize and vines. A group of fifty or more granite *espigueiros* are huddled together on a rocky site below the castle walls, topped by crosses that make them look more like a cemetery than a place for storing grain. On closer inspection they turn out to be odd little slatted granaries, perched on stilts to keep the harvest out of reach of hungry rats.

A very minor road a few kilometres beyond Lindoso crosses the Lima

*The unusual stone
granaries found in this
area of Portual*

*Washday on the riverside
at Ponte de Lima*

to visit **Soajo**, an elderly village in the middle of nowhere with a collection of *espigueiros*, a pillory and its own entrance to the park that does not seem to lead anywhere in particular. The village has two back ways across country to the N101, but it is a good deal easier to continue on along the south bank of the river to **Ponte da Barca**. Although hardly big enough to be called a town, it has an attractive fifteenth century bridge, a characteristically self-important manor house, the Paço Vedro, that takes paying guests and ample space to camp beside the water. However, this does look as if it might get unpleasantly damp during the rainy season.

It is at this point that motorists have to decide whether to visit Bravães before heading northwards to inspect the upper section of the Parque Nacional da Peneda-Gerês, or ignore the area altogether and press on to the coast. As **Bravães** is only slightly out of the way the time it takes would be well spent for anyone interested in ancient buildings. The village is noted for its twelfth-century church of São Salvador, one of the most outstanding Romanesque examples in the country. The main doorway consists of five arches, elaborately decorated with birds, animals and unidentified human forms below a figure of Christ in Majesty. Inside there are a number of frescoes and a slight indication of a Moorish influence.

Arcos de Valdevez, due north of Ponte da Barca, is an atmospheric little place nestling in a bend of the Rio Vez with a splendid old bridge, an eighteenth-century church, an island park and a clutch of inexpensive pensions. From here the N101 presses on to **Monção**, a riverside hamlet on the Rio Minho that masquerades as a spa but could certainly not claim to be tourist orientated. It is known principally as the home of Alvarinho *vinho verde*, the first wine to be exported from Portugal more than five hundred years ago, and for its bread rolls called *Deu-la-Deu*. They are named after the wife of a local mayor who, during a siege in 1368, used the last of the flour to make a batch which she sent out to the attacking forces, assuring them that the townspeople had plenty left over for their own requirements. The enemy took this at its face value and went home to Spain, leaving the lady to become part of military history and the town's coat-of-arms. Monção has two small, mildly attractive churches, the sparse overgrown remnants of its ancient fortress and the Albergaria Atlântico for anyone who plans to spend the night there.

From Monção a rather questionable secondary road follows the Rio Minho along the pleasant valley to **Melgaço**, side stepping now and again to visit one of the nearby hamlets such as Longos Vales with its twelfth-century church. For its part Melgaço has retained some of its ancient fortifications, an understated old church and vivid memories of a siege that was decided by two women champions fighting singlehanded for possession of the stronghold. This took place in the late fourteenth century, when a Spanish female warrior challenged her Portuguese opposite number to a duel, was soundly beaten and forced to surrender along with her supporting army.

Melgaço is only some 10km from the frontier and roughly twice as far from the northern entrance to the Parque Nacional da Peneda-Gerês on the N202, which finds its way eventually to **Castro Laboreiro**, nicely situated up in the mountains beside a small river. It has its own ruined castle, a number of houses built by returning ex-patriots but no facilities for visitors, who stand a good chance of getting lost if they stray too far from the water. A very minor road continues on to the border, where the customs post keeps restricted hours, and joins up with the route that makes for Lindoso on the Rio Lima.

It is a good deal easier and less demanding to drive back to Moncão and continue westwards along the Rio Minho. Here the road winds charmingly down the valley, bordered by pine trees, palms and climbing vines, small cultivated fields and little farmhouses, with a turning off to Monte do Faro, just short of Valença do Minho. There are some very worthwhile views up to the summit which, on a clear day, looks out over the ocean and the green hills of Galicia. A minor road on the outskirts of the town joins up after a few kilometres with the N201, a scenic route through one or two small villages to Ponte de Lima. This, for anyone who choses not to visit the northern section of the park, is only 18km (11 miles) from Ponte da Barca and obviously slightly less from Bravães.

Ponte de Lima is somewhat bigger than expected as befits a busy road junction whose narrow bridge with its variegated arches was once part of the ancient road to Rome. In those days the town was known as *Forum Limicorum* and was totally surrounded by massive stone walls lined with houses on either side. Most of them were demolished at various times in the name of progress and part of the only remaining watchtower has been appropriated by the Biblioteca Publica Municipal. This was founded in 1722 as a permanent home for the archives including the Royal Charter granted to the town by Dona Teresa on 4 March 1125 and confirmed nearly a century later by Afonso II. The old books and scrolls made of thick parchment with Latin and ancient Portuguese lettering are in a good state of preservation and can be seen at the discretion of the librarian. The Igreja Matriz, a stone's throw from the river, was founded in the fifteenth century but renovated three hundred years later and provided with a variety of statues, while its opposite number is home to a small museum. The Pensão São João is about the only place to stay in town but several private homes take in paying guests. Some are rather cheerless, others provide separate accommodation that may be either seedy or quite satisfactory, while the Paço de Calheiros, run by its aristocratic owner, is admirable in every respect.

Ponte de Lima is slightly more than 32km (20 miles) from Braga, marginally closer to Barcelos and only 23km (13 miles) from Viana do Castelo. From here it is a pleasant shortish drive down the coast to **Esposende**, an old fishing port on the northern bank of the Cávado river estuary. The village has both Roman and medieval associations, some elderly buildings including the Chapel of Our Lord of the Navigators, a brace of hotels and a tractor that pulls open carriage loads of tourists backwards and forwards to the nearby beaches. Apart from this it makes very few concessions to visitors, leaving all that sort of thing to **Ofir** on the opposite side of the river.

The beach in this area is wide and sandy, pleasantly under-developed and seldom overcrowded. The large modern Hotel de Ofir on the foreshore has swimming pools, tennis courts and a discotheque while the somewhat smaller Estalagem Parque do Rio, surrounded by pine trees and overlooking the river, is more restrained but offers its guests much the same amenities. Sightseers can visit the little village of Fão, said to have been in existence at the same time as the Roman camp at Belinho, or inspect the sparse remains of Banho monastery, but these attractions fade into insignificence beside the wide variety of sports facilities available. These include boating and sailing, water skiing and wind surfing, fishing for bass near the old Bilhano quay and underwater exploring round the White Horse Rocks at the mouth of the estuary. An ancient legend has it that they got their name after a fleet of ships belonging to King Solomon was driven ashore during a gale. They were carrying horses from the royal stables to be exchanged for gold from Eldorado do Ofir which was being used in the building of his magnificent temple. The gods took pity on the animals struggling in mountainous seas and decided to turn them into stone, to be known thereafter as the Horses of Fão. Be that as it may, there is no connection with the present-day ponies that can be hired for a short trip out into the country. Plans are under way for a golf course near the Hotel de Ofir to compliment the existing 10-pin bowling alley.

Those taking an invigorating early morning stroll along the shore stands a good chance of seeing the *sargaceiros* at work. They are men dressed in white garments reminiscent of Roman togas who use large wooden rakes and nets to gather up seaweed to make fertilisers, just as their forefathers have been doing for hundreds of years. These piles of drying seaweed, like small, round thatched huts, can be seen at various places along the coast, to which A Ver-o-Mar adds its own unique form of agriculture. A series of large sand dunes have been hollowed out and vines planted round the inside edges to prevent them caving in and to provide their owners with a very respectable grape harvest. The flat, moist ground in the middle is turned into sunken market gardens where crops of vegetables like potatoes and cabbage do remarkably well in what would appear to be very unfavourable conditions.

Póvoa de Varzim is a large fishing port, more than somewhat over-blessed with highrise buildings and recreational attractions such as a football stadium and a roller skating rink. It has an unexpectedly attractive pink casino which also plays bingo, a somewhat dilapidated bullring and a handful of totally predictable hotels, restaurants, pubs and discotheques. This is a good place to shop for heavy fishermen's sweaters, filigree articles, pottery and basketwork but has nothing of interest to sightseers with the exception of the weekday fish market, when the catch unloaded by the men is handed over to the women who conduct the auction.

The port's nearest neighbour is **Vila do Conde**, a delightful little place that specialises in making lace. It became so expert in this art that a school, the Escola de Rendas, was opened in 1909 which is very happy to receive visitors at its premises on the Rua do Lidador. Ship-building is another local industry which has persisted since the Age of Discovery. Wooden fishing boats are still produced with tools that are very similar to the ones that were used originally and the yard is open to anyone who is sufficiently interested to call in there during working hours.

The sixteenth-century Socorro Chapel above the shipyard was an Arab mosque before a cross was added to mark its conversion to Christianity, but the Igreja Matriz is more orthodox. It has a carved stone doorway, a disproportionately large belltower and arches inside that are under constant attack from marauding dragons. The Convent of Santa Clara was reconstructed in the eighteenth century but its much older chapel still contains the tombs of Afonso Sanches and his family which were broken into by French troops in search of treasure during the Peninsular War. Fortunately the damage was not too extensive and they can be inspected by enquiring at the school which now occupies the building.

Vila do Conde has nothing very exciting in the way of hotels but there are one or two acceptable restaurants, a motel on the far side of the river and the three-star Parque de Campismo e Caravanismo Rio Alto/Sopete which it shares with Póvoa de Varzim. The town celebrates the Festival of Corpus Christi once every four years when the streets are carpeted with flowers, holds a Procession of Lacemakers annually and observes the Festas de São João at the same time as Oporto. Holidaymakers who feel like a change from the daily cocktail of sea, sun and sand can spend a pleasant day visiting three small towns quite close by. **Rio Mau**, on the N206, is the proud possessor of a small Romanesque church dedicated to St Christopher while **Rates** is well known for its granite church of São Pedro, built in the late twelfth century by Benedictine monks from Cluny on the orders of Henri of Burgundy. It is a bit short on statues but has a multi-arched doorway, a rose window and decorative capitals. Meanwhile **Santo Tirso**, further south and some 24km (15 miles) from Vila do Conde, is the site of the Convento de São Bento, founded in the eighth century, reconstructed five hundred years later and remodelled at leisure sometime after 1659. Having got this far it would be a pity not to drive on to Guimarães and, perhaps, spend the night at the Pousada da Santa Maria da Oliveira in the centre of the town.

Guimarães has never been able to forget completely that it was the first capital of Portugal and still has a castle, one or two small churches and some atmospheric medieval streets to remind it of those far off days. With the passage of time it has expanded to provide space for a number of light industries such as textiles, tanning and the manufacture of kitchenware in addition to the traditional workshops belonging to gold and silversmiths.

*Copper and brass
wares are popular
souvenirs at Esposende*

*The Duke of
Bragança's Palace at
Guimarães*

The town still produces its own special type of linen, and just as in bygone times the flax is grown locally, beaten with wooden slats to make it pliable, bleached in the sun without the aid of chemicals, spun and then woven by hand. The finished articles may be intricately patterned or beautifully embroidered, usually by women working at home. One of the best places to see, and buy, them is the Casa dos Linhos, a long-established linen house in the Alameda de Resistencia opposite the tourist office.

The oldest building in Guimarães is the tenth-century castle, consisting of several towers enclosing a central keep that rises out of the rock on top of a small green hill. It was considerably modernised and strengthened by Henri of Burgundy shortly before the birth of his son Afonso Henriques in 1110 or thereabouts. Unfortunately the castle was vandalised in the nineteenth century and despite having been carefully restored there is nothing of interest to see inside, although it still has an excellent view over the town towards Mount Penha to the south. Beyond the castle walls is the small Romanesque church of São Miguel do Castelo containing a number of ancient tombstones and the font where the future king of Portugal is said to have been baptized.

On the far side of the adjoining lawn is the Paço dos Duques, a palace built by the first Duke of Bragança in the early fifteenth century, abandoned shortly afterwards and later restored almost out of recognition to serve as an official residence and then as a museum. The building is large and fairly conventional with towers and battlements, a centre courtyard and a forest of chimneys, all guarded by a regal statue of Afonso Henriques in a very militant mood. The two main rooms, one of which is the banqueting hall, have eye-catching ceilings and a noteworthy collection of French and Flemish tapestries. Other exhibits include Persian carpets, Portuguese furniture and Chinese porcelain as well as paintings and sculptures, a variety of weapons and old suits of armour.

The Martins Sarmento Museum, which takes its name from the nineteenth-century archaeologist, is predictably full of discoveries he made while excavating the ancient Celtic settlements of *Citânia de Briteiros* and Castro de Sabroso in the hills to the east of Braga. It overflows into the cloister of the Monastery of São Domingos which houses many of the larger exhibits. The Museu de Alberto Sampaio, occupying the medieval cloister of Nossa Senhora da Oliveira, is larger and less specialised, dividing its attention between paintings, ceramics and items of sacred art. Among the most outstanding is a silver-gilt triptych reputed to have been captured by João I from his Castilian opposite number at the battle of Aljubarrota. Also on view are some rather splendid pieces of church plate, a gilded altarpiece, various statues and an old sarcophagus.

The original Igreja Nossa Senhora de Oliveira disappeared many centuries ago, to be replaced by a succession of churches overlooking the Largo da Oliveira with its little free-standing porch that is said to mark the place where there was once a miraculous olive tree. Among the many different versions of the story, the earliest involving Wamba — the seventh-century king of the Visigoths who only accepted the job after a dead branch he thrust into the ground started sprouting — is the most unlikely. Another is the belief that a local merchant called Pearo Esteves brought back a stone cross from Normandy and placed it near a dead tree which immediately burst into life. However the tree succumbed eventually and was replaced by the original cross under its stone canopy.

The Rua de Santa Maria, leading out of the Olive Tree Square, is one of the most atmospheric streets in Guimarães with its well-worn paving stones, elderly arches and houses sporting a variety of carved wood or wrought iron balconies. These can also be seen to good effect in the Largo do Toural, peering out through large windows at its central fountain and wavy two-tone mosaic pavement. Of the several small churches dotted about the old quarter the most memorable is probably the Igreja São Francisco, roughly two blocks from the tourist office, recalling the life of St Francis on the main portal but switching its attention to St Antony inside by means of a series of tiles added to its Baroque altar in the chancel.

In addition to the Pousada da Nossa Senhora da Oliveira and the highrise Hotel Fundador Dom Pedro which has a sauna, a gymnasium, parking facilities and a rooftop bar but no restaurant, there are a few totally forgettable hotels in Guimarães and the Pousada de Santa Marinha da Costa on the slopes of Mount Penha 2.5km ($1^1/_2$ miles) away. It occupies a twelfth-century monastery, surrounds its guests with antiques and offers them small bedrooms converted from the original cells. The town makes little or no attempt to entertain its visitors but the Parque de Campismo Municipal da Penha, although not in the top bracket, has all the basic necessities as well as a swimming pool.

There are several good reasons for visiting **Amarante**, less than 40km (25 miles) southwest of Guimarães. In the first place it makes a pleasant drive through Trofa, a small village where it is sometimes possible to buy attractive souvenirs from the lacemakers hard at work along the roadside. Secondly it is a very picturesque little town full of typical old buildings and thirdly it provides an excellent opportunity for taking a short train ride up to Arco de Baúlhe and back on a delightfully atmospheric narrow-gauge railway.

Amarante has occupied its present site on the Rio Tâmega since 360BC but adopted its present name a good deal later when it took a liking to the Roman governor Amarantus. However this is the only remaining link with the Romans because the town is quite unable to produce anything tangible that was in existence more than five hundred years ago. Even the hermitage of São Gonçalo, who took up residence beside the river in the thirteenth century, has completely disappeared although he is buried in the monastery church that replaced it and was, naturally, named after him.

The river runs through the centre of the town, spanned by a 200-year-old bridge that successfully delayed part of Napoleon's advancing army during the Peninsular War. On one bank elderly houses rise up from the

Traditional costumes are nowadays usually reserved for special occasions

The bridge over the Rio Tâmega at Amarante

water's edge as eddies circle constantly under their overhanging wooden balconies while on the other cars jockey for position at an intersection outside the church. São Gonçalo stands guard with other statues over the nearby Renaissance doorway, looking in slightly better fettle than the effigy on his tomb in a special chapel leading off the chancel. He was designated patron saint of marriages and so many eager hands have been laid on him, asking for his blessing, that part of the carved figure has been badly worn away. The sixteenth-century interior of the church was given a facelift about two hundred years ago but still has its earlier organ front supported by three stalwart figures as well as some attractive carved and gilded woodwork and a Chapel of Miracles which makes a fitting home for votive offerings.

The Albano Sardoeira Museum, upstairs in the monastery cloister which is shared by the town hall, should appeal to anyone interested in modern art and particularly the work of Amadeo de Souza-Cardoso. He was born locally, spent some time in Paris at the beginning of this century, was influenced by Cézanne, formed a close friendship with Modigliani and ran the gamut from Cubism to Expressionism before his death in 1918. With the exception of the eighteenth-century Igreja São Pedro, which has a Baroque façade, a decorative altar and a fine panelled ceiling, the only other local attraction is the Tâmega railway. This is a single-carriage affair that edges its way upstream, stops at the sight of a red flag, keeps a sharp eye open for people and animals on the track, but finds nothing of interest in Arco de Baúlhe so turns round and trundles back again. There is no obvious reason why passengers in need of a little exercise should not get off at one of the unidentified stopping points, explore the valley and hope to find some empty seats for the return journey.

Amarante boasts a clutch of very acceptable hotels in addition to the Pousada de São Gonçano up in the hills on the way to Vila Real and a municipal campsite that has a cafeteria, a modest shop and facilities for swimming, boating and fishing. The town is well known for its sweetmeats, which are certainly on the sugary side, the Romaria de São Gonçalo in early June and its midnight picnics in summer near the bridge with traditional entertainments and food to match. There are two places of interest in the vicinity, both of them accessible from the main road to Oporto. **Travanca**, only 11km (7 miles) away, has a twelfth-century granite church that was once part of a Benedictine monastery. It has some very viewable stone carvings and a fortress tower, but the monastery itself has been turned into a refuge for people who have fallen on hard times.

Paço de Souse, roughly half way to Oporto, also owes its existence to the Benedictine Order but it has a much larger church containing the tomb of Egas Moniz who was tutor to Afonso Henriques. When the prince and his small band of followers were attacked by the King of Léon in 1127 Moniz was sent from the fortress at Guimarães to try to arrange a truce. As a result it was agreed that the Spaniards would withdraw and the prince would, for his part, recognise the king's claim to Portugal. Three years later Afonso Henriques, with an army at his disposal, conveniently forgot his promise and staged another revolt. Moniz considered this to be treason and travelled as a penitant to the Spanish court in Toledo where he offered himself as a hostage and fully expected to be executed. Instead the king was so impressed by this gesture that he was given a free pardon. The story of the event is carved on one side of the tomb with his subsequent funeral on the other.

A minor road from Paço de Sousa rejoins the main highway into Oporto while another strikes out across country to the little spa of Entre-os-Rios, where the Tâmega joins the Rio Douro and accompanies it on the last stage of its journey to the sea. There is no doubt that the upper reaches are far more attractive than the final stretch which is comparatively flat but less prone to flooding since its waters were harnessed to the country's increasingly efficient hydro-electric system.

It is very difficult to decide which is the correct name for the adjacent city, the largest in the country after Lisbon and a centre to be reckoned with since medieval times. The Portuguese call it *Porto* and pretend not to notice when visitors add the initial 'O'. Conversely many maps and official brochures come down on the side of **Oporto**, which most people find much easier to recognise. The whole problem goes back at least to the days of the Romans when there were two towns overlooking the estuary — *Portus*, or simply The Harbour, on the north bank and *Cale* opposite. Together they gave their name to the region known as Portucale, which was part of the dowry of Teresa of Léon when she married Henri of Burgundy.

The English have had a toehold in Oporto since the very early days. Crusaders on their way to the Holy Land stopped off there to do battle with the Moors; Philippa of Lancaster, the daughter of John of Gaunt, married João I in the cathedral and port wine was exported to Britain by British companies both before and after Wellington recaptured the city from Napoleon's forces in 1809. Most of the port wine lodges are in Vila Nova de Gaia on the southern bank of the estuary and positively encourage passers-by to visit the premises, try a glass and, hopefully, buy a bottle or more to take away with them.

Like any other large city Oporto has its fair share of suburbs, some of them decorated with private villas and apartments, others purely industrial whose factories produce tyres and textiles, canned food and ceramics. They have to be crossed by travellers flying in to Pedras Rubras international airport on the northern outskirts, arriving by train at one of the three railway stations or driving in along any of the six major routes converging on the centre from as many different directions. Much of the old city can be explored on foot by anyone who has had the foresight to pack a pair of sensible walking shoes. The area is not very extensive but it is hilly with quite a few narrow, cobbled streets, mosaic pavements and steep alleys fringed with old houses, wrought iron balconies and laundry lines, as well as its wide thoroughfares. Less energetic sightseers can catch a bus, take a taxi or join one of the Cruzeiro das Tres Pontes motor launches for a trip along the river. Cars can also be hired in the city but parking is difficult, traffic moves at a rapid pace and the one-way system is daunting.

Oporto has twelve listed museums and just as many, if not more, historic buildings, monuments and churches in addition to a number of pleasant gardens and scenic vantage points. The last of these include two of the three bridges spanning the Rio Douro — the reinforced concrete Ponte da Arrabida that carries the motorway which will eventually run right down the country and the two-tiered Ponte Dom Luís I, built of iron like the nearby Ponte de Dona Maria railway bridge designed by Gerard Eiffel. The lower level links the old river frontage on the north bank with the port lodges of Vila Nova de Gaia opposite, while the top one connects the upper hillsides on either hand.

The best place to begin a sightseeing tour of Oporto is probably the cathedral, nicely situated on the Terreiro de Sé with an excellent view from the stone terrace in front over the old Ribeira quarter and along the river. It started life as a fortress church in the twelfth century and still has its original rose window, although the Baroque doorway was added much later. The interior was altered quite considerably in the eighteenth century but nevertheless does little to detract from the superb altarpiece in the Chapel of the Holy Sacrament. This was made by leading Portuguese silversmiths in the seventeenth century, whereas the bronze relief of the baptism of Christ in the sacristy is only a little over a hundred years old. The Gothic cloister is the same age as the nation itself but was refurbished at the same time as the rest of the cathedral and partly lined with tiles illustrating Ovid's *Metamorphoses* and the life of the Virgin. Also facing the Terreiro da Sé is the domineering episcopal palace which has now been converted into offices.

Behind the cathedral, on the opposite side of the Avenida Vimara Peres, leading to the Ponte Dom Luís I, the church of Santa Clara is amazingly ornate. The medieval building was completely transformed when money became no object as treasures poured in from Brazil, and every centimetre of the nave and the chancel, as well as the altars, is elaborately carved and gilded. However even this takes second place to the Igreja São Francisco on the Praça Infante Dom Henrique almost overlooking the river a short walk away. It is an incredible sight; the pillars, walls and vaulted ceilings are obscured by a concentrated mass of acanthus leaves, laurels and stylised vines, each with their attendant birds and cherubs and saturated in gold. The high altar is impressively Baroque in keeping with its surroundings but the rose window is original and so is the granite statue of St Francis who has a chapel to himself. The Twelve Kings of Judah have their allotted places on the Tree of Jesse in a chapel on the left.

After such an indigestible feast of riches the Palácio da Bolsa — the Stock Exchange — just next door comes as something of an anticlimax. It was built in the nineteenth century on the site of an ancient monastery and provided with a Moorish Grand Hall inspired by the Alhambra in Granada. Other places to visit in the vicinity include the Casa do Infante, where Henry the Navigator is said to have been born in 1394, the Ferreira Borges Market and the Igreja de Misericórdia in the Rua das Flores, topped with a royal crown. Its prize possession is a religious painting by an unknown artist which includes Manuel I and his whole family and can be seen in the offices next door.

The Museum of Ethnology on the Largo de São João Nova at the far end of the Rua Belmonte is fascinating because nothing is too commonplace or too bizarre to escape its attention. There are Roman mosaics and an early twentieth-century elevator, toys and traditional costumes, wine jars, looms for weaving linen and necklaces made from human hair. Other

A roofscape view of Oporto

Gardens near the Praça da Liberdade and the town hall, Oporto

The two-tiered road bridge, Ponte Dom Luis I, at Oporto, with traditional boats moored off the wine lodges at Vila Nova de Gaia

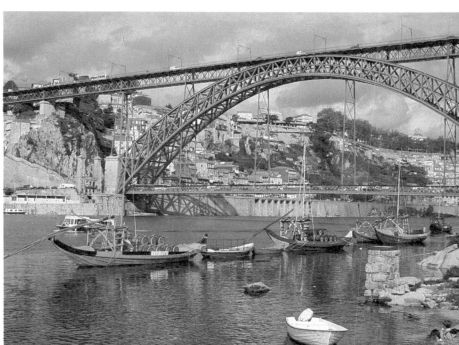

exhibits range from the decorated yokes worn by oxen to furniture, ceramics and items of sacred art. However the Soares dos Reis Museum on the Rua de Dom Manuel II, beyond the Hospital de Sto António, is both larger and more important. It is housed in the Carrancas Palace, built by a wealthy Jewish family at the end of the eighteenth century, occupied briefly by the French during the Peninsular War and later by Wellington who is said to have flushed out Marshal Soult and then eaten the dinner that had been prepared for him.

The museum was named after the sculptor Soares dos Reis and contains several of his marble statues including the *Flor Agreste*, the head of a girl wood carrier which has spawned thousands of typical souvenirs. Not so frequently reproduced is *O Desterrado* — the Exile — and an unflattering likeness of the Count of Ferreira. There are several interesting paintings ranging from Oporto as it was in the late eighteenth century to portraits of Marguerite de Valois and Henri II of France. Also on display are some early Limoges enamels and other examples of sacred art, as well as furniture, ceramics and glass.

A little further along the Rua de Dom Manuel II, on the opposite side of the road, the Palácio de Cristal takes its name from a large glass-covered sports pavilion surrounded by lawns with a lake in the grounds. Nearby, on the Rua de Entre Quintas, the Quinta da Macieirinha Romantic Museum is full of personal effects left behind by Carlos Alberto, at one time King of Sardinia. Part of the building is occupied by the Solar do Vinho do Porto where it is possible to sample various types of port.

One of the most obvious landmarks in Oporto is the Clérigos Tower — at 75m (245ft) among the tallest in Portugal — which has a staircase up to the top with its panoramic view over the city and the Rio Douro. The Baroque church of the same name has a decorative façade and claims to be the first oval church to be constructed in the country. To the east, anyone waiting for a train from the Estaçao de São Bento can pass the time inspecting the picture tiles depicting historic events, methods of transport and glimpses of everyday life prior to 1930 when they were painted by Jorge Colaço.

The main shopping area in Oporto is just north of the station, nudging the Avenida dos Aliados, where the best things to look for are shoes, handmade lace and filigree jewellery, whereas handicrafts of all descriptions are obtainable from the Centre for Traditional Arts and Crafts in the Rua da Reboleira, between the Praça do Infante Dom Henrique and the river. Alternatively the Bolhão Market on the Rua de Sá da Bandeira is colourful and exuberant, brimming over with meat and fish, bread and cheese, flowers, fruit and vegetables.

Oporto's hotels and restaurants are scattered fairly indiscriminately throughout the city and its suburbs with a fair selection either in or close to the old quarter. For comfort in the grand manner the list is headed by the Hotel Infante de Sagres with two comparable but more modern establishments — Le Meridien Porto and the Porto Sheraton Hotel — a longish walk away. A less expensive choice would be the Hotel Corcel, which is agreeably central but a bit noisy and slightly run down. It has no restaurant whereas the Albergaria Miradouro charges a bit more but has an excellent one. Further down the list is the Hotel Malaposta, which has some rooms *en suite*, is cool and quiet with parking round the corner, but no restaurant. For anyone with a tent or a caravan the Parque de Campismo de Prelada is conveniently situated on the Rua do Monte dos Burgos just off the ring road, or via Estrada do Circunvalacao. It is a large, attractive site with trees and hedges, an ornamental lake, shops nearby and buses that run past the entrance.

There is no difficulty whatever in finding a restaurant to suit every individual taste and pocket. They range from the up-market and predictably expensive variety with international menus to little atmospheric establishments serving traditional dishes. The best known of these is *tripas à moda do Porto* a stew made from tripe with calves trotters, herbs and vegetables. It is said to have originated at the time of Henry the Navigator when the townspeople handed over all their meat to supply his ships for an attack on Ceuta and only kept the tripe for themselves. *Bacalhau* or salt cod, is eaten everywhere, the best introduction to it probably being the *bacalhau à Gomes de Sá*. However there are a few foreign restaurants, mainly Italian and Chinese.

Matosinhos, 8.5km (5 miles) up the coast from Oporto, makes a pleasant outing for anyone with time to spare. It is reached along the Avenida da Boavista which ends up in the shadow of the Castelo do Queijo, a fortress built in the seventeenth century to protect the city against pirates and enemy attacks. From here the route follows the shoreline, avoids the docks at Leixões, and finds its way into this modest coastal resort whose somewhat dingy back streets contain a number of good fish restaurants. The main reason for visiting Matosinhos is to see the decorative church of Bom Jesus with its ancient wooden figure of Christ, the focal point of an important pilgrimage that takes place every year at Whitsun. The image is said to have been one of five carved by Nicodemus and thrown into the sea off Judea. When it was washed up on the shores of Portugal the statue had lost an arm but nevertheless resisted every attempt to replace it. Later, according to the legend, an old woman collecting firewood on the beach threw one piece on to the flames but was unable to make it burn. The village elders matched it to the figure and found that it fitted perfectly. The statue is certainly complete and the place where the incident apparently took place is marked by a small chapel and the Cross of Senhor do Padrão.

Espinho, 18km (12 miles) south of Oporto, is the city's most popular holiday playground. It is laid out strictly on the grid system with every kind of sporting facility close to hand. Unfortunately the railway line runs through the resort, more or less parallel to its long sandy beaches, but this does not seem to concern any of its visitors. It has covered swimming pools as well as a large open-air one beside the sea, tennis courts, opportunities for riding and fishing and a casino that is open all the year round.

There is dining and dancing there every night but guests who are planning to gamble are advised to take their passports with them. Golfers have a choice between the 18-hole Oporto Golf Club, opened in 1890 and one of the oldest on the Continent, which has clubs for hire, and the Miramar Golf Club which has 9 holes and can provide trolleys on request. There are a number of hotels of various types, a good many restaurants and the Parque de Campismo da Solverde/Alvatur which provides everything necessary for an enjoyable camping holiday. Although the resort has nothing to offer in the way of historic buildings there is a half-hourly train service to Oporto and access to both the motorway and the N1 for motorists heading south to the Costa de Prata.

In due course a motorway will link Bragança with Oporto, joining the

Port wine maturing in bottles and casks

one already in existence down to Lisbon. In the meanwhile there are major roads from Valença do Minho to both Braga and Oporto, from Braga through Guimarães and Vila Real to the frontier, and from north of Amarante to the provincial capital. Part of the motorway, or *auto estrada*, has already been completed between Oporto and Braga. A network of provincial roads connects all the other towns and larger villages, augmented by local shortcuts which can sometimes be in urgent need of repairs.

Trains operate between Oporto and the surrounding regions as well as to Braga, Guimarães, Chaves and Bragança, although it is necessary to change at Régua for Chaves and at Tua for Bragança. There are some small local lines such as the Tâmega railway up to Arco de Baúlhe but many of these tend to be interesting rather than efficient.

Coaches with multilingual guides are used for sightseeing trips round Oporto, the coach companies run long distance services to Lisbon and the Algarve and there is an extensive network of local buses, some of which apparently do not find it necessary to issue basic timetables.

Additional Information

Places of Interest

Amarante
Albano Sardoeira Museum
Convento de São Gonçalo next to the town hall
Open: 10am-12.30pm, 2-5pm. Closed holidays.
Contains archaeological exhibits, sculptures and paintings.

Tâmego Railway to Arco de Baúlhe
For current timetables enquire at the tourist office.

Barcelos
Ceramics Museum
In the ruined castle
Open: 10am-12noon, 2-5pm. Closed Mondays.

Braga
Casa dos Biscainhos Museum
Rua Biscainhos
Open: 10am-12noon, 2-5pm. Closed Mondays and holidays.
Varied exhibits including Roman relics, paintings, furniture and *objet d'art*.

Nogueira da Silva Museum
Avenida Central
Open: 3-6pm Wednesdays and Fridays.
A personalised collection, interesting but contains some reproductions and copies.

Sacred Art Museum
In cathedral
Open: 9am-12.30pm, 1.30-6pm. Closed Mondays.
Large number of exhibits including some very memorable items.

Guimarães
Alberto Sampaio Museum
Nossa Senhora de Oliveira cloister
Open: 10am-12.30pm and 2-5pm. Closed Mondays.
Mainly paintings and sacred art.

Ducal Palace Museum
Open: 10am-5pm. Closed Tuesdays.
Very decorative apartments with furniture, pictures and porcelain.

Martins Sarmento Museum
Monastery of São Domingos
Enquire locally for opening times.
Prehistoric discoveries from nearby sites.

Oporto
Cathedral
Open 9am-12.30pm, 3-6pm.

Casa do Infante
Rua da Alfandega
Open: weekdays 9am-12noon, 2-5pm.
Not very interesting building where
Henry the Navigator is thought to have
been born.

Igreja de Misericórdia
Rua das Flores
Offices open 9am-5pm
Impressive picture by unknown artist.

Igreja São Francisco
Praça Infante Dom Henrique
Open: 10am-1pm, 2-5pm. Closed
Sundays.
Amazingly decorative Baroque church.

Ethnology Museum
Largo de São João Nova
Open: 10am-12noon, 2-5pm. Closed
Sundays, Mondays and holidays.
Extremely varied selection, both tradi-
tional and fairly modern.

Quinta da Macieirinha Romantic Museum
Rua de Entre Quintas
Open: 10am-12noon, 2-5pm. Closed
Sundays, Mondays and holidays.
Memorabilia of the ex-king of Sardinia.

Soares dos Reis Museum
Rua de Dom Manuel II
Open: 10am-12noon, 2-5pm. Closed
Mondays and holidays.
Largest museum in Oporto, devoted
mainly to pictures and sculptures.

Solar do Vinho do Porto
Quinta da Macieirinha,
Rua de Entre Quintas
☎ 02 60279
Open: Monday to Saturday 11am-
11.45pm. Closed holidays.
Winetasting centre for port.

Stock Exchange
Adjoining Ingreja São Francisco,
Praça Infante Dom Henrique
Guided tours 9am-12noon, 2-5pm
weekdays. 9am-12noon Saturdays.
Marble staircase with statues, and hall
inspired by the Alhambra.

Bolhão Market
Rua da Sá da Bandeira
Open: 7am-5pm weekdays, 7am-1pm
Saturdays.
Large colourful market but practical
rather than quaint.

Centre for Traditional Arts and Crafts
Rua da Reboleira
☎ 02 32 00 76
Open 10am-12.30pm, 3-7pm Tuesday to
Friday
Good place for traditional souvenirs.

Wine Lodges
Vila Nova de Gaia
Most open about 9.30am-12noon, 2-5pm
on weekdays, closing slightly later in
summer. Times can be verified at the
tourist office.

Viana do Castelo
Church of the Misericord
Praça da República
Open: mornings only. Closed holidays.
Contains some excellent tiles.

Municipal Museum
Rua Manuel Espregueira
Open: 9.30am-12noon, 2-5pm. Closed
Mondays and holidays.
Wide selection of exhibits including
archaeology, art and furniture.

Funicular up to the basilica of Santa
Luzia operates daily 10am-6pm.

Vila do Conde
Convent of Santa Clara chapel
Open: 9am-12noon and 2-6pm.
Contains several Renaissance tombs.

Handicraft Centre
Rua 5 de Outubro
Open: 9am-12noon, 2-5pm.

Tourist Information Offices

Amarante
Rua Cândido dos Reis
☎ 055 42980

Barcelos
Rua Duques de Bragança
☎ 053 82882

Braga
Avenida Central
☎ 053 22550

Caminha
Rua Ricardo Joaquim de Sousa
☎ 058 92 19 52

Espinho
Angulo das Ruas
☎ 02 72 09 11

Esposende
Rua 1 de Dezembro
☎ 053 96 13 54

Gerês
Avenida Manuel Ferreira da Costa
☎ 053 65133

Guimarães
Avenida da Resistência ao Fascismo
☎ 053 41 24 50

Moncão
Largo do Loreto
☎ 051 52757

Oporto
Praça do General Humberto Delgardo
☎ 02 31 27 40

Praça Dom João I
☎ 02 37154

Póvoa de Varzim
Avenida de Mousinho de Albuquerque
☎ 052 62 46 09

Valença do Minho
Estrada N13
☎ 051 23374

Viana do Castelo
Rua do Hospital Velho
☎ 058 22620

Vila do Conde
Rua 25 de Abril
☎ 052 63 14 72

Vila Nova de Cerveira
Praça da Liberdade
☎ 051 95787

Vila Praia de Âncora
Rua Miguel Bombarda
☎ 058 91 13 84

Accommodation

Amarante
Pousada de São Gonçano
☎ 055 46 11 13

Barcelos
Albergaria Condes de Barcelos
Avenida Alcaides de Faria
☎ 053 82061

Pensão Bagoeira
Avenida Dr Sidónio Pais
☎ 053 82236

Braga
Parque do Bom Jesus do Monte
(6km east of Braga, off N103)

Hotel do Elveador
☎ 053 25011

Hotel do Parque
☎ 053 22048

Caminha
Pensão Galo d'Ouro
☎ 058 92 11 60

Estalagem da Boega
☎ 051 95 12 31

Caniçada
Pousada de São Bento
☎ 053 57190

Guimarães
Pousada de Santa Maria da Oliveira
☎ 053 41 21 57   ·

Hotel Fundador Dom Pedro
Avenida Dom Afonson Henriques
☎ 053 41 21 75
or 053 41 56 81

Pousada de Santa Marinha da Costa
On Mount Penha 2.5km away
☎ 053 41 84 53

Moncão
Albergaria Atlántico
Rua General Pimenta de Castreo
☎ 051 52355

Ofir
Hotel de Ofir
☎ 053 96 13 83

Estalagem Parque do Rio
☎ 053 96 15 21

Oporto
Hotel Infante de Sagres
Praça Dona Filipa de Lencastre
☎ 02 281 01

Le Meridien Porto
Avenida da Boavista
☎ 02 600 19 13

Porto Sheraton Hotel
Avenida da Boavista
☎ 02 66 88 22

Hotel Corcel
Rua de Camoes 135
☎ 02 38 02 68

Albergaria Miradouro
Rua da Alegria 598
☎ 02 57 07 17

Hotel Malaposta
Rua de Conceicao 80
☎ 02 262 78

Ponte de Barca
Paço Vedro
☎ 058 24117

Ponte de Lima
Pensão São João
Rua do Rosário
☎ 058 94 12 88

Paço de Calheiros
(7km north of Ponte de Lima)
☎ 058 94 13 64

Valença do Minho
Pousada da São Teotónio
☎ 051 2 22 42

Pousada de Dom Dinis
☎ 051 95 16 11

Viana do Castelo
Hotel de Santa Luzia
☎ 058 22191
Hotel Viana Sol
☎ 058 23401

Vila Praia de Âncora
Hotel Meira
☎ 058 91 11 11

3

Costa de Prata

Just as the Costa Verde has earned the right to be called the Green Coast so the Costa de Prata can legitimately claim to have a silver sheen, although it develops red and gold overtones after the grape harvest. It is a long narrow strip of country lying between the Rio Douro to the north and the Rio Tejo, or Tagus, in the south, sharing its borders with all the other main regions apart from the Algarve, while its extensive coastline has an uninterrupted view out across the Atlantic. Most of the area consists of coastal plains threaded with rivers and blanketed by vineyards, woodlands, patches of wheat and maize, occasional orchards and olive groves. Rice paddies make an appearance in the salt marshes round the Ria de Aveiro, a vast lagoon partly cut off from the sea, while further

The Central Canal, Aveiro

south long stretches of silver sand are punctuated with small holiday resorts and backed by grass-covered dunes and the ever-present pines.

Roughly speaking the Costa de Prata can be separated into four different provinces: Aveiro in the north which divides its attention between fishing, modern industries and traditional crafts; Coimbra with its impressive Roman and medieval associations; Leira which has some magnificent buildings, underground caves and atmospheric fishing villages, and Santarém following the Rio Tagus to Abrantes and the Rio Lêzere northwards past the ancient city of Tomar. The whole area is well populated and easily accessible by road from Oporto and Vila Real in the north, from Spain by way of Guarda, Castelo Branco or Marvão, and from Lisbon with a choice between various main roads and the *auto-estrada* that will eventually run the whole length of the country.

Travelling south from Oporto, but ignoring the motorway, drivers with time to spare might deviate slightly at Oliveira de Azeméis to visit **Arouca**. This is a pleasant little mountain village, founded by Julius Caesar, occupied by the Moors and largely reconstructed after their departure. The Convent of Santa Maria dates from the early tenth century. Dona Mafalda, the daughter of Sancho I, became its abbess some 200 years after it was founded and is buried in an ebony and silver tomb near the main altar. The church has its full share of statues, gilded wood carving and a decorated organ loft but most of the pictures, tapestries and other treasures are kept in a museum upstairs in the cloister.

West of Oliveira de Azeméis, where there is a privately owned campsite called the Parque de Campismo La Salette, a number of small roads head for the salt marshes that run parallel to the coast, beyond which are a few small communities with beaches attached. However there is nothing particularly memorable about them so it is probably better, and certainly much quicker, to continue along the N1 down to the turning off to Aveiro. Anyone who overshoots it will have a second opportunity 4km (2¹/₂ miles) further on.

In its younger days **Aveiro** was a busy seaport but Atlantic gales and shifting sands gradually altered the coastline, creating a vast lagoon which left it high but far from dry, surrounded by swamps that were an ideal breeding ground for mosquitoes. In 1808 a channel was forced through to the sea and the town was able to resume many of its previous occupations including fishing and the production of large quantities of salt. Today it claims, somewhat extravagantly, to be the Venice of Portugal, mainly on account of the number of canals and little waterways that wind their way through the built up area. The most attractive of these is the Central Canal, edged with small boats and overlooked by some attractive buildings, a number of which are decorated with coloured tiles.

Aveiro is not over-blessed with historic buildings. The cathedral is, in fact, quite an unremarkable sixteenth-century church that belonged originally to the Monastery of São Domingos. It was given a Barqoue façade and considerably rejuvinated inside, but still has an early Renaissance

Entombment and an ornamental stone cross in a chapel near the entrance. The Convent of Jesus in the Rua Santa Joana, is equally ancient and was subjected to much the same treatment in the eighteenth century. The church is a riot of wood carving and gold as well as scenes from the life of Santa Joana, the daughter of Afonso V, who spent the last years of her life in the convent and was beatified in 1693. She is buried in a splendid marble tomb in the lower choir but there is also a portrait of her in the convent museum. Other items on display include sculptures, paintings and porcelain, while the room where she died has been turned into an oratory.

Anyone staying overnight in Aveiro will find plenty of hotels to choose from, among them the Imperial, an apartment in the Aparthotel Afonso V and slightly cheaper accommodation at the Paloma Blanca, which does not have a restaurant but provides car parking. The two-star camp site at Praia de Barra is the most accessible of several strung out along the coast, many of which provide facilities for swimming, boating and fishing. Praia de Barra is conscientiously building itself up into a popular resort, no doubt to be followed in their own good time by São Jacinto and Costa Nova. The Pousada da Ria, overlooking the lagoon, is hardly more than a restaurant with accommodation attached but it is pleasant and has a garden with an outdoor swimming pool. Murtosa, facing it across the Ria, is a busy little port where seaweed, rushes and fish are unloaded at Bico, a gentle stroll away.

One of the advantages of spending a day or two in Aveiro is that it allows plenty of time for sightseeing in the vicinity. There are boat trips in the summer from the Central Canal to Torreira at the northern end of the lagoon and regular buses to the beach. Alternatively, **Ilhavo**, less than 8km (5 miles) to the south, is said to have been founded by the Greeks and was a fishing port until the river silted up. Nevertheless it has an informative museum full of model boats including the distinctive *moliceiros*, shaped like gondolas with richly painted prows, that are still used to collect seaweed to fertilize the crops. Although it also has a collection of beautiful porcelain this can be seen to better advantage in **Vista Alegre**, a bare 2km further on. The factory where it is made is not open to visitors with the result that it has created a special museum to show how the process gradually evolved. In 1824, when the factory first started production, its output of pottery was fairly basic but then the owner went to Sèvres, near Paris, to find out something about the methods being employed in France. He was fortunate enough to discover deposits of kaolin in his own area and this, coupled with French expertise, enabled the firm to turn out a wide variety of high grade porcelain that is famous throughout Portugal.

The N109 continues its journey south, parallel to the coast, with a turning off at Mira to the beach. Here the wooden houses are built on stilts, clear of the drifting sand, oxen are used to haul in the fishing nets and the catch is auctioned on the spot. In the opposite direction a secondary road heads for Cantanhede, an agricultural centre whose parish church has

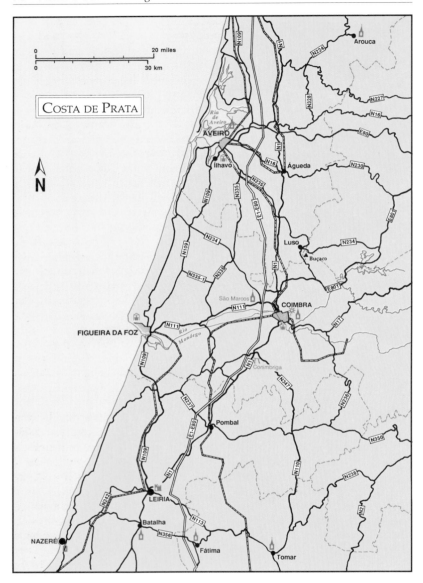

some moderately interesting art work dating from the sixteenth century. However the altarpiece at Varziela, just off the road, is intricately carved and somewhat more impressive.

The whole road down from Aveiro to Figueira da Foz is rather dreary, partly on account of the impoverished-looking villages that run into one another along much of the route. However this is relieved by the strange

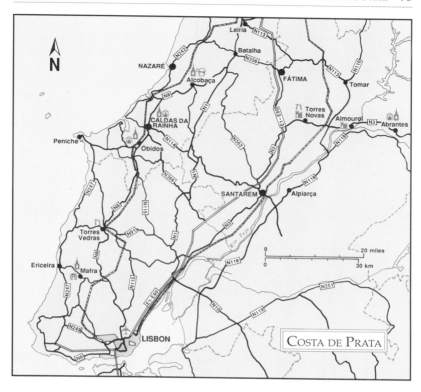

juxtaposition of sometimes squalid little houses and comparatively modern villas smothered in coloured tiles. These may vary from one wall to the next, include pictorial scenes and may even be repeated right round the garden. Some of the architecture is very imaginative, although there is nothing aggressively modernistic or too obviously inspired by the Moors.

At first sight **Figueira da Foz** is not particularly inviting, largely because of the amount of highrise building that is going on. Its site at the mouth of the Mondego River has been occupied for the best part of two thousand years but there is nothing to show for it apart from a number of archaeological exhibits in the municipal museum. The present town dates from the nineteenth century and concerns itself almost entirely with fishing and tourism. Most holidaymakers congregate on the magnificent sandy beach that curves round Figueira Bay, where the first British troops landed in 1808 on their way to the battle grounds at Rolica and Vimeiro, south of Óbidos. Apart from the fishing boat harbour there are moorings for pleasure craft, facilities for sailing, tennis and fishing, a golf course under construction, and a casino. A honey-coloured fort stands guard near the tennis club at the river mouth, the Casa do Paço near the yacht harbour, has some pictorial Dutch tiles, while coins, ceramics and old photographs vie for attention with archaeological exhibits in the nearby Museu Municipal do Dr Santos Rocha. The town has some attractive gardens like the Santa Catarina Park, where there is a restaurant and a swimming pool, one or two easily forgettable churches and the sparse remains of some defensive walls at Buarcos on the far side of the bay. Accommodation ranges from the Grande Hotel da Figueira on the seafront, through the Clube de Vale de Leão 6km (4 miles) away, which has apartments but no restaurant, to a not very prepossessing motel with a snack bar on the N109. There are also four different campsites, the nearest of which are the Municipal Park on the outskirts of the town and the Parque de Campismo de Quiaios/Quitar beside the sea at Praia de Quiaios, beyond the lighthouse.

Inland from Figueira da Foz, upstream from the concentration of rice paddies in the lower Mondego valley, **Montemor-o-Velho** is distinguished by the imposing remains of a hilltop fortress, built in the eleventh century to protect Coimbra from the Moors. After this danger had passed it became a bone of contention between Afonso II and his sisters, Teresa and Mafalda, who had inherited it from their father. At last the pope intervened and settled the potentially destructive family feud by simply handing the stronghold over to the Templars and leaving Teresa in control of the town. At various times thereafter the walls, towers and battlements were strengthened and generally improved but no-one bothered very much about the palace, with the result that most of it has fallen down. The church of Santa Maria de Alcáçova, near the keep, was given a facelift in 1510 and is still quite attractive, as is the view from the ramparts over yet more rice fields to some distant hills.

The countryside dries out considerably as the road continues along the valley towards Coimbra through São Martinho de Avore and São João do Campo, neither of which is in any way remarkable. However, a minor road to the north near these two villages leads to the monastery church of São Marcos which escaped the unwelcome attentions of some irate inhabitants a hundred or more years ago. It dates from the fifteenth century and could almost be described as a mausoleum for the da Silva family and a young soldier, Fernão Teles de Meneses, who was the first to be buried there. His tomb is the most outstanding, elegant and superbly carved under its stone canopy, although two of the other three are certainly rather more ornate. The main doorway and the altarpiece are both original and even the few well-intentioned alterations carried out comparatively recently do not detract greatly from the medieval atmosphere.

Coimbra, basking on its hillside above the Rio Mondego, is the third largest city in Portugal and undoubtedly one of its most historic towns. It was known to both the Romans and the Moors and became the nation's capital when Afonso Henriques moved down from Guimarães in 1139. By the time Afonso III transferred his court to Lisbon a little more than one hundred years later it had developed into a thriving community, surrounded by orchards and vineyards and sufficiently important for the established university to be resited there in the fourteenth century. This ancient seat of learning has had a very chequered career. Initially it was tossed backwards and forwards between Lisbon and Coimbra like a shuttle-cock until finally it came to rest in the hilltop palace in 1537. João III did all he could to promote the university whereas, after his death twenty years later, the Cortes tried just as hard, but unsuccessfully, to close it down. The Marquês de Pombal, in his turn, sacked several members of the faculty on the grounds of corruption, extended the range of subjects and introduced a series of new rules and regulations which he considered to be long overdue. Today it is Portugal's leading university with several thousand students who still observe many of its ancient customs and traditions in a setting that manages to blend the past and the present most effectively.

The old city of Coimbra should really be explored on foot, starting perhaps from the Almedina Arch on the Rua Ferreira Borges, a twelfth-century fortified gateway left over from the medieval walls. Behind it a maze of narrow roads and twisting alleys, assisted by antiquated stairways like the Escadas de Quebra Costas, or Broken Ribs Steps, find their way up to the Sé Velha on the Rua Borges Carneiro. This is the old cathedral, built in the twelfth century when Coimbra was the capital of Portugal and generally considered to be the finest Romanesque example of its kind in the country. Said to have been converted from an Arab mosque, it has all the makings of a fortress on the outside with the addition of a blue and white dome and an enormous arched window over the main entrance. The interior is spacious, admirably uncluttered and very dignified with an ornate altarpiece created by two Flemish sculptors who incorporated the Nativity, the Resurrection and the Assumption of the Virgin. The Chapel of St Peter is lined with tiles and contains a sadly damaged altarpiece by Jean de Rouen, one of the many foreign artists attracted to the Coimbra School of Sculpture in the sixteenth century. The cloister is a good deal older while the chapterhouse contains the tomb of Dom Sisinando, a Moor who was converted to Catholicism, became the first Christian governor of the city and died in 1091.

Slightly further up the road is the Machado de Castro Museum, housed in the original episcopal palace and reached by way of an attractively decorated courtyard. The ground floor is filled with noteworthy sculptures, among the most outstanding of which are statues of the Virgin Mary, an Entombment of Christ and an extremely graphic interpretation of The Last Supper. Somewhat out of context, unless he was a Crusader, there is a fascinating medieval knight on horseback, shouldering his mace and gripping the reins of a remarkably docile looking pony, which is also dressed up ready for action. The first floor of the museum is devoted to paintings and a variety of exhibits such as gold and silverware, French furniture, Chinese porcelain and Persian carpets. The Arab Salon has a Mudejar ceiling, the Bishop's Chapel is decorated with silk and tiles while elsewhere the assorted knick-knacks that belonged for the most part to the

saintly Queen Isabel have predictably religious associations. The base-
ment consists of a number of cellars built by the Romans underneath their
substantial forum and are now used to house a few relics from prehistoric
times.

Behind the museum and its small attendant church the new cathedral,
or Sé Nova, looks out somewhat gloomily on to the Largo da Feira,
perhaps because it has nothing of any particular merit inside. Its nearest
neighbours are a selection of large buildings belonging to the university.
The most eye-catching of them has a marble façade etched with various
figures and assorted mathematical instruments surrounding the large
glass doors that open on to a matching courtyard. To one side of this whole
uniform complex a statue of Dom Dinis, who founded the university in
Lisbon in 1288, takes a sideways look at the Aqueducto de São Sebastião
as it stretches away in a series of arches to make contact with the local
prison. On the way it passes the large Botanical Gardens whose entrance
is in the Alameda Dr Julio Henriques. They were laid out in a strictly
formal manner on the orders of the Marquês de Pombal, with terraces and
geometrically sited flowerbeds containing some exotic plants, a selection
of trees but not much in the way of grass or water.

The old heart of the university is in the opposite direction, on three sides
of the vast palace courtyard with a statue of João III looking across,
without any apparent signs of approval, at the refurbished remains of his
ancient residence and ignoring the view spread out behind him. The
approach is through the decorative Porta Férrea, which replaced the
original fortified gateway and faces the Capela de São Miguel, a small
Manueline chapel that has been rather too enthusiastically restored.
Apart from being mildly viewable, and keeping the odd treasure in its
Sacred Art Museum, the main feature here is an ornamental doorway
with twisted pillars, crowns and at least one coat-of-arms. Then, just next
door, behind its own decorative entrance, is the superb library, presented
by João V and without any doubt the jewel in the university crown. The
three interleading rooms are lined throughout with carved, highly coloured shelves filled with splendid old books, the ceilings are painted,
elaborate inkwells stand on beautiful inlaid tables and even the strictly
functional steps were designed to match.

At the far end of the courtyard an uninspiring tower, built less than
three hundred years ago, replaces part of the original palace, a vast
proportion of which had simply been pulled down. Nearby a stairway
leads up to the Sala dos Capelos, now the ceremonial hall, which was once
the throne room. It turns out to be a good deal less impressive than the
library despite its painted ceiling and the various royal portraits hanging
on the walls.

Foremost among the other places of interest in and around the old town
is the Church of Santa Cruz in the Praça 8 de Maio, not all that far from the
Almedina Arch down the Rua Visconde de Luz. The monastery was built
in the sixteenth century on the site of a much earlier church and although

it has not worn particularly well there are many noteworthy things to
see inside. The first two kings of Portugal, Afonso Henriques and
Sancho I, are buried in ornate tombs on either side of the high altar,
having been moved there in 1520 from the graveyard outside. Also well
worth seeing are the beautifully carved and gilded choir stalls decorated with the Cross of the Order of Christ, unidentified castles and
galleons that played their part in the Age of Discovery. A group of early
paintings are kept in the sacristy beyond which is the Silent Cloister
with scenes of the Passion inspired by Dürer. To the rear of the church
is a strange hangover from the sixteenth century known as the Jardim
de Manga, or Garden of the Sleeve, which does not appear to serve any
useful purpose. It is neither a garden nor a conventional pavilion but
rather more of a folly said to have been thought up by João III in an idle
moment, using his sleeve to make a rough sketch of the sort of design
he had in mind.

   The opposite bank of the Rio Mondego, reached across the Ponte
Santa Clara from the Largo da Portagem, has something for almost
everyone. Opposite the large university stadium a short road leads to

Traditional folkdancing in colourful costumes

the former Santa Clara-a-Velha Convent, or rather what little is still left of it. Constant flooding over more than six hundred years has inundated the original Gothic church, now partly submerged with hardly more than its rose window and the tops of the arches rising above the water and the encroaching weeds. The New Convent of Santa Clara, built to replace it in the seventeenth century on higher ground at the end of the Calçada Santa Isabel, is enormous by comparison. Most of the buildings have been taken over by the army but the Baroque chapel is open to visitors except during services. This is more or less a shrine to the much revered queen, St Isabel, whose body was removed from the old convent and buried in a silver tomb in the chancel. Nearby a wrought iron grille protects the queen's original tomb on which she is shown wearing the habit of the Poor Clares. In addition to some of her clothes which are preserved in the sacristy, there is a late nineteenth-century statue of her in the church and a series of panels illustrating her last short journey up from the river bank.

Between the two convents, on the Rossio Santa Clara, the Portugal dos Pequenitos Park is a magical place for children. It is, as its name implies, a cross section of Portugal in Miniature with many famous landmarks cut down to size along with typical buildings representing several countries that were once part of its extensive overseas territories, as well as the little Museu da Criança, which is a museum designed specially for children.

Adults may prefer the Quinta das Lágrimas further down the Rua António Augusto Gonçalves. It is a small wooded park belonging to the Villa of Tears where Inês de Castro was murdered in about 1355. She was a Spanish lady-in-waiting who caught the eye of Afonso IV's son Pedro after his wife died. The couple are said to have married secretly in the Church of São Vincente in Bragança, which was an unfortunate mistake because his father either authorised or agreed to her murder, possibly in order to prevent any close ties developing with Spain. When Pedro succeeded to the throne he settled his score with two of the men who killed her in the typically barbaric fashion that earned him the title of Pedro the Cruel. Then he had her body exhumed, forced the court to acknowledge her and finally decreed that they should be buried side by side in the abbey church at Alcobaça. The present villa, dating from the eighteenth century, is not open to the public but the owners sometimes allow visitors to walk through the grounds and inspect the Fonte dos Amores where the star-crossed lovers are believed to have spent much of their time.

Coimbra has a number of other less well publicised attractions including the Mosteiro de Celas, not far from the Avenida Bissaia Barreto. It is a twelfth-century Cistercian convent with an attractive cloister and an altarpiece by Jean de Rouen that was added four hundred years later. A statue of Pope John Paul II who visited the city in 1982 is sited on the way up to the university and there are various little churches dotted about behind the small regiment of fairly modest hotels strung out along the waterfront. The best of these is probably the Hotel Astória, while the Residencial Parque just down the road is somewhat cheaper. Anyone who would prefer to stay outside the city might consider the Hotel Dom Luis, 2.5km (4 miles) away along the N1. People with tents or caravans will find a two-star campsite on the Rua General Humberto Delgado next to the municipal stadium on the outskirts.

The best places to shop in Coimbra are in the tangle of little streets in the vicinity of the Praça Comércio although hand-painted pottery can be found almost everywhere. Other good buys are glass from Marinha Grande, the porcelain of Vista Alegre, leather goods and lace. Some of the modest restaurants specialise in local dishes such as mutton cooked in red wine, roast kid and particularly suckling pig, cooked in a brick oven and so tender that it can be carved by tapping it with the edge of a plate. The main celebration in Coimbra is the Festival of the Queen Saint, held every other year during the first fortnight in July, whereas the students hold their annual Queima das Fitas in May.

Less than 28km (17 miles) northeast of Coimbra is the enchanted **Forest of Buçaco** which owes its existence to a group of Benedictine monks who built a hermitage there nearly fifteen hundred years ago. From the eleventh century onwards it was a retreat for the clergy of Coimbra Cathedral and in 1622 Pope Gregory XV threatened to excommunicate any woman found loitering in the vicinity. Six years later the Barefoot Carmelites added a monastery, walled in the whole area and planted a variety of trees brought back by the early explorers, such as maples and Mexican cypresses, setting them among the existing oaks and other indigenous varieties. These were then given additional protection by Pope Urban VIII who extended the threat of excommunication to anyone found guilty of damaging them. However this did not bother the Duke of Wellington who defeated the French under Massena at the Battle of Buçaco in 1810. Following the dissolution of the monasteries in 1834 the area was turned into a national park and the Forestry Department continued the good work, adding species such as Japanese camphor trees, monkey-puzzle trees, Oriental spruces, sequoias and Himalayan pines. These were augmented with mimosa, magnolias and other flowering shrubs with a ground cover of hydrangeas, ferns and flowers like lily of the valley.

Predictably an impressive hunting lodge was built for the royal family next to the remains of the monastery where Wellington spent the night in a cell before going out to do battle with the French army. When the monarchy was abolished in 1910 the palace was turned into an hotel, still with its magnificent staircase, decorative tiles, suits of armour and sumptious furnishings. Admittedly the plumbing can be a bit temperamental at times and the peace and quiet invaded by coachloads of tourists anxious to absorb the atmosphere, but nevertheless the Palace Hotel do Buçaco, is an ideal place from which to explore the forest and the surrounding area.

Although there are one or two roads through the park the best way to see it is undoubtedly on foot, starting from one of the many entrances or from the car park in front of the hotel, which is nicely situated in the

The elaborately carved window in the cloister of the Convento de Cristo, Tomar

The participants in Tomar's famous festival carry on their heads these tall piles of bread decorated with paper flowers

middle. From here one option would be to head northwards along a marked path, past the ancient hermitage of Our Lady of the Assumption to the Fonte Fria. This is an underground spring that spills out of a small grotto and cascades down a long stone stairway to a pool surrounded by lovely flowering shrubs. From here a stream flows between banks of ferns, hydrangeas and rhododendrons to the Fern Valley Lake which is con-

The spectacular and colourful Tabuleiros Festival is held every other year at Tomar

nected by a series of woodland paths to exits like the Mountain Gate and the Battlements Gate, besides providing several alternative routes back to the hotel.

Another excellent choice would be past the Avenida dos Cedros, lined with the famous Buçaco Cedars, to a convoluted Way of the Cross, dating from the seventeenth century. Here a series of small chapels containing tableaux recalling scenes on the road to Calvary mark the route to the Cruz Alta which has a remarkable panoramic view over the whole area. The cross can also be reached by road from the hotel, past a waterfall that tumbles down into the Font de São Silvestro, leaving the park through the Queens Gate to call at a small military museum that concerns itself exclusively with the final stages of the Peninsular War. It concentrates, quite naturally, on the Battle of Buçaco which took place quite close by on a site marked with an obelisk surmounted by a star. The park with its fountains, grottoes and little isolated hermitages covers about 100 hectares (260 acres) but is one place where nobody need be afraid of getting lost. Detailed maps of the whole area are available from the Palace Hotel and also from the Tourist Office in **Luso**, a pleasant little spa about 3km (2 miles) away to the north. The town can also offer a variety of less expensive but quite adequate hotels, one of which has a large swimming pool, as well as facilities for tennis and fishing but unfortunately no official campsite at the moment.

South of Coimbra, a turning off the N1 to Condeixa leads to the ruins of *Conimbriga*, the most important Roman site in Portugal. It was a fortified Celtic settlement as long ago as 800BC, set on rising ground between two narrow gorges which made it comparatively simple to defend but provided no easy means of escape for the inhabitants when the Romans launched their first attack about 200BC. However, it was not until roughly two centuries later that the Emperor Augustus gave it his undivided attention and work started on building it up into an attractive town with an aqueduct, a forum, temples, baths and private villas.

Conimbriga grew and prospered for the next three hundred years but when the Roman Empire started to crumble round the edges it was decided to improve the defences and many of the existing buildings were pulled down to create new fortifying walls. Despite this feverish activity they were unable to prevent the Swabians capturing it in the mid-fifth century, upon which everybody moved out to the neighbouring settlement of *Aeminius,* which eventually blossomed into Coimbra. So far only a small proportion of the town has been excavated but there is plenty to see, both on the site itself and in its informative museum near the entrance on the old Roman Way that passed through en route from Lisbon to Braga.

Outside the ramparts, the House of the Fountains was virtually destroyed to provide building materials for the walls. However it still has its central courtyard with flowerbeds and water jets, once surrounded by columns, and the remains of a handful of different rooms with fascinating mosaic floors. The designs include everything from hunting scenes and a four-horse chariot to Perseus holding the head of Medusa, a reluctant donkey, sea creatures and wading birds. The House of Cantaber, beyond the gates, is even larger and more opulent, approached through a colonnade, with private apartments grouped round their individual pools, a dining area, a specious courtyard and elaborate cold, warm and hot water baths. There are also a few lead pipes that predate modern central heating systems by nearly two thousand years. Elsewhere among the excavations are the remnants of the forum and the temple, an occasional villa, the communal bath house and assorted piles of rubble that were originally taverns, shops and the homes of artisans who earned their living in the town. All the relics that have so far been recovered are on display in the museum. Among them are sculptures, mosaics, jewellery and pottery as well as a whole variety of everyday items.

There are two options open to motorists heading south from the ruins. The N1, homing in on Pombal with its restored medieval castle where the famous Marquês died in 1782, is the most direct route to Leiria, while the N110 makes for **Tomar** in the southeastern corner of the region. The best reason for choosing this longer, round-about road is to visit the magnificent Convento de Cristo, built especially for the Knights Templar. The Order was founded during the First Crusade but moved down from its original castle at Soure in 1150 when the Grand Master, Gualdim Pais, decided that Tomar would be preferable. He built a church and started work on a hilltop castle but this proved to be unsatisfactory and was abandoned in favour of the present site.

The first part of the convent to be built was the Templars' Rotunda, or Charola, inspired by the Temple of the Dome of the Rock in Jerusalem, with a high altar in the middle encircled by the aisle. When the Templars were forcibly disbanded in 1314 their role was taken over by the newly created Order of Christ whose governor, Henry the Navigator, added a small chapel dedicated to St Thomas Becket, the martyred Archbishop of Canterbury. The exuberantly decorated nave is largely surrounded by cloisters, each with its own individual atmosphere and function. The Claustro Principal is both simple and impressive and is said to have been where Philip II of Spain was proclaimed King of Portugal during the fracas that followed the death of Sebastião I on an ill-advised expedition to North Africa. Next to it is the Renaissance Cloister of Santa Barbara with its famous Manueline window, a seething mass of sculptured ropes, anchor chains, seaweed, ship's cables and coral with a royal crown and the Cross of the Order of Christ, all calling to mind the caravels that left Portugal on their famous voyages of discovery in the sixteenth century.

The Hostelry Cloister, the sacristy and the Ablutions and Burial Ground Cloisters are all open to visitors but the rest of the buildings are strictly out of bounds, and these unfortunately include the twelfth century keep and the old chapterhouse. By way of compensation the lovely Capela de Nossa Senhora da Conceição on the way down to the town can be seen by anyone who is sufficiently interested to call in at the Tourist Office for the key.

Other places of interest in Tomar include the late-fifteenth century church of São João Baptista, liberally decorated with flora and fauna on the outside, which has an arresting limestone pulpit and some very worthwhile paintings including a *Baptism of Christ* triptych which is kept locked up in the baptistry. A small Gothic synagogue in the Rua Dr Joaquim Jacinto is of comparable vintage while the church of Santa Maria do Olival in the Rua de Santa Iria stands on the site of a castle built by Gualdim Pais who is buried inside.

Every second year, alternating with the Festival of the Queen Saint in Coimbra, Tomar holds its Tabuleiros Festival. It is a ceremony associated with the Brotherhood of the Holy Spirit, founded by the saintly Queen Isabel, and designed to provide food and sustenance for the poor. It begins with a series of processions through the streets in early July. All the participants, who are numbered in hundreds, are virgins dressed in white and carrying *tabuleiros* — flat receptacles — on their heads piled high with loaves of bread. These are attached to sticks nearly as tall as the girls themselves and decorated with wheat, green leaves and brightly coloured paper flowers. The next day cartloads of bread and wine are distributed among the city's deserving families, after which everyone joins in the general rejoicing with traditional music and dancing, feasting and firework displays. The Fair and Festival of St Irene is more concerned with dried fruit and local handicrafts and takes place in the second half of October.

Most of the local hotels, among them the Hotel dos Templários, overlooking the public gardens, tend to be noisy and are usually fully booked at festival time. However there is alternative accommodation within easy reach such as the Pousada de São Pedro, beside the large Castelo de Bode Dam a few kilometres away to the south-east. On the other hand, anyone confined to a wheelchair would find life much easier at the Estalagem Vale da Ursa, to the northeast, between Águas Belas and Cernache de Bonjardim on the N238.

Abrantes, on the north bank of the Tagus beyond the Castelo de Bode Dam, can also provide accommodation at the Hotel de Tourismo. It is a pleasant small town, conveniently situated on the N3, which played host to both Junot and Wellington during the Peninsular War, although its old fortress was not much good to either of them, having largely disintegrated a century or two before. It is worth strolling up through the flower-filled alleys to the fourteenth-century keep and the Church of Santa Maria do Castelo. This contains a number of tombs and the Museu de Dom Lopo de Almeida with its collection of sculptures, archaeological odds and ends and a variety of Spanish tiles.

Downstream from Abrantes the fairytale castle of Almourol stands all by itself on a little rocky island in the middle of the Tagus. It was built by the Templars towards the end of the twelfth century on the site of an ancient Roman fortress and is swathed in legends which have all the most acceptable ingredients — a local giant, beautiful princesses and valiant

The Sanctuary of Fátima, now an important place of pilgrimage

The monastery church of St Mary Victorious, Batalha

knights who conducted themselves in the manner of Douglas Fairbanks in his most dashing Hollywood productions. Reality at close quarters comes as a bit of a letdown because there are no cauldrons bubbling ominously over great log fires, duelling swords or sumptuous apartments. However a boatman is on hand at the landing stage to ferry visitors across and, once inside the towers and ramparts, steps lead up to the top of the keep for anyone who is prepared for a long climb in order to admire the view. Meanwhile, further downstream, Torres Novas draws attention to its castle walls, some rather odd caves and the remains of a Roman villa complete with its original mosaics, about 3km (2 miles) to the south.

Due west of Tomar along the N113, there is a turning off to **Ourém Velha** that has a castle which was practically rebuilt in the fifteenth century for Dom Afonso, the son of the first Duke of Bragança, whose simple crypt is in the nearby parish church. Marginally further on, at Pinhel, another secondary road branches off in the same direction for a scenic run to **Fátima**, one of the most famous sanctuaries in Christendom. Prior to 13 May 1917 very few people had heard of a small place called Cova da Iria, tucked away in hilly country between Tomar and Batalha. On that day three young children had a vision of the Virgin Mary in an oak tree while they were herding sheep. She told them that everyone should pray for peace but warned of the dangers ahead if her message was ignored.

The children, Lúcia, Francisco and Jacinta, had the same vision on the thirteenth of each subsequent month until October when a crowd of seventy thousand saw what has since been called the Miracle of the Sun. It apparently began to revolve after a heavy shower of rain and looked as if it might hit the earth like a ball of fire. In due course the Pope recognised the validity of the miracle of Our Lady of Fátima and a massive basilica was built on the site. It contains the graves of Francisco and Jacinta, who died in 1919 and 1920 respectively, while Lúcia, who was the only one who actually talked to the Virgin, became an inmate at the Carmelite convent in Pontevedra.

Large notices make it clear that the massive sanctuary with its central tower, colonnades and gigantic esplanade has little to offer sightseers. Visitors are told to respect the feelings of pilgrims, to cover their legs and shoulders and remember that they are on holy ground. Somewhat more prosaically, they are also warned not to forget to lock their cars. There are times when the site is almost deserted and it is possible to walk through unhindered, pausing beside an oak tree which has replaced the one in which the Virgin appeared to the children as well as its attendant chapel of Our Lady of Fátima. At other times it is crowded with upwards of one hundred thousand pilgrims, many of whom approach the basilica on their knees. The great pilgrimages on the anniversary of the miracles are marked by solemn masses, torchlight processions and all-night vigils, the blessing of the sick and prayers for forgiveness, recalling the Virgin's warning that the punishment for sin is war.

Except around the twelfth and thirteenth of each month between May and October it is not too difficult to find an hotel in Fátima, beginning with the Hotel de Fátima, which is fairly large and fully equipped, down to the much smaller Residencial São Paulo, which has no restaurant but, like many of the others, can find space to park the car. Nor is there any problem when it comes to souvenirs because they are available in their thousands in most of the shops and wayside stalls. The majority are definitely shoddy but the faithful tend to agree with a local priest who told an irate customer that it is the association and not the quality that counts.

Batalha, 18km (11 miles) west of Fátima, has a great deal of historical interest. After the death of Fernando I in 1383 without a son and heir his widow, Leonor Teles, assumed the monarchy, egged on by her lover Count Andeiro. This did not suit the King of Castile, who had married Fernando's daughter Beatriz, so he promptly claimed the throne on her behalf and demanded that she should be acknowledged immediately as Queen of Portugal. Members of the Portuguese nobility who objected to becoming vassals of Spain rallied behind Fernando's illegitimate half-brother, João of Aviz, who was then proclaimed king.

The inevitable climax came at the battle of Aljubarotta in 1385. The Portuguese army, augmented by a contingent of English archers provided by Richard II, dug themselves in alongside the road to Lisbon. By nightfall the advancing Spaniards had been routed and the independence of Portugal assured for the next two hundred years. The site is marked by the chapel of São Jorge on the N1. There is also an iron statue of a baker's wife who played her part in speeding the defeated Castilian soldiers on their way by hitting them with a shovel.

Before the battle João I vowed that he would build a church if the outcome was satisfactory and three years later work started on the monastery of St Mary Victorious some 4km (2¹/₂ miles) to the north. Today it is far better known as the superb monastery of Batalha. The church of golden coloured stone is a complicated symphony of pinnacles, flying buttresses, open balustrades, blind arcades, statues and stained glass. This is at total variance with the majestically simple Gothic nave that soars without any unnecessary clutter up to its high vaulted ceiling. On the right is the Founders Chapel where João I and his wife, Phillipa of Lancaster, are buried side by side in appropriately palatial surroundings in company with four of their children. These include Dom Fernando who spent the last years of his life as a hostage in North Africa where he died in Fez of dysentery. Henry the Navigator's tomb is on the right although he also has a more modern counterpart in the church of Santa Engrácia in Lisbon.

The Royal Cloister, to the left of the nave, is suitably ornate with slender, decorative columns and sculptured screens that make full use of everything from fleur-de-lys to the newly-created Cross of the Order of Christ. Leading off this are both the comparatively restrained Cloister of Afonso V, decorated with his coat-of-arms and that of his father, Duarte, and the chapterhouse with its Tomb of the Unknown Soldiers. Both of them died during World War I, one in France and the other in Africa. Not far from the Lavobo dos Monges, in the northwest corner of the Royal Cloister, the old refectory has been turned into a small museum that spends part of its time selling souvenirs. Finally, an intricately carved, early sixteenth-century doorway leads off an exterior porch beyond the nave into the Capelas Imperfeitas, or Unfinished Chapels, which João and Phillipa's son Duarte planned as a mausoleum. Work continued in a desultory fashion for the best part of a hundred years, during which Manuel I transferred his attention to Belém, and was finally abandoned by João III.

Strategically positioned beside the monastery is a large equestrian statue of Nun' Alvares Pereira, the commander of the Portuguese forces at the battle of Aljubarotta, during which he employed tactics that had been perfected by the English during the Hundred Years' War. Beyond it the Pousada Mestre Afonso Domingues is pleasantly sited in its own small garden, but there is not a lot of accommodation available and consequently it is usually fully booked at the height of the season. In this case the Quinta do Fidalgo, on the other side of the main road, makes a perfectly acceptable alternative.

North of Batalha on the N1 and only 11km (7 miles) away, **Leiria** has two rivers — the Liz and the Lena — and a splendid medieval castle to its credit. The hilltop site was occupied even before the Romans put in an appearance. Afonso Henriques built a stronghold to protect his emergent nation against a surprise attack by the Moors who still occupied both Lisbon and Santarém, but this was sacked by the Arabs and had to be rebuilt on more than one occasion. Dinis and his queen, St Isabel, spent a short time in the palace he had added inside the ramparts and which still has its original staircase leading up to a large rectangular hall whose arcaded balcony commands a wide view over the town below. Other attractions inside the walls are the twelfth-century keep, also built by Dom Dinis, and the ruined chapel of Nossa Senhora de Pena. There is nothing very much to see in the cathedral on the Largo da Sé but the shops are well supplied with local handicrafts including multicoloured pottery from Cruz da Légua, decorative glass from Marinha Grande and other items that originate in the Serra do Aire. Leiria has quite a few hotels and restaurants. The Hotel Eurosol and the Hotel Eurosol Jardim are unashamedly commercial in the modern manner. They share everything including the telephone number, a diningroom in the former and a snack bar in the latter, a communal garage and a swimming pool and are located on the southern edge of the town.

There are several minute coastal resorts strung out along the beaches west of Leiria, each with its own name but very little else. São Pedro de Moel has developed rather more rapidly than most and is reached by way of Marinha Grande and the Pinhal do Rei, a pine forest planted by Dom Dinis in the early fourteenth century, which supplied timber for the ships used by early explorers like Bartolomeu Dias, Cão and Vasco de Gama. **Nazaré**, some 21km (13 miles) down the coast, is a different matter

The Costa de Prata offers attractive campsites

Oxen hauling fishing boats onto the beach at Nazaré

altogether. It claims to have been a busy fishing village in the days of the Phoenicians; adding that its name comes from a statue of the Virgin supposedly brought back from Nazareth in the fourth century by an itinerant monk.

These days Nazaré combines fishing with a lucrative tourist industry, providing a wide but not very up-market selection of hotels for holiday-makers and an extensive beach littered with portable awnings and col-oured sun umbrellas. The Bairro dos Pescadores is the fishermen's quarter where a succession of narrow cobbled streets and alleys make their way down the hillside, lined with whitewashed cottages and festooned with laundry. The Sitio quarter, strung out along a cliff top to the north of the town, can be reached by road or by funicular. Its main attractions, apart from the view, are a small chapel with a splendid legend and the seven-teenth-century church of Nossa Senhora de Nazaré at the far end of the Rua Dom Fuas Roupinho, facing the main square. It has a Baroque doorway and quantities of tiles in the transept illustrating well-known events from the Old Testament.

The tiny chapel poised above the sea is encrusted with tiles recalling an ancient legend concerning Fuas Roupinho who is remembered chiefly for a sea victory off the lonely Cabo Espichel, south of Lisbon, in 1180. On this occasion he was chasing a deer which suddenly disappeared over the edge of the cliff. Realising that he could not pull up his horse in time he prayed to Our Lady of Nazaré for help and she performed the necessary miracle. A stairway down to the crypt is said to contain a deer's footprint, leading one to hope that she may have taken pity on the poor hunted animal as well. Out at the end of the promontory a lighthouse has replaced an old fort, beyond which there are steps down to the farthest point. It has a splendid view of the Atlantic rollers thundering over the jagged rocks below but it should on no account be attempted by anyone without a head for heights. In fact, holidaymakers who prefer the sea in a more gentle mood would probably find São Martinho do Porto, on its little sheltered bay a few kilometres down the coast, a good deal more to their liking. Nazaré is one of the last places in Portugal where a few women of uncertain age still wear their traditional dress as a matter of course. It is functional rather than picturesque, consisting of voluminous dark pleated skirts with a knitted shoulder cape worn over an ordinary long sleeved blouse.

Visitors in search of a campsite have several to choose from in the area. The municipal Parque de Campismo da Praia de Pedrógão to the north has a three-star rating with all the expected facilities while the site at São Pedro de Muel is smaller but can provide a limited amount of accommo-dation. Nazaré offers two alternatives — the Parque de Campismo do Valado/Orbitur and the larger, slightly better equipped Parque de Campismo e Caravanismo Vale Paraiso 2km (1^1/$_4$ miles) from the town, with the addition of an unclassified site called the Parque de Campismo Colina do Sol at São Martinho do Porto. Anyone planning to visit

Alcobaça, 14km (9 miles) inland on the N8, could try the local one-star municipal site that offers very little apart from the basic amenities.

The monastery of Santa Maria at **Alcobaça** has been described as one of the finest groups of Cistercian buildings anywhere in Europe. Although this is a somewhat extravagant claim there is no doubt that the vast abbey is unusually impressive. It was founded by Afonso Henriques, the first king of Portugal, to fulfil a vow he made to St Bernard in 1147 after his armies had driven the Moors out of Santarém. Work began some thirty years later and before long the monastery was a force to be reckoned with, owning large tracts of land, villages and fishing ports, wielding considerable power throughout the country, influencing schools and the university of Coimbra and accumulating a great deal of wealth in the process. Nevertheless, it did not manage to escape the attention of French troops under Junot during the Peninsular War and a quarter of a century later the monks were obliged to leave when all the existing monasteries were eliminated.

A considerable amount of rebuilding and rejuvenating was carried out during the eighteenth century but the main doorway and the rose window are both original, watched over by a number of statues including São Bernardo and São Bento, who are comparative newcomers to the scene. Inside, the exceptionally long narrow nave with its rows of massive pillars has nothing in the way of decorations to detract from the extremely ornate tombs of Pedro the Cruel and Inês de Castro on either side of the transept. They lie with their feet towards the centre so that when they have to stand up to be counted they will be facing each other. Both tombs were badly damaged by French soldiers searching for hidden treasure but despite this they still have their attendant angels and scenes from the bible reflecting paradise and the jaws of hell as they are expected to appear on Judgement Day. Inês de Castro's tomb is supported by dogs with human faces, at least one of whom is believed to have been among her murderers at the Villa of Tears in Coimbra. The death of São Bernardo, recalled in minute detail, shares a small chapel near the tomb of Dom Pedro with those of Afonso II and Afonso III.

On the opposite side of the nave the Cloister of Silence contains a fourteenth-century lavabo or washing basin, beyond which is the splendid refectory. Here, according to contemporary reports, the monks gorged themselves while listening to passages from the bible read to them from a pulpit, reached up a stairway built into the wall. The adjoining kitchen is immense, with huge open fireplaces and a stream running through to ensure that any fish reaching the table would be deliciously fresh. Stairs lead up from the cloister to the monks' dormitory above the storeroom next door to the chapterhouse. The construction of the monastery is illustrated with tiles in the Kings' Hall, to the left of the main entrance, with statues of a succession of Portuguese monarchs carved by the monks.

Alcobaça is a quiet, attractive little town of narrow streets and elderly houses which supports at least two major industries. The Atlantis Crystal Factory produces beautiful handmade glass which can be bought from its own shop on the Avenida Professor Joaquim Natividade near the river as well as throughout the country and in several places overseas. A wine cooperative on the outskirts, about 1km ($^1/_2$ mile) up the road to Batalha, has its own Museu de la Junta Nacional de Vinho with wine presses, casks and other equipment and quantities of bottles full of the local produce. In addition there are pottery workshops in the town, fabrics such as chintz and damask are readily available while the open air market offers a wide range of fruit and vegetables.

The hotels in Alcobaça are nothing special but the Hotel Santa Maria, near the abbey could serve as a base for visitors who want to explore the Serra do Aire, whose main towns are Porto de Mós with its hilltop castle and Mira de Aire, well known for its handicrafts. However the main reason for visiting the area is to inspect some of the many underground caves in the vicinity. The biggest of these are the Old Windmill Caves, or Grutas dos Moinhos, discovered in 1947, which cover a distance of more than 4km ($2^1/_2$ miles) although only a small section is open to the public. Seemingly endless steps lead from one grotto to another with names like the Red Chamber, the Pearl Chapel and the Church Organ, down to the Great Lake and the Black River which has a tendency to flood during the rainy season. Fortunately there is a lift back to the surface. The Money Caves near São Mamede are so called because a group of bandits are reputed to have tossed a traveller down into them before they remembered to remove his money bags but so far there is no record of anyone finding them.

A short distance away the Alvados Caves are noted for their honey-coloured walls and massed stalactites and stalagmites whereas the Caves of Santo António have equally predictable attractions but in a delicate shade of pink. At ground level the countryside is not particularly attractive, consisting mainly of chalky ground with eucalyptus and olive trees protected by dry stone walls. South of Porto de Mós a right-hand turning off the N362 calls in at Fráguas on its way to Rio Maior. This is an unexceptional little town with a long, uncomplicated history and a shimmering expanse of salt spread out on fields of interlocking pads to dry off in the sun. From here it is only 30km (20 miles) or so to Santarém.

Legend has it that in 653 the body of a young nun called Iria was thrown into the river by a monk who had murdered her and was washed up near the Roman settlement of *Scalabis*. Opinions vary as to whether this was during its occupation by the Visigoths or some time later in the reign of Dom Dinis, but at all events one of the kings concerned decided to call the town Santa Iria, which over the years became **Santarém**.

Because of its position on the banks of the Rio Tagus Santarém has had its fair share of problems. It was captured by the Moors, recovered by Afonso Henriques in 1147, patronised by both the court and the Cortes, used as winter quarters for the French troops under Masséna and fought

Santa Maria Monastery, Alcobaça

over during the Civil War before peace returned in 1834. Under the circumstances it is a little surprising to find that it has managed to preserve anything at all.

The church of Nossa Senhora da Graça, on the Rua Braamcamp Freire, dates from the late fourteenth century with a doorway similar to the one at Batalha and a beautiful rose window carved out of a single block of stone. The interior is refreshingly simple, having a carefully restored nave and a number of tombs, the most striking of which belongs to Pedro de Meneses. He was the first governor of Ceuta after it was captured by João I in the early fifteenth century in an effort to reduce the number of pirate raids from North Africa. One of the members of his family married Pedro Álvares Cabral, the navigator who discovered Brazil and who is buried under the floor in one of the small chapels.

More or less round the corner the Igreja da Marvila is lined with early seventeenth-century tiles, an extremely popular form of decoration that is repeated along the corridors of the Jesuit Seminary in the Praça Sá da Bandeira at the far end of the Rua Serpa Pinto. It was built on the site of a royal palace and still does its best to look like one. The church has a painted ceiling and a great deal of marble but otherwise has little of interest to offer. Much the same applies to the Igreja de Santa Clara, a tidy step away down the Rua 31 de Janeiro, which started life as part of the thirteenth-century convent founded by Dona Leonor. The church contains both her original tomb and its 300-year-old counterpart sited below the rose window. Still further on, to the right of the Praça Egas Moniz, there is an excellent view over the town from the São Bento Belvedere.

Santarém's Municipal Museum is housed in what was originally the church of São João Alporão at the opposite end of the Rua Serpa Pinto. The nave is full of sculptures, pieces of Arab and Roman pottery, assorted stonework, unrelated odds and ends and a variety of old tombs. One of them belongs to Duarte de Menses who died protecting Afonso V during a skirmish with the Arabs in North Africa. Sadly the only part of him that survived the battle was a single tooth but that was sufficient for his wife to perpetuate his memory with an elaborate sarcophagus recalling his position as governor of Alcácer-Seguir. Facing the museum is a fifteenth-century clock tower known as the Torre das Cabaças, while round the corner, at the far end of the Avenida 5 de Outubro, an attractive garden has been created inside the ancient Arab fortress. It takes its name from the Sun Gate, or Portas do Sol, and has an uninterrupted view of the Tagus and the Ribatejo Plain beyond.

Quite apart from its historical associations Santarém is known as a bullfighting centre and is famous for its annual festivities. The National Agricultural Fair and the International Folklore Festival are held in the first half of June while the Great Fair of Our Lady of Sorrow takes place on the second Sunday in October followed by a gastronomic extravaganza at the end of the month. The events staged in the bullring, just off the main Lisbon road, between Easter and the end of October, are spectacular, the more so because the bull is never killed. The *cavaleiros* are dressed in eighteenth-century costumes with embroidered coats, breeches, plumed hats, knee boots and silver spurs and ride stallions attired in the manner of medieval warhorses. Their job is to tire out the bull after which the *moços-de-forcado* are brought on to remove it from the ring. Their leader tries to catch the animal by its horns but failing that he simply pushes against its shoulder while the others hang on to its tail.

Across the Tagus and only about 10km (6 miles) away, **Alpiarça** is worth visiting on account of its Casa dos Patudos Museum. This vast mansion on the outskirts, close to the Lisbon road, belonged to José Relvas, a statesman who had both the time and money to indulge his love of art. The house is magnificently furnished and contains some fine tapestries and carpets, pictures by foreign artists as well as Portuguese paintings and sculptures and a collection of beautiful porcelain from a number of countries throughout Europe and the Far East.

There are no hotels of any consequence either in or around Santarém although the Hotel Abidis has its points and so does the Residencial Muralha. However, anyone in search of something a bit larger could always try the Hotel Malhoa in **Caldas da Rainha**, 40km (25 miles) away. It is a pleasant, well-established town, founded in 1484 by Dona Leonor, the wife of João II. She was on her way to Batalha when she noticed some peasants bathing in hot sulphur pools along the roadside. On discovering that they were doing it for their health she decided to see if the water would help her rheumatism and found it so beneficial that she at once interrupted her journey. The place where she turned back is Tornada, less than 6km up the road, so called because it means 'return from a trip'.

The thermal hospital in the centre of the town was ordered, financed and administered by the queen who was also responsible for the church of Nossa Senhora do Pópulo in the Plaça 25 de Abril. It is a rather severe, world-weary building on the outside but the interior is lined with cheerful blue and yellow tiles that are carried through into the baptistry where there is a heavy, decorative font. The large Dom Carlos I Park in the vicinity of the baths is equipped with tennis courts, a small boating lake, a shaded campsite and the Museu de José Malhoa full of modern paint- ings, sculptures and pottery. Marginally further afield, between the Rua Rafael Bordalo Pinheiro and the Avenida Visconde de Sacavém, the Ceramics Museum reflects nearly every aspect of this traditional industry which has flourished since the nineteenth century. Other attractions include small pottery workshops and the colourful open air Mercado da Fruta that takes up most of the Praça da República.

A minor road connects Caldas da Rainha with Foz do Arelho, 8km (5 miles) to the west on the Lagoa de Obidos, neatly situated on the edge of this large lagoon but within easy reach of the sea. It has a wide sandy beach, some not too obtrusive buildings and small boats for hire but nothing that could be described as remotely sophisticated. The country-side around is pleasantly agricultural with orchards and vineyards scarred here and there by clay pits providing the raw material for the ceramics industry.

Óbidos, 5km (3 miles) south of Caldas da Rainha, is a tiny picture book village, totally delightful in winter when there are not many people about but seething with camera-wielding tourists at other times of the year. The fact that it is well scrubbed and painted, draped in bougainvillaea, wisteria and geraniums and enclosed by impeccably restored Moorish walls adds to its charms. The narrow main street has a paved strip down the middle edged with cobble stones that acts like a magnet to pedestrians.

Everything about Óbidos is small, including the Pousada do Castelo which has taken over the remains of a fifteenth-century castle destroyed in the Lisbon earthquake of 1755. It can only find space for about twenty guests at any given time so it is essential to book in advance. There are one or two other places to stay such as the Estalagem do Convento, while the tourist office may be able to suggest a few private homes with rooms to let.

In the early days Óbidos was a fortified coastal town but the sea receded, turning the wide bay into a large lagoon, with the result that it became far less important from the military point of view. However it has always been an attractive little place and so enchanted the young Queen Isabel in 1228 that her husband, Dom Dinis, made her a present of it. The idea caught on and his example was followed by every subsequent monarch until the mid nineteenth century when Dona Maria II became queen in her own right, thereby owning it automatically.

The church of Santa Maria at the end of the main street was where the ten-year-old Afonso V married his even younger cousin Isabel in 1444. It has changed considerably since then, having been provided with an interior coating of seventeenth-century tiles, a painted ceiling and a finely carved Renaissance tomb. The adjacent Municipal Museum acts as a storehouse for various religious paintings and sculptures rescued from other churches in the area after the earthquake. It also has a few archaeological exhibits and a room devoted to the Peninsular War with a relief map of the region where Wellington won his first victory over the French in 1808. Except for the church of São Pedro, the ancient Porta da Villa, which is still the main entrance to the town, and a view from the ramparts, there is little more to see apart from a pillory in the main square and a handful of small shops festooned with souvenirs. Just outside the town a sixteenth-century aqueduct stretches away into the distance surrounded by trees, a few orchards and a collection of small farms.

Due west of Óbidos, **Peniche** is, first and foremost, an important deep-sea fishing port, its sheltered harbour overflown by seagulls while the catch is being unloaded and driven to the local canning factories. It hardly rates as a popular holiday resort. The beaches are not particularly inviting, the sea has gouged out large caverns in the battered cliffs and accommodation is somewhat limited. That having been said, Peniche also has a number of attractions which deserve an honourable mention at the very least. The most obtrusive of them is a stalwart sixteenth-century fortress

Decorative pottery is popular in many regions of Portugal

The monastery at Mafra

that served as a prison until 1974, was then converted into a distribution centre for refugees from Angola and is now providing houseroom for a local museum whose exhibits do little to relieve the atmosphere.

Some four hundred years ago the peninsula was an offshore island but as the sea retreated a narrow isthmus built up naturally, connecting it to the mainland. For anyone with time to spare there is a pleasant excursion out to the lighthouse by way of Papoa, which has its own windmill and the remains of the Forte da Luzo, built to compliment the fortress in Peniche. The road follows the coastline round to Remédios, clustered about an attractive little chapel full of picture tiles, and beyond it there is a splendid view of the ocean over an isolated rock, known as the Nau dos Corvos because it looks like the prow of a ship, to the Berlenga archipelago, some 12km ($7^1/_2$ miles) away.

Most of these so-called islands are hardly more than rocks and partly submerged reefs but **Berlenga Grande** is big enough to support a bird sanctuary, a few fishermen's cottages and a seventeenth-century fortress which has been turned into a pension. There is a ferry service out to the island from Peniche between June and September, a small campsite near the dock, a rather basic shop and restaurant-cum-bar to match. Rowing boats are available explore the many caves and grottoes while the clear water makes it a happy hunting ground for divers and fishermen as well as yachtsmen who can drop anchor in the shadow of the Fuerte de São João Baptista, which has a tiny landing stage of its own.

Before heading south from Peniche those interested in old churches would do well to pause in **Atouguia da Baleir**. As a village it is totally forgettable but the church of Nossa Senhora da Conceição with its twin belltowers has a beautifully carved altarpiece while the church of São Leonardo contains a memorable painting of the saint and an unusual version of the Nativity. A minor road doubles back to join the coastal route to the south, bypassing a series of modest holiday resorts before turning inland to Torres Vedras. The most tourist conscious of these is Porto Novo although the only place to stay is the Hotel Golf Mar, which has both an indoor and an outdoor swimming pool, a 9-hole golf course and two tennis courts.

Torres Vedras is known mainly for its wine, its four-day Carnival before the beginning of Lent and the fact that Wellington set up his historical line of defence in the area to protect Lisbon from the French. Apart from this it has a mildly viewable church of São Pedro, a sixteenth-century fountain and the remains of a castle that was restored several times before it was finally demolished by the earthquake of 1755. Holidaymakers thirsting after knowledge, and prepared for a long walk to acquire it, should get hold of a pamphlet called *The Lines of Torres Vedras*, published by the British Historical Society of Portugal. It contains all the relevant information about this early version of the Maginot Line which turns out to be a seemingly endless succession of trenches and their protecting walls.

There are not many campsites along the coast below Praia de Santa Cruz and even fewer hotels apart from a modest selection in Ericeira. This is a pleasant fishing village known primarily as the port of departure for Manuel II and his family when they sailed into exile in 1910. However it is only 11km (7 miles) from **Mafra** which combines the perfectly acceptable Albergaria Castelão with an eighteenth-century palace and a monastery designed to outdo anything else Europe had to offer. The result was certainly impressive, spread over 4 hectares (10 acres) numbering its rooms in hundreds, it doors and windows in thousands and the total cost in millions of cruzados. It was never very popular with the Portuguese royal family but did remarkably well as a temporary barracks for both British and French troops during the Peninsular War, after which part of the complex was turned over to the local army.

Mafra already had a castle at the beginning of the eighteenth century but this was blown up by João V who had sworn to build a new religious masterpiece if his apparently sterile queen gave him an heir. Dona Maria was born in due course and the project was completed in 1735. The overall design is not at all original. The large marble basilica has pride of place in the centre of the seemingly interminable façade, measuring 220m (722ft) with wings at either end topped by outsized domes. Meanwhile the monastery buildings are arranged round their own courtyard tucked away behind the church. The twin belltowers are linked by a double row of columns and have more than a hundred bells between them, which fortunately do not reverberate sufficiently to dislodge the saintly statues from their niches high up in the walls. The interior is a kaleidoscope of coloured marble, ranging from black and red to pastel shades, complimented by attractive altarpieces, bronze candelabra and six matching organs that were added in the early nineteenth century.

The palace is less harmonious, filled with unexceptional furniture to replace the original pieces that João VI took with him when he sought refuge in Brazil during the Peninsular War and forgot to bring back afterwards. One of the most impressive apartments is the Baroque library with its collection of well over thirty thousand books. The conducted tours also include the kitchens and the monks' hospital, the pharmacy, one or two cells and a fairly run-of-the-mill museum of sacred art. Many of the statues and altarpieces were created by the Mafra School of Sculpture, founded by João V, whereas a large proportion of the ceramics came from Sobreiro, a few kilometres away on the road to Ericeira and better known these days for its miniature village designed especially for children. From Mafra, which strictly speaking is south of the unmarked border between the Costa de Prata and the Costa de Lisboa, there are optional routes down to the Serra de Sintra and to Lisbon.

The Costa de Prata is well served by highways, secondary roads and byways that cover almost every part of the region. Trains from Lisbon to the north of the country call at several of the main centres augmented by bus services to the major resorts, although these are less frequent in the

A typical Portugese windmill near Óbidos

The sandy coastline at Praia de Santa Cruz

outlying areas. The roads on the whole are well maintained but a reasonable amount of care should be taken when exploring off the beaten track. The weather in the area is usually very pleasant, seldom dropping below 10°C (50°F) in the winter or climbing much above 19°C (67°F) in August because of the cool onshore breezes from the Atlantic.

Anyone who enjoys seafood would be in their element in this part of the country. A chowder, known as *caldeirada* is one of the local specialities, varying from place to place, especially in Aveiro where it is made with eels. Peniche is noted for its lobsters and sardines, Martinho do Porto relies more on red mullet while, slightly inland, the Bairrada district north of Coimbra offers roast suckling pig and Leiria concentrates on sausages. Most of the traditional sweet dishes are made with eggs and sugar although Torres Vedras produces tasty bean cakes known as *pastéis de feijao* while Alcobaca concentrates more on its fresh fruit.

Although souvenirs can be bought nearly everywhere the designs change subtly from one community to another. The little pottery figures from Caldas da Rainha are distinctive and so are the faience wine jugs from Aveiro, Marinha Grande is the place to look for hand-painted glass while Nazaré has heavy fishermen's sweaters. Peniche has revived the ancient art of bobbin lace making which is practiced in the Workhouse of the Daughters of Fishermen on the Rue do Calvario and can be bought in the Avenida do Mar, whereas the weavers of Óbidos are sometimes to be seen at work on their traditional cotton carpets. In fact there are plenty of attractive, useful articles for anyone who has the time and the inclination to look for them.

Additional Information

Places of Interest

Abrantes
Museu de Dom Lopo de Almeida
In church of Santa Maria do Castelo
inside castle walls
Open: 10am-12.30pm, 2-5pm. Closed Mon.
Sculptures, tombs and some tiles.

Alcobaça
Monastery of Santa Maria
Guided tours 9am-5pm.
The largest church in Portugal with magnificent tombs and monastic quarters open to the public.

Museu de la Junta Nacional de Vinho
On outskirts
Open: 9am-12.30pm and 2-5.30pm.
Wine museum belonging to the local co-operative.

Almourol
18km (11 miles) west of Abrantes
Boat trips to and round the ancient stronghold in the middle of the Tagus, April to October in good weather.

Alpiarça
Casa dos Patudos Museum
On outskirts, off the Lisbon Road
Open summer: 2-7pm Thursdays. 10-11am, 1.30-6pm Saturdays, Sundays and holidays.
Winter: 10-11am, 1.30-5.30pm Saturdays, 3.30-5.30pm Sundays and holidays. Closed 1 January, 2 April, 1 May, and 25 December.
Large mansion with private collection of furniture, pictures, china and other articles.

Arouca
Monastery church and museum
Open: 9.30am-12.30pm and 2.30-3.30pm.
Closed Mondays and day after a holiday.
Royal tomb. Several treasures in the cloister.

Aveiro
Museum in the Convent of Jesus
Rua Combatentes
Open 10am-12.30pm and 2-5pm. Closed Mondays.
Decorative church with treasures on display near Santa Joana oratory.

Boat trips from the Central Canal Mid-June to mid-September 10am-5pm. Arranged by the tourist office.

Batalha
Monastery and Museum
For opening times enquire at the tourist office behind *pousada* next door.

Buçaco Forest
North-east of Coimbra

Military Museum
Near Queens Gate
Open: 9.30am-5.30pm. Closed Mondays and holidays
Exhibits mainly concerned with local battle during Peninsular War.

Maps of walks through the forest obtainable from the Palace Hotel and the tourist office in nearby town of Luso.

Caldas da Rainha
Ceramics Museum
Between Avenida Visconde de Sacavem and Rua Rafael Bordalo Pinheiro
Open: 10am-12.30pm, 2-5pm. Closed Mondays and holidays.
Attractive and sometimes amusing examples of local ceramics.

Malhoa Museum
In Dom Carlos I Park
Open: 10am-12.30pm, 2-5pm.
Mainly modern pictures, sculptures and pottery.

Coimbra
Botanical Gardens
Alameda Dr Julio Henriques
Open: 9am-7pm.
Formal gardens with trees and some exotic plants.

Cathedral
(Sé Velha) Rua Borges Carneiro

Machado de Castro Museum
Rua Borges Carneiro
Open: 10am-1pm, 2.30-5pm. Closed Mondays.
Exceptionally fine collection of Portuguese sculptures and other exhibits.

Convent of Santa Clara-a-Nova
Calçada Santa Isabel
Open: 9.30am-12.30pm, 2-5.30pm.
Closed Mondays, holidays and during services.
Chapel containing the tomb of Queen Isabel.

Mosteiro de Santa Cruz
Praça 8 de Maio
Open: 9.30am-12.30pm, 2-6pm.
Royal tombs, fine wood carving and pictures.

Portugal in Miniature
Rossio Santa Clara
Open: 9am-7pm April to September, 9am-5.30pm October to March.
Garden with scaled down buildings designed mainly for children.

University Library
Ring doorbell to obtain entry.
Three outstanding rooms with beautiful furniture and old books.

Museum of Sacred Art
In the Manueline Chapel
Open: 9am-12noon, 2-5.30pm.

Sala dos Capelos
Open: 9am-12.30pm, 2-5.30pm.
Original throne room with painted ceiling and royal portraits.

Conimbriga
15km (9 miles) southwest of Coimbra
Open: 9am-1pm, 2-8pm in summer.
9am-1pm, 2-6pm in winter.
Ruins of Roman city with remains of villas and interesting mosaics.

Museu Monográfico
On the site
Open: 9am-12noon, 2-6pm. Closed
Mondays and holidays.

Figueira da Foz
Museu Municipal do Dr Santos Rocha
Rua Calousta Gulbenkian
Open: 9am-12.30pm, 2-6pm. Closed
Mondays and holidays.
Archaeological exhibits, coins and old
photographs.

Ilhavo
Marine Museum
On northern outskirts
Open: 9am-12.30pm, 2-5.30pm. Closed
Mondays and holidays.
Nautical exhibits and the fishing indus-
try.

Leiria
Castle
Open: 9am-7pm summer, 9am-6pm
winter.
Contains rather subdued palace and
ruins of a small chapel.

Mafra
Palace and Monastery
Open: 10am-1pm, 2-5pm. Closed
Tuesdays and holidays.
Guided tours include, some royal
apartments, small museum of sacred art
and sections of the monastery.

Óbidos
Municipal Museum
In the church square
Open: 10am-1pm, 2-5pm. Closed
Mondays.
Mainly exhibits from churches damaged
in the 1755 earthquake.

Peniche
Fortress
Open: 1-7pm. Closed Mondays.
Contains small museum with archaeo-
logical exhibits and local arts and crafts.

Sea trips to the Berlenga Islands June to
September.
Full information available in the har-
bour.

Workhouse of the Daughters of Fishermen
Rua do Calvario
Open: weekdays when lacemakers are
at work.
Examples also seen in the
Industrial and Commercial School,
Avenida 25 de Abril.

Santarém
Archaeological Museum
São João Alporão
Rua Serpa Pinto
Open: 10am-5pm. Closed Monday
mornings and holidays.
Interesting display of items including a
Gothic tomb.

Serra do Aire
An attractive series of underground
caves, within more or less easy reach of
each other:

The Grutas dos Moinhos Velhos
Between Mira de Aire and Porto de Mós
Open: 9am-9pm May to October. 9am-
6pm November to April.
A number of colourful galleries with lift
back to the surface.

São Mamede Caves
Near the village. Enquire locally for
times.

Alvados Caves and Santo António Caves
On the N361
Open: 9am-9pm April to September.
9am-6pm October to March.
Underground chambers with attrac-
tively coloured rock formations.

Tomar
Capela de Nossa Senhora da Conceição
On the road to the Convento de Cristo
If closed collect the key from the tourist
office.

Convento de Cristo
Open: 9.30am-12.30pm and 2-6pm.
Closed Mondays.
A massive monastery centred on the
twelfth-century Templars' Rotunda.

Torres Novas
Ruined Roman Villa Cardilio
3km to the south
Enquire at the house next to the site.

Torres Vedras
The nearby Lines of Torres Vedras
constructed by Wellington during the
Peninsular War.
For details see a pamphlet issued by the
British Historical Society of Portugal.

Vista Alegre
Porcelain Museum
South of Aveiro, at porcelain factory
Open: 9am-12.30pm and 2-5.30pm.
Closed Saturdays, Sundays and holidays.
For a guided tour telephone in advance
034 22261.

Tourist Information Offices

Abrantes
Largo de Feira
☎ 041 22555

Aveiro
Praça da República
☎ 034 23680

Batalha
Largo Paulo VI
☎ 044 96180

Alcobaça
Praça 25 de Abril
☎ 062 42377

Buçaco
Posto de Turismo Luso
☎ 031 93133

Caldas da Rainha
Praça da República
☎ 062 34511

Coimbra
Largo de Portagem
☎ 039 25576 or 23886

Fátima
Avenida Dr José Alves Correia da Silva
☎ 049 51139

Figueira da Foz
Avenida 25 de Abril
☎ 033 22610

Leiria
Jardim Luis de Camoês
☎ 044 32748

Mafra
Avenida 25 de Abril
☎ 061 52023

Óbidos
Rua Direita
☎ 062 95231

Peniche
Rua Alexandre Herculano
☎ 062 72271

Santarém
Rua Capelo Ivens
☎ 043 23140
Portas do Sol
☎ 043 23141

Tomar
Avenida Dr Cândido Madureira
☎ 049 33237

Torres Vedras
Rua 9 de Abril
☎ 061 23094

Accommodation

Abrantes
Hotel de Tourismo
Largo de Santo Antonio
☎ 041 21261

Alcobaça
Hotel Santa Maria
Rua Dr Francisco Zagalo
☎ 062 43295

Aveiro
Imperial Hotel
Rua Dr Nascimento Leitão
☎ 034 22141

Aparthotel Afonso V
Praceta Dom Afonso V
☎ 034 29640

Paloma Blanca
Rua Luis Gomes de Carvalho
☎ 034 22529

Pousada da Ria
☎ 034 48332

Batalha
Pousada Mestre Afonso Domingues
☎ 044 96260

Quinta do Fidalgo
☎ 044 96144

Hotel Eurosol
Hotel Eurosol Jardim
Rua Dr José Alves da Silva
☎ 044 24101

Buçaco Forest
Palace Hotel do Buçano
☎ 032 93101

Caldas da Rainha
Hotel Malhoa
Rua Antonia Sergio
☎ 062 84 21 89

Coimbra
Hotel Astória
Avenida Emídio Navarro
☎ 039 22055

Residencial Parque
☎ 039 29202

Hotel Dom Luis
Quinta da Varzea
☎ 039 84 15 10

Fátima
Hotel de Fátima
Rua João Paulo II
☎ 049 52351

Recidencial São Paulo
Rua de São Paulo
☎ 049 51572

Figueira da Foz
Grande Hotel da Figueira
Avenida 25 de Abril
☎ 033 22146

Clube de Vale de Leão
Estrada do Cabo Mondrago
☎ 033 26601

Ilhavo
Paço da Hermita
☎ 034 32 24 96

Mafra
Albergana Castelo
Avenida 25 de Abril
☎ 061 52320

Óbidos
Pousada do Castelo
☎ 062 95105

Estalagem do Convento
Rua Dom João de Ornelas
☎ 062 95217

Porto Novo
Hotel Golf Mar
☎ 061 98157

Santarem
Hotel Abidis
Rua Guilherme de Azevedo
☎ 043 22017

Residencial Muralha
Rua Pedro Canavarro
☎ 043 22399

Tomar
Hotel dos Templários
Largo Cândido dos Reis
☎ 049 32121

Pousada de São Pedro
Castelo do Bode
☎ 049 38159

Estalagem Vale da Ursa
(northeast of Tomar on N238)
☎ 074 67511

4

COSTA DE LISBOA

The capital city of **Lisbon**, or Lisboa to be strictly accurate, is not particularly impressive at first sight. It is relatively compact with hardly any skyline to speak of because it rises and falls over a series of low hills on the northern bank of the Tagus, roughly 10km (6 miles) upriver from the sea. The outlying areas consist of comparatively modern suburbs, several of which are already past their best, while even some of the older districts towards the centre give off an almost tangible aura of genteel decay. However it only takes a few hours of determined sightseeing to discover a very different side to Lisbon and appreciate why the Phoenicians called it *Allis Ubbo*, or 'delightful little port', in about 1200BC.

From its earliest days the city has been blessed with an ideal natural harbour in the Mar de Palha, a veritable inland sea behind the mouth of the Tagus, which was relatively simple to defend and provided a sheltered anchorage for warships as well as merchantmen. The port changed hands any number of times as the country was overrun by one group of invaders after another. Eventually it was recaptured from the Moors by Afonso Henriques, the first king of Portugal, in 1147 with the aid of a miscellaneous party of crusaders who stopped off to help on their way to the Holy Land. A little over a century later it replaced Coimbra as the nation's capital. Everything was more or less straightforward after that, culminating in Vasco da Gama's discovery of a sea route to India followed almost immediately by the annexation of Brazil. Untold wealth began to flood into Portugal and Lisbon soon became the major trading centre of what was then the world's leading maritime power. Business flourished and splendidly ornate buildings added to the general air of euphoria.

On 1 November 1755 southern Portugal was hit by a violent earthquake, which was so powerful that it was even felt in England, underground in the lead mines of Derbyshire. Buildings in Lisbon collapsed like packs of cards, burying their occupants under mounting piles of rubble. Hundreds of wax candles burning in the churches to mark All Saints Day set fire to the woodwork, sending the congregations rushing frantically for safety along the river bank where vast numbers were drowned by a huge tidal wave that was forced inland from the Atlantic. It engulfed the lower town, inundated the docks and added to the sum total of the disaster which was said to have destroyed two thirds of the city.

The task of rebuilding the capital was left in the capable hands of the future Marquês de Pombal who decreed that the new streets should be 40ft wide with pavements on either side and the replacement buildings uniformly functional and devoid of any unnecessary adornments. Part of the result is the elegant if slightly unimaginative **Praça do Comércio**, also ✳ known as the Terreiro do Paço after a royal palace which had occupied the site since the early sixteenth century. It faces the river, not far from the Estacão do Cais do Sodre — one of the main railway stations — and the south terminal ferry with its regular services across the Tagus. The other three sides of the square are occupied by matching classical buildings with pinkish-red façades above their tall arcades, housing a number of commercial concerns and administrative departments in addition to the main post office.

In the centre of the Praça do Comércio, once the scene of bullfighting but now a giant parking space, is the bronze equestrian statue of José I who was on the throne at the time of the earthquake. Behind it a much decorated triumphal arch, added after the dictatorial Pombal was no longer in any position to object, leads to the Rua Augusta that forms part of the grid pattern separating it from the Rossio. Not far from the arch, in the direction of the post office, is the spot where Carlos I and his eldest son were assassinated in 1908.

The **Rossio**, or to give it its full title, the Praça Dom Pedro IV, is rather ✳ less impressive but a good deal more decorative. The Dona Maria II National Theatre has taken the place of the old Palace of the Inquisition, where horrific atrocities were committed in the name of religious justice. It overlooks a Baroque fountain surrounded by flower sellers who, when it rains or the wind is in the wrong direction, take refuge under coloured umbrellas in an effort to keep dry. Midway between the fountain and its companion at the opposite end a statue of Pedro IV, who was also Pedro I of Brazil, comes in for a lot of unwelcome attention from masses of pigeons who also descend on any passers-by carrying a likely-looking bag of food. Nearby is the **Praça dos Restauradores**, distinguished by its lofty ✳ obelisk dedicated to the men who led a revolt against Spain in 1640. A Moorish-type building with typical horseshoe arches, more or less round the corner, is in fact the entrance to the local railway station.

One of Lisbon's less widely publicised museums, the Geographical Society's **Museu Entográfico do Ultramar**, in the Rua Portas de Santo 🏛 Antão behind the National Theatre, consists of all sorts of bits and pieces brought home as souvenirs from far-flung outposts of the empire. These include carvings from the Congo, Angola and Mozambique, musical instruments and even a shrunken head or two. The parallel Avenida de Liberdade, described by local taxi drivers as Lisbon's Champs Élysées, runs in an arrow-straight line up to the Praça Marquês de Pombal, flanked by hotels and restaurants, places of entertainment, shops and offices. The square, actually a perfect circle vaguely reminiscent of the Étoile in Paris, with streets radiating from it like the spokes of a wheel, has a massive

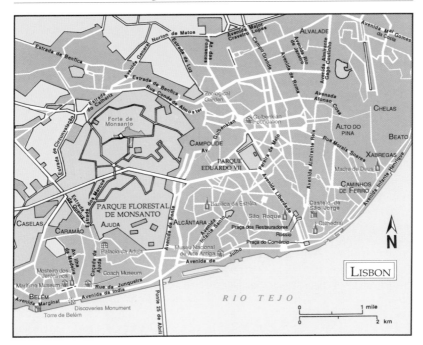

white centrepiece recalling the marquês and his most outstanding achievements. It is ringed with manicured gardens, small islands planted with palms and various other trees, a constant flow of traffic and buildings that are predictable and generally rather bland.

One of the best places to start exploring is the Bairro Alto, a somewhat hilly district to the west of the Rossio, with narrow streets many of whose elderly houses could do with a clean and a fresh coat of paint. Apart from fashionable boutiques, a seemingly inexhaustible supply of restaurants and *fado* bars and almost as many little shops that specialise in anything from sweetmeats or leather goods to books and manuscripts, there is at least one church especially worthy of note. From the outside the **Igreja São Roque** is not very prepossessing, possibly because its sixteenth-century façade was among the casualties in 1755, but the interior is another matter altogether. Scenes from the Apocalypse run riot across the wooden ceiling above the nave while a painting of the vision of St Rock shares one of the small chapels with an array of colourful 400-year-old tiles. Nevertheless its *pièce de résistance* is the Chapel of São João Baptista (St John the Baptist), a perfect example of the way in which the country's rulers and their enormous wealth were quickly parted. João V ordered it from Rome where it was built, consecrated by Pope Benedict XIV and then dismantled and shipped to Lisbon where it was duly reconstructed near the high altar. When it had been crammed to capacity with marble, lapis

A bird's eye view of a square in Lisbon

The Rossio, Lisbon, with the statue of Pedro IV

lazuli, ivory, amethyst, alabaster and gold, everything that was left over found its way into the **Museum of Sacred Art** next door. There are richly decorated vestments, a mitre encrusted with Brazilian rubies, silver plate and medieval paintings as well as a fourteenth-century statue of the Virgin and Child.

A few blocks away, clinging tenaciously to the hillside, is the ruined **Convento do Carmo**, founded after the battle of Aljubarrota in 1385 and shaken to pieces by the earthquake. Some of the walls and arches are still standing and have been incorporated into an archaeological museum stocked with everything from Bronze Age pottery and oddments discarded by the Visigoths to assortments of coins and ancient tombstones. There is also a likeness of Afonso Henriques, the founder of the nation, which may or may not be the oldest sculpture of him still in existence. Slightly further south, towards the river, the **São Carlos Opera House** and the **Museu Nacional de Arte Contemporânea** almost, but not quite, face each other across the Rua Serpa Pinto. The latter is devoted to paintings from the late nineteenth and early twentieth centuries with a selection of sculptures thrown in for good measure, none of which is particularly memorable.

The ancient district of Alfama, on the opposite side of the Rossio, is presided over by the **Castelo São Jorge**, poised on the top of its own small mountain peak high above the city. The site was chosen by the Phoenicians, developed by the Romans and the Visigoths, adapted by the Moors and up-dated by Afonso I. Today its businesslike ramparts, towers and battlements have been expertly restored but serve no useful purpose apart from guarding a collection of terraces and gardens and providing visitors with a variety of panoramic views. The *alcázar* was transformed into a royal palace in the fourteenth century but abandoned within two hundred years, although parties of schoolchildren still make valiant attempts to recapture the original atmosphere. Young knights, shouting at the top of their voices, brandish wooden swords while the opposing Arabs, resplendent in newspaper headdresses held in place with string, refuse to admit for a moment that defeat is even remotely possible.

Nestling in the shadow of the castle is the ancient quarter of Santa Cruz. It is a jumble of narrow streets hemmed in by elderly houses whose wrought iron balconies are festooned with laundry while the doors have Judas windows that were so necessary in the olden days to spy on the world outside. Another local attraction is the **Museu da Marioneta** filled with puppets, both the Portuguese variety and examples from the Far East, which came in useful for making political comments before plays using marionettes were banned by Dr Salazar.

Somewhat further afield, and built as its name implies outside the city walls, is the **Monastery of São Vincente de Fora**, completed in the early seventeenth century. Its lofty white façade has no intention of being overlooked whereas the interior is relatively unadorned apart from the Baroque altar and eight attendant wooden sculptures that are all as large as life. Hunting scenes were used to decorate the cloister while the former monks' refectory has been converted into a royal pantheon where many of the kings and queens of Portugal are buried. Nearby, the **Igreja da Santa Engrácia** is also a national pantheon but with somewhat less majestic connections, recalling Henry the Navigator and Vasco da Gama. The church, in the form of a Greek cross, took a considerable time to build, the finishing touches having been added as recently as 1966. There is even an elevator up to the dome for anyone who wants to get a pigeon's eye view of the city. Twice a week, on Tuesdays and Saturdays, the Feira da Ladra, or local fleamarket, clutters the adjacent Campo de Santa Clara with stalls full of everyday articles at reasonable prices. It is not a place to look for hidden treasures but it is noisy and colourful and worth a brief visit if you happen to be in the area.

The Alfama, lying between the castle and the river, is a totally unselfconscious labyrinth of narrow streets and alleys, linked in places by decrepit stairways, that survived the earthquake mainly because it is built on rock. The Arabs settled there and called it Alhama, drawing attention to their public baths fed by hot springs near the Largo das Alcaçarias, but these have totally disappeared together with practically all the elegant town houses built later by the returning Christians. However a few can still be seen, especially in the vicinity of the Rua da Regueira. It is definitely an area to explore on foot, calling for a fair amount of energy, comfortable shoes and reasonable precautions against pickpockets and other petty thieves.

Any cars, trams or other vehicles that do manage to force their way into the Alfama spend a disproportionate amount of time fuming in traffic jams — and it takes even longer to park. Fortunately most of the major attractions are within convenient walking distance of each other, starting with the **Cathedral** on the Rua Augusto Rosa, a short stroll from the Praça do Comércio and the waterfront. The Sé, as it is called, was originally built for Gilbert of Hastings, the first bishop of Lisbon, with the obligatory fortified towers and a large rose window over the main entrance, but it has been considerably restored and renovated several times since then. The interior is dark and rather disappointing while the sacristy has been turned into a museum whose treasures include a casket containing relics of St Vincent. According to popular belief two ravens, or possibly crows, escorted a boat containing the body of the saint into Lisbon from Valencia, where he was martyred, via the Sagres peninsula whose headland was promptly named after him. He was proclaimed patron saint of the city but displaced later by St Anthony of Padua, a local resident who became a missionary during the thirteenth century and was canonized shortly after his death. The little church of **Santo António da Sé**, directly facing the cathedral, occupies the site where he was born and his festival is celebrated with enormous enthusiasm during the third week in June.

There are some sparse remains of a Roman theatre in the vicinity of the Sé but they are of considerably less interest than the **Museu-Escola de**

⛩ **Artes Decorativas**, housed in a seventeenth century palace that belonged to the counts of Azurara further up the hill. The decorative arts on display include some magnificent furniture as well as tapestries and rugs, silverware, ceramics and glass. An added attraction is that craftsmen of varying descriptions have their workshops just next door, producing copies of traditional articles, employing the same methods that were used by their predecessors.

✳ Another place that is well worth visiting is the **Miradouro de Santa Luzia**, an attractive flower-filled square with splendid views, set into a section of the ancient Moorish ramparts bordering on the Largo do Limoeiro. It takes its name from the church of Santa Luzia whose walls are covered with tiles depicting some of the outstanding historical events in the history of the city. Among them is a tribute to Martim Moniz, a knight who lost his life preventing the Arabs from closing one of the castle gates ⛩ in the face of an attack by Afonso I. Finally, the **Military Museum**, occupying the old arsenal overlooking the docks, is mainly of interest to those who are keen on weapons and other aspects of war.

⛪ To the east of the Alfama, and not too far away, is the much restored and ⛩ richly decorated **Igreja da Madre de Deus** and its attendant **Azulejo Museum**. Not a great deal remains of the early sixteenth century convent, founded by Dona Leonor, the widow of João II, although the marble basin for holy water in the sacristy is thought to have belonged to her. Several early paintings in the chancel came from the original church but the scenes from the life of St Francis were added subsequently, when the building was enlarged. The Baroque altarpieces are drenched in gold and there are tiles everywhere, even down in the crypt which has its own altar of gilded wood. Part of the convent buildings round the cloisters are home to the ⛩ Tile Museum, where examples going back more than four hundred years provide the starting point for a collection that traces the history of *azulejos* up to the present day. Some are frankly unattractive, a few are amusing and many are colourful but the most eye-catching is a massive view of the Lisbon waterfront as it was before the earthquake altered it completely.

Having exhausted most of the possibilities on offer upriver from the Praça do Comércio it is logical to start exploring in the opposite direction. The first place of interest beyond the Praça Duque de Terceira, apart from ⛩ a large covered market, is the **Museu Nacional de Arte Antiga**, in the Jardim 9 de Abril. It is one of the most absorbing of all Lisbon's many museums and, for some people, more than one visit is needed to appreciate it properly.

In pride of place, at all events among the Portuguese Primitives, is a set of half a dozen panels depicting the Adoration of St Vincent. The groups consist of knights, monks and fishermen surrounding various members of the nobility. Foremost among them are Henry the Navigator and other assorted princes, representatives of the House of Bragança and Isabella of Aragon while Afonso V and Queen Isabel kneel to receive the saint's blessing. The artist, Nuno Gonçalves, also put himself in the picture, along

Flower seller in the Rossio, Lisbon

with a Moorish knight, a Jew and even a beggar.

As well as the works of Portuguese painters a number of foreign artists are also represented including Holbein, Dürer and Zurbarán, along with Bosch's *Temptations of St Anthony* which the saint seems to have resisted without any apparent effort. Other sections of the museum are devoted to arts and crafts from nearly every country that traded with Portugal during her golden age. There is embroidery, inlaid wood and ivory from India, Chinese porcelain, Japanese artwork and carvings from Africa. Gold and silver extravagancies, developed for the court at Versailles and coveted by its opposite number in Lisbon, have a section to themselves. A large proportion of the magnificent articles on display date from the late eighteenth century, having been ordered by José I to replace similar treasures that were lost in the earthquake. One of the most outstanding examples of religious art to have escaped intact is a splendid monstrance created by Gil Vicente, the medieval poet and goldsmith, which once belonged to the monastery at Belém. Also on view are carpets, furniture and pottery as well as tiles and ornate wood carvings in a small chapel that was once part of the Convent of Santo Alberto, a former occupant of the site. Other landmarks within a radius of half a dozen blocks or so are the **Basilica da Estrêla** and the Necessidades Palace, which now provides a home for the Foreign Ministry. The former is a late eighteenth-century construction, notable for its towers and marble statues, founded by Dona Maria I who is buried near the high altar.

A touch further downstream is one of the modern sights of Lisbon — the remarkable **Ponte 25 de Abril**, built in the early 1960s. It is a steel suspension bridge measuring 2,278m overall — which is about $1^1/_2$ miles — incorporating the longest single span in Europe. For the benefit of anyone interested in such details the official description points out that the 1,013m (3,323ft) span is suspended from two massive pylons and soars 70m (230ft) above the surface of the Tagus. There are two levels, the upper one for road traffic while the lower is designed to take a double railway line. The whole construction is watched over by a monumental statue of Christ in Majesty, copied from the one in Rio de Janeiro, with a lift up to the top of the pedestal nearly 400ft above the water. From here there are panoramic views over the capital, the estuary and the Serra da Arrábida down to Setúbal.

The Avenida de Brasilia follows the north bank of the river, past a ferry station and a well-patronised pleasure boat harbour, to the dazzlingly white **Padrão dos Descobrimentos**. This monument to the age of discovery was completed marginally ahead of the Ponte 25 de Abril in 1960, the five hundredth anniversary of the death of Henry the Navigator. It represents the bows of a stylised caravel with the prince standing at the prow, wearing his familiar voluminous hat and holding a small ship under full sail. Lined up along the decks behind him on either side are many of the people who were associated with the emerging empire, some of them easily recognisable like Manuel I, but others are unfortunately obscure. It would be nice to think that they include famous explorers such as Dias, da Gama and Magellan as well as other leading figures of the day. Inside the monument there is a cultural centre with exhibition halls and an auditorium for audio-visual presentations. The whole structure is surrounded by a wavy black and white mosaic pavement whose centrepiece is an enormous compass dial containing a colourful map of the world.

Only a short walk away along the river bank is the **Torre de Belém**, an extremely decorative fortress that was completed in 1521. At that time it stood almost in the middle of the Tagus, off what was the Restelo beach where caravels rode at anchor, taking on men and supplies before sailing out into the unknown. Its primary functions were to discourage enemy privateers and collect harbour dues, both of which meant posting lookouts in the strategically placed sentry boxes under their matching ornamental domes. The main tower has several Moorish characteristics and overlooks an extensive terrace, used originally as a platform for cannons and a statue of Our Lady of Safe Homecoming. Two floors below were the damp, unpleasant and very unhealthy dungeons. These days the Belém Tower is reached by way of a short, stubby causeway and anyone who is prepared to climb up to the balcony is rewarded with an uninterrupted view of the Padrão dos Descobrimentos with the Ponte 25 de Abril in the distance.

In the olden days, before the Tagus narrowed down to its present size, the northern bank barely skimmed past the **Mosteiro dos Jerónimos**, a magnificent Manueline pile on the opposite side of the Avenida da India. It started life in 1460 as a modest hermitage, founded by Henry the Navigator, where monks belonging to the Order of Christ attended to the temporal needs and spiritual wellbeing of seafarers. However, in 1499, when Vasco da Gama returned to Belém having discovered the sea route to India, Manuel I imposed a 5 percent tax on the cargoes of spices and precious stones that followed in his wake and earmarked it for the building of a new monastery on the site. The initial construction was completed by 1517 after which a succession of artists and architects added their own individual touches before the end of the century. In some ways the result is almost magical.

The south portal, overlooking the river, is an exuberant mixture of slender turrets, statues and reliefs illustrating episodes in the life of St Jerome. It is flanked by tall decorative windows and surmounted by the Cross of the Order of Christ which invariably appeared on the sails of the caravels during the age of discovery. Beyond the dome, which all but dwarfs the twin spires on the left, are the old convent buildings that were extended and considerably transformed in the nineteenth century.

The interior of the church is amazingly spacious, partly because the nave and the aisles are of uniform height, emphasised by the lines of matching, well-decorated columns that support the vaulted roof. The royal tombs in the transepts are unusually restrained although each one is balanced on the backs of two rather endearing, polished marble el-

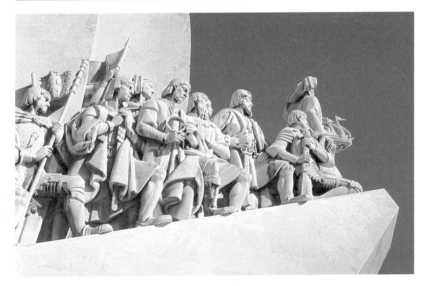

The Padrão dos Descobrimentos (Discoveries Monument), Lisbon

Torre de Belém, Lisbon

The Monastery of Jerónimos, Lisbon

ephants. Vasco da Game is also buried there, and so is the poet Luís de Camões, appropriately crowned with laurel leaves, whose epic *Os Lusíadas* was written to commemorate the famous voyage of discovery to India. The overall effect is at variance with the high altar, a stupendous example of somewhat over-enthusiastic gilt Baroque. On the other hand the cloisters are exceptionally beautiful, built one above the other with delicate stone tracery, a considerable amount of carving and a door through to the upper choir with its original wooden stalls.

Despite all the wealth and attention lavished on it in the early days the fortunes of the monastery altered considerably, going from bad to worse in the space of about one hundred years. Revenues dwindled with the changing situation in the country and eventually the monks were forced to explore every possible avenue in an attempt to keep their establishment going. By some miracle the building survived the earthquake of 1755 with only superficial damage but there was no money in the national coffers afterwards to spend on care and maintenance. At the beginning of the nineteenth century army units moved into part of the convent and when the monasteries were dissolved a few years later it was turned into a home for orphans. Shortly after this the west wing was largely rebuilt and extended and now houses the city's **Maritime Museum** and the **Planetarium**.

The exhibits in the Museu de Marinha are many and varied, tracing the country's long and frequently impressive association with the sea. In the entrance to the main section there are statues, cannons and three anchors from the *Nina*, one of the ships that accompanied Columbus across the Atlantic to San Salvador. Elsewhere, apart from stately galleons there are scale models of other ancient warships and merchantmen as well as twentieth-century surface vessels and submarines. The fishing fleets are represented by various types of craft which operated along the coast and in the river estuaries while, in a class by itself, is the reconstructed state-room of the royal yacht *Amelia*.

Visitors with an eye for detail can inspect a variety of uniforms, pour over ancient charts — some of them are original — and admire the seaplane *Santa Cruz* which crossed the south Atlantic in 1922. Other attractions include navigation instruments of all types and descriptions and articles of modern warfare such as mines, shells and torpedoes. As one would expect it receives just as many enthusiasts as the nearby **Museum of Popular Arts** where the contents range over the whole gamut of folk art and traditions.

In the old riding school that once formed part of the Palace of Belém the **Coach Museum**, founded by Queen Amelia in 1905, is one of the finest in the world. In addition to more than seventy different vehicles — everything from state carriages to sedan chairs — there are silver harnesses, stirrups and spurs, uniforms worn by the drivers and footmen and a figure known as the *estafermo* which riders attempted to prod with a lance before he could lash out at them with his whip.

By far the most magnificent coaches are lined up at the far end of the main hall, heavy and highly ornamented with large sculptured lions, cherubs and prancing horses, in which kings and princes rode in procession to ceremonial events such as coronations. Other, less ostentatious models are gilded, beautifully painted and upholstered in velvet and damask, much of which shows all-too-obvious signs of wear. Members of the court also had their splendid conveyances but on the orders of the Marquês de Pombal these became increasingly less decorative. The smaller hall on the right-hand side is full of interesting examples, thoughtfully labelled in English as well as Portuguese which makes identifying them a good deal easier.

Other attractions in the vicinity that are worth remembering, especially if time is no object, are the **Chapel of St Hieronymus**, the former **Colonial Gardens** and the **Casa dos Pastéis de Belém**, a cake shop that has been making delicious cakes, served hot with cinnamon and sugar, for more than 150 years. In addition the Calçada da Ajuda climbs up the hill behind the Museu Nacional dos Coches to the **Palacio Nacional de Ajuda**, a comparatively modern royal residence with some interesting tapestries, assorted furniture, sculptures and a selection of not particularly memorable pictures. It stands on the edge of the enormous Parque Forestal de Monsanto, an area of untamed countryside, full of winding roads and improvised picnic sites.

On its way into the city the Avenida Calouste Gulbenkian sweeps under the Aguas Livres Aqueduct which spans the Alcântara Valley. Although it has a Roman look about it the 200ft-high aqueduct took from 1728 to 1748 to build, and still provides Lisbon with fresh water.

Not unnaturally the Avenida Gulbenkian leads directly to the **Calouste Gulbenkian Foundation** where a section of the building is devoted to a superb museum of art presented to the nation by the Armenian multi-millionaire. The area it occupies is not very large but nothing in it should be overlooked. 'Mr Five Per Cent', as he was known as a result of a 5 per cent investment in the oil fields of Iraq, was a connoisseur who was only interested in perfect and authentic items. He knew what he wanted and was able to pay the price so that each item in his collection is a superb example of its kind.

The logical place to start is probably in among the antiquities, beginning with an Egyptian alabaster bowl that is nearly 3,000 years old. There are treasures from ancient Greece and Rome, with coins, medals and antique jewellery. Carpets from the Middle East vie for attention with glass and pottery along with copies of the Koran and fifteenth-century poetry. The Orient is also well represented by Chinese porcelain and lacquered articles from Japan.

Outstanding examples of European art include Rubens' *Portrait of Hélèn Fourment*, Rembrandt's *Portrait of an Old Man*, works by van Dyck, Romney, Gainsborough and Turner as well as *The Bridge at Mantes* by Corot and Manet's *Child with Cherries*. There are also sculptures and tapestries, elegant French furniture, bronzes, gold and silverware and Art Nouveau jewellery. The foundation has made a special point of fostering modern Portuguese art which has a whole section to itself. Some of the exhibits are frankly uninspiring but collectively they give a clear idea of how local events dictated changes in style, especially under Salazar. Amadeo do Souza Cardoso, who died in 1918, worked in Paris and was influenced by Cézanne before developing his own particular brand of Expressionism. Other names to look for are Eloy, Botelho, de Silva, Pomar and Ribeira and, more recently, Paula Rego whose contributions have a strange, brooding quality about them.

Anyone beginning to wilt under a surfeit of elderly buildings, churches and museums would be well advised to look for a change of scene in the **Eduardo VII Park**, named after Britain's Edward VII who visited Lisbon in 1902. It is within easy strolling distance of the Calouste Gulbenkian Museum, just to the north of Marquês de Pombal Square. The landscaped gardens are pleasant and relaxing, especially in the Estufa Fria, or cold greenhouse, where wooden slats are used to protect a variety of ferns and exotic-looking plants. Set in amongst them are some attractive little grottoes, an occasional fishpond and one or two modest waterfalls. Anything that needs hothouse conditions, such as orchids and some types of cacti, is relegated to the large Estufa Quente which, as a result, can be extremely colourful.

One of the many exhibits in the Coach Museum, Lisbon

Although quite a few birds live in the Parque Eduardo VII a far greater number are on view in the privately-owned **Zoological Gardens**, a tidy walk away beyond the aqueduct. There are more than 3,500 inhabitants all told, mostly familiar species, whose dens and cages are surrounded by tree-filled gardens. Local families use it as a convenient picnic spot whereas visitors tend to gravitate towards the Miradouro dos Minhos, a small mill at the top of a rise overlooking the Monsanto Park with Benfica's Luz football stadium slightly to the northwest. Due north, and a bit further off, is the National Costume Museum, tucked away in the suburb of Lumiar opposite the local cemetery. Known as the **Museu do Trajo**, its periodical exhibitions highlight changes in fashion since the Middle Ages while the **Museu de Teatro** is more concerned with theatrical costumes, stage sets and other such matters. They share a delightfully wooded park that was laid out at the end of the eighteenth century.

Heading back towards the city centre the only other tourist attractions are the **Municipal Museum**, whose contents are historically interesting but hardly rivetting enough to hold the attention of casual visitors, and the dark red bullring which can, and frequently does, cram in more than 8,000 noisy spectators. Meanwhile sightseers with time on their hands have several other small churches to choose from as well as the main **Botanical Gardens** to the west of the Avenida da Liberdade and the **Vasco de Gama Aquarium** at Dafundo on the N6 beyond the Torre de Belém. It augments its tanks of sea plants, fish and shellfish, a colony of turtles and resident seals with a display of sea creatures that have been preserved and put on display upstairs.

Because Lisbon is so hilly it requires a certain determination to do all one's sightseeing on foot, especially if time is limited. Places that look quite close together on the map may well be separated by a small, steep valley which means negotiating long flights of steps or clambering up a series of narrow, twisting alleys, particularly in the area round the Castelo de São Jorge. It is not always possible to squeeze in with a car and parking can be a very real problem. However there are several alternatives for getting from one point to another, all of them simple and inexpensive.

The most convenient and easiest solution is to take a taxi. They are relatively cheap, the drivers try to avoid traffic jams wherever possible and will often point out places of interest along the route. Waiting time is obviously extra but very few journeys inside the city limits will come to more than about 400 escudos plus a 10 per cent tip. At the moment every taxi in Portugal has black bodywork and a greenish-turquoise roof which makes them easy to recognise, but apparently they are all to be resprayed yellow in 1992 on instructions from the EEC. This is causing a lot of aggravation among the owner drivers who resent spending the money and are amazed that the beaurocrats have nothing more important to worry about.

The metro also has a lot to recommend it and is very simple to use although it does not cover a great deal of ground. Tickets cost 40$00, but work out cheaper in bulk, and are obtainable from the various underground stations, each one a hive of feverish activity during the rush hour. Maps of the city with details of the various routes covered by public transport are available from some newsagents and make it quite simple to work out an itinerary.

Buses and trams accept the same tickets which can be bought from the conductor, if there is one, or from the driver in cases where everyone gets on at the front. Anyone planning to use either system to a large extent can save a few escudos by buying a block of them from a booth on the Avenida Fontes Pereira de Melo, near the point where it joins the Praça Marquês de Pombal, but there is no particular fare because this varies according to the distance involved. Occasionally an incline is so steep that the local transport finds itself classed as a funicular. A case in point is the Calçada da Glória where, for a set price, you can cover the short distance between the Avenida da Liberdade and the Rua São Pedro de Alcântara. Other little funiculars are the Bica, operating between the Rua de São Paulo and the Calçada do Combro in the Bairro Alto, and the Lavra which hauls itself up through a straight-jacket of houses on the northwest side of the Rua Portas de Santo Antão. In addition the Santa Justa street lift, built about a hundred years ago, rather in the manner of the Eiffel Tower, is another useful shortcut with some quite extensive views.

The port area of Lisbon is entirely functional with docks and warehouses, steel mills, cement works and refrigeration plants, which leaves precious little space for waterside restaurants and atmospheric little bars. However there are boat trips along the Tagus during the holiday season and regular ferries across the river from three different points that give passengers an entirely different view of the capital. One is adjacent to the Praça do Comércio, the south ferry station is only slightly downstream while the Belém ferry runs from a point almost opposite the Coach Museum to Porto Brandão on the estuary.

Lisbon has plenty to offer quite apart from sightseeing. There are classical concerts, especially during the winter, the Hot Clube de Portugal in the Praça da Alegria caters for jazz enthusiasts at the weekends while a whole range of bars, discotheques and night spots feature everything from African rhythms to *fado*, leaving the casino in Estoril to provide gambling and floorshows. Spectator sports include football and bullfighting as well as motor racing, in addition to which there are swimming pools and the Lisbon Tennis Club, with activities such as deep sea fishing off the coast a short drive away.

Shops come in all shapes and sizes, dealing in every conceivable variety of appropriate merchandise. The Amoreiras Complex, described by some as a monstrosity, is a highrise concrete and glass construction consisting of apartments, shops, restaurants and places of entertainment. The Rua Augusta is considered to be a good place for fashion articles while the surrounding area is awash with traditional crafts such as gold and silverware, tapestries, porcelain and pottery. Other things to look out for are leather shoes, belts and bags as well as embroidery and antiques, books, old maps and manuscripts. At the opposite end of the scale are the Ribeira Market on the Avenida 24 de Julho and the Feira da Ladra. Souvenirs in the lower price bracket are quite predictable, the least obvious of them being small pots of sweet basil connected, for some reason, with St Anthony.

Most of the local festivals have saintly connections. St Anthony opens the proceedings in mid-June with two days of merrymaking accompanied by sardines, red wine, bunting and balloons. Ten days later the Feast of St John calls for similar decorations, processions and a bonfire or two, after which there is hardly time to recover before St Peter is accorded much the same treatment, leaving just twenty-four hours to clear up before 1 July.

As befits a modern European capital Lisbon has a good many sophisticated restaurants where both the food and the clientele are very much at one with their surroundings. However there are even more atmospheric little places serving traditional dishes, other establishments where the menus originated in far-flung outposts of the empire like Mozambique, Goa or Brazil, and a plethora of bars and cafés which may be quite delightful or simply dismal and depressing, frequently with food to match.

Some of the best places to eat are in the Alfama and the Bairro Alto. In the expensive bracket are the Tágide, off the Rua Garrett, with superb views and mouthwatering specialities, and the nearby Tavares that has never quite recovered from the fact that it started out as a café in the late eighteenth century. For atmosphere and good food at more down to earth prices there are few places to beat the Alfaia, off the Rua de São Pedro de Alcânt, or the Bota Alta in the vicinity of the Church of St Rock, which is very popular and usually bursting at the seams.

Further afield, the Caseiro in the Rue de Belém does a very tasty line in fish. Tourists from Brazil should feel at home in the Comida de Santo on the Rua da Escola Politécnica near the Botanical Gardens, which is marginally less expensive than the Conventual, a few blocks away in the Praça das Flores, meanwhile English visitors in search of familiar surroundings can choose between Restaurante 33, on the Rua Alexandre Herculano and the Saddle Room in the Praça José Fontana, a brisk walk away on the far side of the Parque Eduardo VII. When it comes to ordering traditional dishes in typical small restaurants *bacalhau* is as much part of Portugal as *paella* is of Spain. It is made from dried, salted cod and there are said to be 365 different ways of preparing it, with an extra recipe thrown in for Leap Year. Fish stews such as *caldeirada* are almost as popular and broad beans make frequent appearances although other vegetables and salads are usually conspicuous by their absence.

It is not an easy matter to select a handful of hotels from the considerable number that are available in the capital, however there are a few which deserve an honourable mention. The tallest, and currently the most expensive, is the Lisboa Sheraton which is reputed to cost more than its counterpart in New York. It has everything including a heated open-air swimming pool. In the same category is the older Ritz Inter-Continental, overlooking the Parque Eduardo VII. Also in the luxury class is the elegant Avenida Palace which was a happy hunting ground for spies of all nations during World War II. The entrance is just round the corner from the Rossio but there is no longer a private way through to the station next door.

Slightly less luxurious is the Tivoli Lisboa with such obvious advantages as tennis, swimming, a solarium and parking for the car. The Tivoli Jardim next door is probably better value, especially as guests can use all the same sports facilities. York House, by comparison, is slightly out on a limb on the way to Belém. The main part of the building was an early seventeenth-century convent whose former chapel has been turned into a dining room, still with its font and marble plaques, pewter plates and candlesticks. The cells once occupied by novices are naturally small and rather cramped but there are suites and larger rooms facing on to an attractive courtyard. The annex across the road has a French turn-of-the-century atmosphere with fussy decorations and lots of red plush.

The Hotel Roma is strictly functional with a swimming pool, a gift shop and the ability to whisk large parties on package tours through the cafeteria for breakfast and then load them on to sightseeing coaches in double quick time. The main advantages are that it is relatively inexpensive, has a garage and is quite close to an underground station. Other places worth considering are the Albergaria Senhora do Monte in the Calçade do Monte, north of the Alfama, and the rather more accessible Residência Horizonte. The latter is unexceptional but efficient whereas the delightful Senhora do Monte may occasionally run out of hot water, but makes up for it by being in a residential area where the local roosters act as alarm clocks in the morning.

Visitors who are planning to spend any length of time in the capital, or who prefer to arrange a self-catering holiday, can rent furnished accommodation in the city while those camping or towing a caravan can choose between the Monsanto Camping Park within easy reach of the *auto-estrada* or a variety of other campsites along the Atlantic coast.

The Costa de Lisboa is a fairly small region on either side of the Tagus, sandwiched in between the Costa de Prata to the north and the infinitely larger Planicies, stretching as far south as the Algarve. River ferries operating from the Lisbon waterfront near the Praça de Comércio converge on Cacilhas on the opposite bank whereas the Ponte 25 de Abril is the only road bridge between Vila Franca de Xira and the Atlantic. Once on the other side the main highway heads directly for **Setúbal** on the Rio Sado beyond the Serra da Arrábida. It is the third biggest port in the country with a large fishing fleet, a pleasure boat harbour, various industrial interests and a full quota of tourist attractions.

Historically Setúbal has just as much to boast about as Lisbon although, unlike the capital, it does not claim to have been founded by Ulysses. However there are traces of an Iron Age settlement and evidence that it

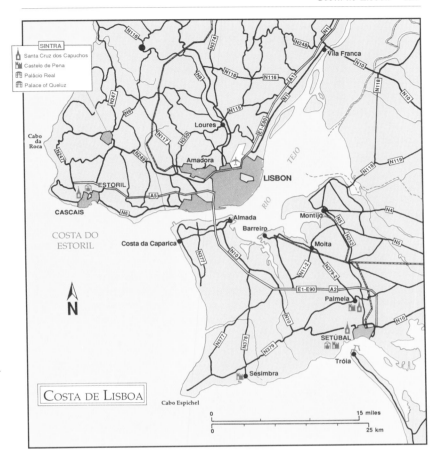

was an important Roman town whose main function was salting fish. For some reason it was bypassed by the Moors and only fortified in the fourteenth century, after which it developed rapidly with its first railway station opened in 1860 and gas lighting installed two years afterwards.

Today Setúbal tends to sprawl along the water's edge, its old fishermen's quarter contrasting sharply with an ever-increasing number of highrise buildings and wide, sometimes tree-lined avenues. It is dominated by the Castelo de São Filipe, built some four hundred years ago on the instructions of Philip II of Spain. He had only recently invaded Portugal and found it necessary to keep a sharp eye on his new subjects as well as protecting the coastline from attacks by the English fleet. Apart from the well-preserved ramparts and a small chapel decorated with eighteenth-century tiles there is not much to see except the view. However, a fairly modern *pousada* has been built inside the walls and is pleasant if somewhat lacking in atmosphere.

Predating the castle by about a hundred years, the Church of Jesus, in the Praça Miguel Bombarda, is the work of Diogo Boitac who went on to design the magnificent Mosteiro dos Jerónimos in Belém. It has the same high vaulting spanning the nave and the aisles, supported by spiral columns that look like giant sticks of barley sugar. Tiles have been used to decorate the walls of the nave and the chancel, showing scenes from the life of the Virgin Mary. The cloister has been converted into a museum which contains, among other things, some rather impressive gold and silver treasures including an antique processional cross. The upper galleries are particularly memorable for a series of paintings depicting the life of Christ from the manger to the grave while the lower galleries are decorated with tiles, some of which are nearly five hundred years old.

The Regional Museum of Archaeology and Ethnology, overlooking the most easterly strip of garden in the Avenida Luisa Todi, has a collection that any magpie would be proud to own. There are prehistoric items from the Bronze Age, ancient coins, pottery, traditional costumes and a whole range of local crafts. Industry and agriculture are both represented, along with working models fashioned out of wood and iron and tiny replicas of fishing boats. Meanwhile the Fishing and Oceanographic Museum in the next block concentrates on a wide variety of sea creatures and other aspects of marine life.

The Igreja de São Julião on the Praça de Bocage is an attractive little church that was damaged in the Lisbon earthquake and had to be extensively rebuilt. Its foundations are thought to be as old, or even older, than those of the Igreja de Santa Maria da Graça, believed to date from the thirteenth century but reconstructed three hundred years later when the carved altarpiece was added. It is just opposite the Região de Turismo de Setúbal which occupies part of the Casa e Capela do Corpo Santo, an elegant town house with its own private chapel. The Casa de Bocage, the birthplace of the satirical poet Manuel du Bocage in the Rua Edmond Bartissol, is another local landmark with a Gallery of Visual Arts and a library containing several of his works.

Setúbal, although too commercial to be a popular holiday playground, has other things to offer such as a marina, a somewhat larger fishing harbour where the night's catch is sold off every morning, a football stadium, a bullring and a busy market. In addition ferries, carrying cars and other passengers, leave at regular intervals from the commercial dock for **Tróia**, less than half an hour away. This is a rapidly developing tourist resort with hotels, apartment blocks, shops and villas, situated at the end of a long sandspit on the far side of the river.

Tróia was originally a Phoenician settlement appropriated by the Romans, who called it *Cetóbriga*, before it was destroyed by an earthquake in 412AD. Roughly 2.5km (1^1/$_2$ miles) along a sandy path are the remains of the town, only part of which has so far been excavated. The ruins are not particularly memorable, consisting mainly of a burial ground, salt vats and the vestige of a temple which was obviously decorated with frescoes in its day. For anyone less interested in these antiquities than in the modern amenities on offer there is a golf course, plus swimming pools and plenty of night life as well as pleasant beaches on the seaward edge of the pine-encrusted dunes.

Slightly to the north of Setúbal a large castle with a long and turbulent history broods over the picturesque white town of **Palmela**. It is said to be Roman in origin although the Arabs may have been responsible for its second line of defence and certainly left behind a mosque that was converted to Christianity before being shaken to bits in the earthquake of 1755. The Duke of Viseu, who was involved in a plot to assassinate João II, was stabbed to death in the royal bedchamber while his collaborator, the Bishop of Évora, was thrown into the dungeon below the keep where he was found dead shortly afterwards.

The former monastery of the Knights of Santiago inside the battlements is now the Pousada Castelo de Palmela, with a superb view over the surrounding plains patterned with olive trees. It is most attractively furnished and has a heated swimming pool and a glassed-in cloister full of exotic plants as well as accommodation on the ground floor. There is plenty of parking space, also fishing and sailing within easy reach. The attendant church of Santiago has little in the way of decorations apart from the order's coat-of-arms and the tomb of its last master, Jorge de Lencastre, in a bay off the north aisle. On the other hand the Church of St Peter, just outside the ramparts, is lined throughout with tiles recalling his exploits as a fisherman and his eventual death by crucifixion, as well as an especially graphic portrayal of Christ walking on the waters of the Sea of Galilee.

A few kilometres to the southwest of Palmela are the delightful twin towns of **Vila Nogueira de Azeitão** and **Vila Fresca de Azeitão**, surrounded by orchards, vineyards and olive groves. Both have plenty to recommend them. The former grew up in the shadow of a Dominican monastery, now almost non-existent, and the Tavora Palace, dating from the sixteenth century, but these days it is better known for its wines. The firm of José Maria de Fonseca is one of Portugal's leading exporters and is delighted to show visitors over the premises any morning or afternoon during the week.

On the other hand the gardens of the Quinta de Bacalhôa in Vila Fresca are closed every morning and also on Sundays and holidays, their trees, shrubs and tiled pavilion hidden from view behind solid stone walls and a heavy green wooden gateway. On the far side of the gardens, at 86 Rua Almirante Reis, is a small but fascinating tile factory where it is possible to inspect the whole process from start to finish. The methods used have not changed since the seventeenth century and nor have the colours, consisting of various shades of blue, yellow, green and sepia. The special clay is rolled out on beds of sand to prevent it sticking and cut into squares which are then left to shrink, a process that takes longer in winter than it does in summer. They are then glazed, fired and painted, after which they are fired again. The finished tiles are all exactly the same size, except where they have been altered to follow a curved edge for some special project, and may have individual designs or be part of an elaborate picture. Orders are accepted for anything from a reproduction of a famous masterpiece to a copy of a photograph, the price and the length of time taken depending on the size and the amount of work involved.

One of the best places to stay while exploring the Serra da Arrábida is the Estalagem da Quinta das Torres, a slightly shabby country mansion not far from the winery. It is an impressive sixteenth-century building, oozing old-world charm, with beautiful family furniture, pictures and objects d'art. There are tapestries in the diningroom, Troy can be seen burning on the tiles in the gallery and the courtyard, guarded by four square towers, has a Renaissance fountain off-set by orange trees. Guests are served breakfast in their rooms but for anyone who wants to be self contained there are also two bungalows in the grounds complete with their own kitchenettes. However, credit cards are not currently accepted. Alternatively there are one or two hotels in Sesimbra, just along the coast, in addition to some rooms in private houses and five different campsites in the surrounding area.

A pleasant coast road skirts the cliffs to the west of Setúbal interspersed with little sandy beaches, particularly at Figueirinha and Portinho da Arrábida, which are suitable for windsurfing, sailing and underwater fishing. Beyond them steps lead down to the Lapa de Santa Margarida where traces of prehistoric occupants were found in the grotto. From here the road turns inland, has a change of heart and rejoins the ocean at **Sesimbra**, a wholly delightful little fishing port strung out along the edge of the bay.

The town, which has every intention of becoming a popular holiday resort, struggles up the hillside in a jumble of little streets and alleys, stone steps and houses gaily decorated with flowers and multi-coloured laundry. Fishermen disentangle their lines in the middle of the road when they cannot be bothered to go down on the beach, fish hang out to dry in the most unlikely places, having been bought at auction on the quayside, and no-one takes any notice of cars until the last possible moment. Beyond the harbour with its large fleet of trawlers, some with an eye or a star painted on the bow, there is a small but extremely busy shipyard where the vessels are built, painted and repaired. The castle, on its bare hilltop above the town, was captured from the Moors in the twelfth century but is hardly worth inspecting at close quarters because there is nothing inside apart from the local graveyard and some fallen masonry.

Modern developments are beginning to nibble at the edges of the old village and during the summer the beach on either side of the antiquated Santiago Fort is covered with variegated umbrellas and bodies toasting in the sun. Tucked away behind the fort are two small churches of no particular merit, a modest archaeological museum and the municipal library, housed in what was once a chapel attached to a fifteenth century

A decorative tile picture may be designed to order at Vila Fresca de Azeitão

Relaxing on the rocks on the Costa de Lisboa

hospital. The countryside around is partly agricultural, with an occasional marble quarry and large tracts of deserted moorland that are ablaze with flowers in the spring. Slightly to the east the Serra do Risco, which is part of the Parque Natural de la Serra da Arrábida, is popular with hill climbers and ramblers who enjoy walking across wide open spaces with nothing to distract their attention from the view.

The most westerly point in the area is Cape Espichel, a windswept promontory complete with a lighthouse and the Sanctuary of Nossa Senhora do Cabo, built nearly three hundred years ago, whose Baroque interior is filled with *ex-votos*. It stands at the end of a large, dusty quadrangle flanked by long lines of arcaded, double-storey buildings where generations of pilgrims could find food and lodging for the night. Nearby is the tiled Ermida da Memória while the little beach of Lagosteiros, down at sea level, once played host to dinosaurs who left their footprints quite close by.

A choice of minor roads wander up to the Lagoa de Albufeira, a lagoon of very respectable proportions, set back from the foreshore and surrounded by pine trees. It is a good place for sailing, fishing and windsurfing with a number of useful campsites in the vicinity. From here a secondary road makes contact with the main highway before it crosses the Ponte 25 de Abril into the capital. Once on the other side there is a choice between the N6 and the N7, both of which head for Estoril. However little would be achieved by planning a sightseeing drive along the coast because it is over developed, over populated and entirely devoid of tourist attractions.

For many years now **Estoril** has been looked on as a playboy's paradise where the rich, and occasionally the famous, spend their time playing golf, deep sea fishing, gambling, going horseracing or to motor races. The casino is a large complex with practically no character, an expensive restaurant, somewhat mediocre floorshows and opportunities to win or lose a fortune at anything from roulette to baccarat. There is also a regiment of one-arm bandits. The streets are lined with palms, flowers bloom in the park and the beach is adequate but rather overcrowded while most of the hotels are luxuriously equipped and charge accordingly.

A great many visitors have switched their attention to **Cascais**, once a traditional fishing village but now heavily veneered with all the trappings of tourism. Little horsedrawn vehicles are available for trips around the town, stalls along the seafront are festooned with knitwear and articles made from coral and shells, while the newsagent offers a wide selection of English books and magazines, post cards and yesterday's papers in several different languages.

Since the days of its youth, when the Romans, the Visigoths and Moors all favoured it with their attention, Cascais has played its part in the history of the country. It was sacked by the Duke of Alba in 1580 and barely had time to recover before an equally devastating attack by the English in 1597. It suffered in the Lisbon earthquake but when the members of the court decided that it would be a good place to spend the summer of 1870 architects were called in to build a royal residence and several most attractive houses. Hotels followed in their wake, restaurants started to appear, shops were opened and its future was assured. The Museum of the Counts of Castro Guimarães, housed in the family's nineteenth-century mansion, has a very viewable collection of furniture, carpets and silverware as well as bronzes, pottery and some interesting old books. Other local attractions include the church of Nossa Senhora da Assunçao, the open-air market on Wednesdays and the daily fish auction down by the beach. Among its many comfortable hotels are the Albat Roz, the less expensive Hotel Baia overlooking the sea, and the small Cas Da Pérgola, which does not have a restaurant.

From Cascais a coast road keeps company with the sea round to Guincho, where windsurfing is popular but bathing is dangerous, and carries on to the Cabo do Roca, the most westerly point in Europe. It has both a lighthouse and a tourist desk where visitors can buy a certificate to prove that they have actually been there. Beyond are any number of sandy beaches and little sheltered coves much beloved by fishermen. Among the various species to be found in the area are mullet, bream, bass and sole as well as mussels, squid, cuttlefish and crabs. Praia da Adraga has both sand and a variety of caves while Praia das Maçãs, slightly further north, is larger and more crowded, due in part to a small tram that plies backwards and forwards to Banzão during the summer months. One of its closest neighbours is the picturesque village of Azenhas do Mar, clinging like a limpet to the side of a cliff with swimming pools carved out of the rocks below.

Colares, a few kilometres from the coast, is said by experts to be the home of some of the finest red wine in Portugal. This is due to the fact that the vines are planted in sand dunes to a depth of more than 4m (13ft), as against the normal 1m (3ft), and protected from the elements by fences made from canes. The grapes also provide a distinctive yellow liqueur — *aguadente* — that is strong and heavily scented and should always be served well chilled. About half way along the road from Colares to Sintra, set in magnificent woods, a pair of very ordinary iron gates lead to the Quinta de Monserrate, an estate which Byron described as one of the loveliest places he had ever seen. Both the extensive grounds and the house itself, which looks more like an Arab palace than the home of a wealthy Englishman, have a history that is just as intriguing.

The story began in 1790 when an English Huguenot merchant called Gerard de Visme bought a ruined chapel on the site and replaced it with a pseudo Gothic castle. Four years later this was taken over by William Beckford who immediately set about creating a classical landscape with a massive waterfall and a flock of sheep to give it an authentic atmosphere. In 1856 Francis Cook, who had made a fortune out of a drapery business in London, bought the property and employed a workforce of over 2,000 to transform both the house and grounds. During the next five years

Fishermen preparing their lines near Sesimbra

The harbour at Sesimbra, crowded with multi-coloured fishing boats

Cascais

The tiled interior of the Palácio Real at Sintra

plants, trees and shrubs were imported from all over the world, the head gardener at Kew advised on landscaping and three Etruscan tombs, similar to four others that found their way into the British Museum, were placed at strategic vantage points. The Cook family owned the property until 1946 when a change of fortune persuaded them to sell it to the Portuguese government.

In the years that followed the estate deteriorated rapidly until Alan Paterson, a director of the Ontario Botanical Gardens in Hamilton, offered to help with the job of restoring it. As a result a team of six was sent over from Canada to assist Gerald Luckhurst, the English landscape gardener who had been apointed to take overall charge of the project. There is still a lot of work to be done but even so the palace and parklands of Monserrate are certainly worth visiting.

Although the Portuguese monarchy adopted **Sintra** as an ideal summer resort more than five hundred years ago they were by no means the first to appreciate its many qualities. The area was occupied in prehistoric times, the Romans built villas there and the Moors added a hilltop fortress of their own which was captured by Afonso Henrique in 1147. This was largely restored in the nineteenth century by Fernando of Saxe Coburg-Gotha, the consort of Maria II and a cousin of Prince Albert, the husband of Queen Victoria.

Fernando also built the Castelo da Pena just next door, on the ruins of an ancient monastery. It is an excessively extrovert construction, part Moorish, part Gothic and part Renaissance with Baroque overtones, that would look equally at home in Bavaria where similar flights of fancy were appearing at almost the same time. The monastery's Manueline chapel and cloister were kept virtually intact but are somewhat overwhelmed by the seemingly endless succession of royal apartments that have been left untouched, apart from cleaning and normal maintenance, since the last occupants fled the country in 1910. The park was also largely the work of Fernando II, a promotion to kingship bestowed on him after the birth of a son and heir. It is a happy blending of tall trees and flowering shrubs, topped by a sixteenth-century cross and a large statue of a man in armour, presumably the architect Baron von Eschwege, standing guard over his handiwork. The Chalet da Condessa, decorated with imitation trees made of wood and cork, was built in 1870 for a Swiss-German opera singer who Fernando took under his wing after the death of the queen.

Sintra is really three towns in one — the old quarter or Vila Velha, the more modern section known as Estefânia and the elderly village of São Pedro. The centrepiece of the Via Velha is yet another palace, instantly identified by two enormous chimneys — looking like a cross between oast houses and giant liqueur bottles — built over the kitchens. This Palácio Real is, in fact, a not very remarkable hotchpotch of different styles, altered and enlarged at intervals without any overall plan except to provide additional space. Among its most striking features are the glazed sixteenth-century tiles, especially those in the chapel and the dining hall.

A flight of well over one hundred birds, each carrying a flower and a scroll, decorate the ceiling of the Magpie Room. According to legend they were painted on the orders of João I after the queen surprised him in the act of presenting a rose to one of her ladies-in-waiting. No doubt there is some less fanciful explanation, especially as another room is similarly adorned with swans, but nobody with the true facts has been prepared to spoil a good story.

The parish church of São Martinho on the Largo da Republica was all but destroyed in the earthquake of 1755 and has little of interest to offer. However, tnere are several craft shops in the vicinity for people in search of souvenirs, a museum of toys at the far end of the Rua Gil Vicente and a Regional Museum which divides its attention between modest prehistoric finds, a few Roman relics and a miscellaneous collection of pictures. The highly ornamental Fonte Mourisca in the Liberdade Park, overlooking the Volta do Duche, could quite easily be Moorish but was actually designed by a local sculptor in 1922.

Seteais Palace, on the eastern outskirts of Sintra, was built for a Dutch consul in the late eighteenth century and bought shortly afterwards by a Portuguese nobleman. Its name, Seven Sighs, reflects the disappointment caused by the lenient terms imposed on the French under the Sintra Convention, signed at the palace in 1808 by the Duke of Wellington. It is now a very up-market hotel, the Hotel Palácio de Seteais, well aware of its various attractions but the staff are not always as gracious as their elegant surroundings. A pleasant alternative is the Hotel Tivoli Sintra.

The open horse-drawn carriages that ply for hire in the square outside the Palácio Real are ideal for visiting the Castelo da Pena. However they are more expensive than the local coaches which offer tours that also include a visit to the monastery of Santa Cruz dos Capuchos. It is a fascinating little place, hardly more than a hermitage, surrounded by enormous boulders with minute cells hollowed out of the rock and lined with cork. It has its own refectory and little chapel decorated with tiles but no obvious aids to easy living.

São Pedro, which to all intents and purposes is part of Sintra, has a medieval church dedicated to St Peter with the insignia of the Bishop of Lisbon embedded over the main doorway. The fair which takes place on the second and fourth Sunday of every month, and can trace its origins back to the Reconquest, is large, noisy and.colourful, dealing in everything from brushes and brooms to flowers, fruit and vegetables. From here it is a short, undemanding drive down the N249 to the Palace of Queluz, an extremely elegant royal residence, inspired by the country home of the Marquês de Castelo Rodrigo and frequently compared to Versailles.

A tour of the palace includes the Ambassador's Hall, decorated with marble and mirrors, and the Don Quixote Room where the exploits of Cervantes' famous hero are re-enacted round the walls. The Music Room where the queen and her daughters staged impromptu concerts is just

The exuberant carving on the Pena Palace at Sintra

Azenhas do Mar

next to the throne room which makes a valiant effort to rival the Hall of Mirrors at Versailles, lit by superb Venetian chandeliers. Even the quarters allotted to the Royal Guard are decorated with eighteenth-century tiles inspired by Chinese and Brazilian landscapes.

The formal gardens surrounding the Palace of Queluz also have a distinctly French air about them, having been modelled on those created by Le Nôtre and adapted where necessary by Jean-Baptiste Robillon and his Dutch associate Joseph van der Kolk. They are laid out with lakes and fountains, ponds and little waterfalls, complimented by statues and marble urns. The shrubs and low hedges are carefully manicured and there is even a sizeable canal lined with tiles which could be flooded whenever the royal family was in residence and felt like taking a boat out on the water. A restaurant has been installed in the palace kitchens where the prices are high, the food adequate and the surroundings full of atmosphere but somewhat contrived.

The countryside round Sintra is perfect for walking, either just wandering about or heading for one of its less obvious attractions. A case in point is Janas, slightly inland from Azenhas do Mar, whose circular, whitewashed church is an ancient place of pilgrimage. It is dedicated to São Mamede, the patron saint of livestock, whose sixteenth-century likeness can be seen inside. Further to the north, but still only 11km from Sintra, the village of Odrinhas has the remains of a Roman villa, a mosaic pavement in a good state of repair, a small archaeological museum and a medieval burial ground.

The traditional inhabitants of the area, known as the Saloio from the Arabic for countryman, are mainly farmers and craftsmen, following in the footsteps of their Mozarab forefathers — Moors who were converted to Christianity after the Reconquest. They tend to be swarthy, of medium height and the men frequently wear a woollen cap, rather like a Dickensian nightcap, with a tassel at the point that falls over to rest on one shoulder. Several craft workshops have made enviable names for themselves such as Eduardo Azenha's pottery at Santa Suzana, Manuel Silvestre Lobinho's basketwork in Gouveia and the marble and stone cutters of Montelavar and Pero Pinheiro, none of whom appear to object to visitors.

Neither restaurants nor accommodation of any description is available in the majority of tiny hamlets, linked by a cobweb of country lanes and cart tracks. However most of the local campsites have cafeterias, although one glaring exception is the Parque de Campismo dos Capuchos near Sintra. For anyone planning to travel with a tent or a caravan a good choice would be either the one at Praia Grande on the coast south of Praia das Maçás, the Parque de Campismo do Guincho-Orbitur 7km from Cascais or the municipal site at Oeiras 17km west of Lisbon. There are some reasonably priced hotels in Sintra and Cascais but, on the whole, anyone who has to watch their *escudos* would be unlikely to find much to choose from in Estoril.

Nobody should have any problems getting to the Costa de Lisboa or travelling round the area afterwards. Lisbon's international airport is in direct contact with the United States and Canada, as well as other European cities, with additional internal services. It takes less than half an hour by taxi from the airport at Portela on the northern outskirts of the capital into the city centre or there are buses to the Praça Marquês de Pombal and the Rossio.

There are three main railway stations in Lisbon. Trains from France, Spain and northern Portugal use the Santa Apolónia terminus on the river. Local services from the Sintra area operate to and from the Rossio whereas the Estoril coast is linked to the Cais do Sodré station near the Praça do Comércio. Anyone arriving from southern Portugal has to leave the train at Barreiro, on the opposite bank of the Tagus, and complete the trip by ferry, an arrangement that also applies to passengers from Palmela and Setúbal.

As well as the metro and all the buses, trams and taxis in Lisbon there are frequent bus services to Setúbal which has local links with the surrounding area, especially Palmela, Sesimbra and the Cabo Espichel. A car tour of the Setúbal peninsula can be completed very comfortably in one day but it would probably be necessary to make two trips to the Serra de Sintra in order to explore the coast and visit all the different palaces and gardens in the vicinity.

Additional Information

Places of Interest

Cabo Espichel
Westerly point on the Setúbal Peninsula

Sanctuary of Nossa Senhora do Cabo
Out-of-the-way church with Baroque interior and many ex-votos.

Cascais
Fishing village/tourist resort. Sandy beaches and a busy fish market between the Praia da Ribeira and the Praia da Rainha.

Church of Nossa Senhora da Assunção
With tiles and paintings.

Museum of the Counts of Castro Guimarães
Open: 10am-5pm. Closed Mondays.
Furniture, pictures and *objet d'art*.

Lisbon
Ajuda Palace
Calçada da Ajuda
Open: 10am-5pm. Closed Mondays.
Comparatively modern royal residence with nineteenth-century furnishings.

Archaeological Museum
Largo do Carmo
Open: 10am-1pm and 2-5pm. Closed Mondays and holidays.
Archaeological finds that are less impressive than the ruined monastery where they are housed.

Arte Antiga Museum
Jardim 9 de Abril
Open: 10am-1pm and 2.30-5pm. Closed Mondays and holidays.
Magnificent exhibits from all parts of the ancient empire, pictures and French silverware.

Belém Tower
Avenida do India
Decorative ancient fortress on the banks
of the Tagus.

Botanical Gardens
Rua do Salitre
Pleasant gardens with a variety of
plants, pools and walkways.

Castelo de São Jorge
On the hill above the Alfama district
Some walls and towers with gardens
and superb views over the city.

Cathedral (Sé) Rua Augusto Rosa
Ancient church twice damaged by
earthquakes, now considerably restored.

Coach Museum
Rua de Belém
Open: 10am-5pm. Closed Mondays.
One of the world's most outstanding
collections of coaches.

Contemporary Arts Museum
Rua Serpa Pinto
Open: usually 10am-1pm, 2-5pm.
Closed Mondays.
A run-of-the-mill collection of late
nineteenth-century and early twentieth-
century exhibits.

Costume Museum (Museu do Trajo)
Largo Júlio de Castilho
Open for temporary exhibitions of
fashion from the Middle Ages onwards.

Craft Workshops
Rua Augusto Rosa
Traditional workshops near Museum of
Decorative Arts.

Cristo Rei Statue
Large figure of Christ on the south bank
of the Tagus facing the city with a lift to
the top of the pedestal.

Decorative Arts Museum
Rua Augusto Rosa
Open: 10am-1pm, 2.30-5pm. Closed
Sunday and Monday.
Includes furniture, rugs, glass, ceramics,
silver and embroidery.

Estrêla Basilica
Calçada da Estrêla
Impressive church with twin towers and
noteworthy marble statues.

Feira da Ladra
Campo de Santa Clara
Large and colourful open-air market
held on Tuesdays and Saturdays.

Fronteira Palace
Praça General Humberto Delgado
Variable opening hours and quite
expensive entrance fee to a few rooms
and the gardens.

Gulbenkian Foundation
Parque de Palhava
Includes the Calouste Gulbenkian
Museum and Museum of Modern Art
Open: 10am-5pm Tuesdays, Thursdays,
Fridays and Sundays, 2-7.30pm
Wednesdays and Saturdays from July to
October. 10am-5pm Tuesdays to Sun-
days November to June. Always closed
Mondays.
The former houses the magnificent
collection donated by the Armenian
millionaire while the latter consists of
contemporary Portuguese art works.
Both museums have cafeterias.

Jerónimos Monastery
Avenida da India
Magnificent former monastery with
elaborate portals and arresting interior.

Madre de Deus
Reconstructed church with exceptionally fine gilt woodwork, many interesting pictures and an absorbing tile
museum.

Maritime Museum (Museu de Marinha)
Jeronimos Monastery buildings,
Avenida da India
Open: 10am-5pm. Closed Mondays and
holidays.
Statues, models, documents, a few
uniforms, and other items of nautical
interest.

Military Museum (Museu de Artilharia)
Near Santa Apolónia Railway Station on
the river
Open: 10am-4pm Tuesdays to Satur-
days. 11am-5pm Sundays. Closed
Mondays.
Arms and armour of all descriptions.

Municipal Museum (Museu da Cidade)
Jardim do Campo Grande
Open: 10am-1pm and 2-6pm. Closed
Mondays.

History of Lisbon with everything from tiles to pictures.

Museu Etnográfico do Ultrama
Rua Portas de Santo Antão
Open: 11am-1pm, 3-5pm. Closed Tuesdays, Saturdays, Sundays and holidays.
Comprehensive collection of items from the Portuguese overseas territories.

Padrão dos Descobrimentos
Slightly upriver from the Belém Tower Brilliant white monument to Portugal's early discoverers.

Parque Eduardo VII
Praça Marquês de Pombal
Extensive park with hothouse and cold greenhouse both full of exotic plants.

Parque Florestal de Monsanto
Large, uncultivated area to the west of the city with roads, rides, paths and picnic spots.

Popular Arts Museum
On the river near the Belém Tower
Open: 10am-12.30pm, 2-5pm. Closed Mondays and holidays.
Displays of folk arts and traditions as well as everyday articles from all over the country.

Puppet Museum (Museu da Marioneta)
Largo Rodrigues de Freitas
Open: 11am-5pm. Closed Mondays.
Wide variety of puppets and occasional performances.

Ribeira Market
Avenida 24 de Julho
Large, permanent covered market overlooking the river.

Santa Engrácia
Rua dos Corvos
Open: 10am-5pm. Closed Mondays.
Tall, recently completed church, now national pantheon.

Santa Justa Street Lift
Near the Rossio
Openwork construction rather like the Eiffel Tower connecting two levels of the city and providing some quite extensive views.

Santa Luzia
Largo do Limoeiro
Tiled walls in the church depict the history of Lisbon.

São António da Sé
Opposite the cathedral
Small, elegant church incorporating the room where St Anthony of Padua was born in 1195.

São Roque
Largo Trindade Coelho
Sixteenth-century church with magnificent chapels, artwork and outstanding museum of sacred art.

São Vicente de Fora
Near Campo de Santa Clara
Part of the ancient monastery and church where members of the royal House of Bragança are buried.

Theatre Museum
Largo Júlio de Castilho
Opening times vary.
Designs, photographs and costumes connected with the local theatre.

Vasco da Gama Aquarium
On N6 at Dâfundo, beyond Belém
Open: noon to 6pm. Closed 1 May.
Comprehensive collection of sea creatures, both alive and preserved.

Zoo
Praça General Humberto Delgardo
Open: 9am-8pm in summer and 9am-6pm in winter.
Wild animals in a large park filled with trees and flowers.

Palmela
On the northern slope of the Serra da Arrábida, 5km from Setúbal
The remains of an ancient castle attached to former monastery of St James, part of which is now a *pousada*.

Queluz
On the N249 from Lisbon to Sintra
Guided tours 10am-1pm and 2-5pm. Closed Tuesdays.
An extremely elegant royal palace surrounded by beautiful formal gardens. Decorative apartments possibly inspired by Versailles.

Quinta de Monserrate
2km west of Sintra
A Moorish-looking palace and grounds being restored.
Open every day of the year.

Setúbal
Large industrial centre, port and holiday town on the Rio Sado, well known for its oysters.

Casa de Bocage
Rua Edmond Bartissol
Birthplace of the poet with a selection of his works.

Castelo de São Filipe
Sixteenth-century castle part of which is now a *pousada*.

Church of Jesus
Praça Miguel Bombarda
Open: 10am-12.30pm, 2-6pm. Closed Mondays and holidays.
Flamboyant doorway and eyecatching interior. Part of the original convent houses the municipal museum.

Museum of Regional Archaeology and Ethnology
Avenida Luisa Todi
Open: 9.30am-12.30pm, 2-5.30pm. Closed Mondays and holidays.
Prehistoric exhibits, working models and items made from cork.

Sesimbra
Coastal resort 26km (16 miles) west of Setúbal, popular with underwater swimmers and fishermen. Colourful harbour with twice-daily fish auction.

Castle with towers and ramparts but nothing of interest inside.

Shipyard where trawlers are built and repaired.

Sintra
Favourite summer residence of the kings and queens of Portugal, 28km (17 miles) west of Lisbon.

Castelo da Pena
Guided tours 10am-4.45pm, closed Mondays.
Idiosyncratic castle on hill above town built on the site of an ancient monastery.

Fully equipped with some lovely items and some hideous black German furniture.

Castelo dos Mouros
A Moorish fortress near the Pena Palace, somewhat restored in the nineteenth century
Some traces of the early occupants and extensive views. Closed on Mondays.

Palácio Real
Guided tours 10am-5pm. Closed Wednesdays and holidays.
Fourteenth-century royal residence with later additions. Interesting decorations and legends.

Monastery of Santa Cruz dos Capuchos
Open: 9am-12noon and 2-5pm daily.
Sixteenth-century hermitage 5km (3 miles) to the west of Sintra

Troia
At the end of a sandspit facing Setúbal. A popular holiday resort reached by ferry or motor boat across the estuary.

Cetóbriga
The ruins of a Roman town about 2km away. Not a great deal to see so far. To view apply to the caretaker.

Vila Fresca de Azeitão
A small village south-west of Palmela

Quinta de Bacalhôa
Open: 1-5pm daily. Closed Sundays and holidays.
Private mansion surrounded by beautiful gardens filled with trees, shrubs and tiles.

Semão Arte
Rua Almirante Reis
Small tile factory which can be visited during working hours.

Vila Nogueira de Azeitão
Small town with some elderly buildings, noted for its wine and cheese.

J. M. da Fonseca Wine Company
Almost opposite Távora Palace
☎ (01) 208 0227
Open: 9am-12noon and 2-5pm, Monday to Friday for winery visits.

Tourist Information Offices

Lisbon
Praça dos Restauradores
☎ 01 36 36 24 or 36 63 07
At the airport
☎ 01 89 36 89

Cascais
In the town hall, Praça de Outubro
☎ 01 268 01 76

Estoril
Arcadas do Parque
☎ 01 268 01 13

Sesimbra
Avenida dos Náufragos
☎ 01 223 3304 or 223 1926

Setúbal
Rua do Corpo Santo
☎ 01 065 24284

Sintra
Praça da República
☎ 01 923 1157

Accommodation

Cascais
Albatroz
Rua Frederico Arouca
☎ 01 28 28 21

Hotel Baia
Avenida Marginal
☎ 01 28 10 33

Cas da Pérgola
Avenida Valbom
☎ 01 284 00 40

Estoril
Casa da Rocheira
Avenida da Bélgica
☎ 01 268 0217

Lisbon
Lisboa Sheraton
Rua Latino Coelho

☎ 01 57 57 57

Ritz Inter-Continental
Rua Rodrigo de Fonseca
☎ 01 69 20 20

Avenida Palace
Rua 1 de Decembro
☎ 01 36 01 51

Tivoli Lisboa
Avenida da Liberdade
☎ 01 53 01 81

Tivoli Jardim
7 Rua Júlio César Machado
☎ 01 53 99 71

York House
Rua das Janelas Verdes

Hotel Roma
Avenida de Roma
☎ 01 76 77 61

Albergaria Senhora do Monte
Calçada do Monte
☎ 01 86 28 46

Recidência Horizonte
Avenida António Augusto de Aguiar
☎ 01 53 95 26

Palmela
Pousada Castelo de Palmela
☎ 01 235 1226/1395

Setúbal
Pousada de São Filipe
☎ 065 23844

Sintra
Hotel Palácio de Seteais
8 Avenida Barbosa Bocage
☎ 01 923 3200

Hotel Tivoli Sintra
Praça da República
☎ 01 923 35 05

Vila Nogueira de Azeitão
Estalagem da Quinta das Torres
☎ 01 208 0001

5

Montanhas

Montanhas is the second largest region in Portugal, losing out to Planicies by a short head. It is also the only one of the six with no outlet to the sea, being cut off by the Costa Verde and the Costa de Prata in the west, separated from Planicies by the Rio Tejo, or Tagus, to the south and sharing a common frontier with Spain in the north and east. However it makes up for its lack of beaches with varied and often impressive scenery, lakes, nature reserves and atmospheric towns and villages. The area consists of three different provinces — Trás-os-Montes, the isolated 'land beyond the mountains' on the far side of the Rio Douro, Beira Alta whose two main towns are Viseu and Guarda, and Beira Baixa which shares some of the highest mountain peaks in Portugal but levels out when it reaches the fertile plains along the Tagus.

Much of the region is steeped in mystery, ably assisted by imagination and strange granite carvings of animals dotted about the northern countryside which may have had some religious significance in pagan times. Not all the local spirits are friendly so it is customary to frighten them away in the closing stages of the year with horrific masks and ancient incantations. If one, more crafty than the rest, manages to weave a spell or two before retreating there are witches and warlocks who will deal with the problem in return for a small gift, but not for money.

The Romans looked in from time to time but did not go in for a great many building projects apart from an occasional town and a collection of forts to protect their gold mining interests within striking distance of the Rio Tâmego. The Moors do not appear to have been very enthusiastic either and left behind little of note, apart the remains of some fortifications in one or two strategic centres. On the other hand the Christians went to work with a will, building fortified castles and churches that bore the brunt of Spanish invasions, Portuguese reprisals and French and English confrontations during the Peninsular War.

The three main crossing points from Spain into Montanhas are at Vilar Formoso on the road from Cuidad Rodrigo to Guarda, San Martin del Pedroso, dealing with traffic from Zamora to Bragança, and Feces de Abaixo, roughly mid-way between Verin and Chaves, with a few minor alternatives in between. Any number of little roads approach both sides of the border, then either change direction or peter out completely.

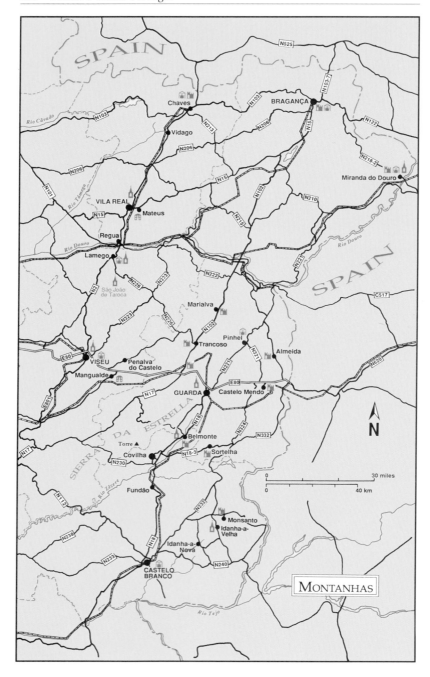

Bragança town centre

Bragança is one town that does owe its existence to the Romans, having been fortified by Julius Caesar, but it lost its identity when it was constantly besieged and battered by the Christians and the Moors. In 1442 João I made his illegitimate son Afonso the Duke of Bragança and two hundred years later his descendant was placed firmly on the throne as João IV, in opposition to Philip II of Spain. From then onwards the family ruled Portugal until the monarchy was abolished in 1910. They also strengthened the country's ties with England when Catherine of Bragança married Charles II, exchanging a massive dowry for promises of aid in time of trouble should the occasion arise. Their castle, which started life in the twelfth century, was considerably enlarged and up-dated but its owners spent very little time there once they had so many other royal palaces at their disposal. Nevertheless it is still an impressive building with towers and battlements, a drawbridge and a military museum housed in the keep. The church of Santa Maria is a comparatively recent addition, having replaced an earlier building nearly three hundred years ago. On the other hand the Domus Municipalis next door is said to be the oldest town hall in Portugal, where elders congregated during the Middle Ages to sort out local disputes.

Bragança's cathedral is something of a disappointment and can safely be ignored in favour of the Museu do Abade de Baçal on the Rua do Conselheiro Abilio Beça. This occupies the former bishops' palace and has something of interest for nearly everyone. On the ecclesiastical side there are beautifully embroidered vestments, church plate and a superb altar front, fashioned in leather nearly a thousand years ago and decorated with flowers. Archaeologists will probably be more interested in the pagan and Roman relics, in addition to which there are instruments of torture beloved by the Inquisition and even an extensive coin collection. For visitors who are planning to stop over in Bragança to explore the old town and the area round about, the Pousada de São Bartolomeu is probably the best bet, with the Hotel Bragança as an acceptable alternative. So far there are no official campsites in the immediate vicinity.

The Montezinho Parque Natural blankets the whole area to the north of Bragança and although there are a number of minor roads and several minute hamlets it is likely to prove more attractive to hikers and ramblers than it is to motorists. Vinhais, on the edge of the park to the west of Bragança, has its own modest prehistoric relics and the ruins of a thirteenth-century castle, neither of which is particularly spectacular. Nor is the hamlet of Rio de Onor, cut in half by the border with Spain which is very correctly marked with a chain and thereafter studiously ignored by the villagers on either side.

A more rewarding day out would begin at **Miranda do Douro**, reached by way of the N218 which turns off the main road just short of the frontier and follows it down to the Rio Douro. The town's most obvious landmark is its ruined castle, blown up during the Seven Years' War but still brooding over a deep gorge which has been flooded as part of an extensive hydro-electric system. The underground power station can be inspected ❊ by anyone who is interested and has had the foresight to obtain permission from the authorities in Oporto.

The two major attractions in Miranda do Douro are the cathedral and the Terra de Miranda Museum in the main square. The former, built of granite in the sixteenth century, has a magnificent carved and gilded altarpiece depicting the Assumption of the Virgin Mary, watched by the Apostles, as well as ornate choir stalls and a dozen or so interesting pictures in the sacristy. However its *pièce de résistance* is the Menino Jesus da Cartolinha, standing in a glass case in the south transept. The Child Jesus is splendidly dressed, having several changes of clothing made for Him by the townspeople, and an assortment of jewellery, but is never seen without a silk top hat. Meanwhile the museum highlights every aspect of daily life in the community, from traditional costumes to farm impliments and a child's playpen to Spanish pottery.

The small Pousada de Santa Catarina is quiet and comfortable but anyone thinking of staying there in mid-August would be well advised to book in advance. The Festas de Santa Bárbara on the third Sunday of the month pulls in the crowds, many of whom come to watch the ancient Pauliteiros Dance. The young men taking part dress themselves up in white skirts, embroidered jackets and black hats trimmed with ribbons and flowers, and brandish sticks which they use in place of swords. Nobody seems to know exactly when the custom originated, or even why, but that does not detract from their enjoyment. Miranda do Douro is also an excellent place to do a bit of shopping because the goods on offer include a variety of local arts and crafts as well as the usual souvenirs.

From Miranda do Douro the N221 wends its way to Mogadouro over relatively flat country with little to see apart from grazing lands and a few trees. Although there is nothing particularly memorable about the village or its derelict castle it does offer rather unusual souvenirs. The Centro Cultural in the Avenida da Espanha sells tiny reproductions of both the castle ruins and typical village houses, correct down to the smallest detail. They are not outlandishly expensive and a few grouped together make an interesting display and a good talking point.

Visitors with time to spare might enjoy following the border down to Freixo de Espada-à-Cinta, which has quite a viewable church, returning by way of Torre de Moncorvo, preferably along the N220. This is a mildly attractive route with a long-focus view of the town surrounded by arid mountain peaks. The local church is larger than one would expect and not at all prepossessing but it is worth having a quick look round inside. From here two equally serpentine options make for the N102 which is the most obvious route back to Bragança. On the other hand the N215 branches off to the left through Vila Flor with its little, very personalised museum, to Mirandela, whose three companion villages — Romeu, Vale de Couço and Vila Verdinho — are small, colourful and tucked away among the cork oaks and chestnut trees. Thereafter the N213 carries on to Chaves.

Anyone with rheumatism, stomach troubles or suffering from an attack of nerves is encouraged by the local brochures to try the healing waters of this modest little spa, which also offers fishing and dancing. The Romans were the first to discover the natural thermal springs at **Chaves**, which they called *Aquae Flaviae*, and Trajan liked it well enough to build a bridge

The castle and walls of the fortified town of Bragança

over the Tâmega in 98AD which is still going strong today. The town was captured by the Moors and after they had been driven out it was fortified as a warning to the Spaniards in Verín to stay on their own side of the border.

In its younger days the bridge had one or two additional arches but otherwise it looks very much the same as it did when Roman soldiers paced backwards and forwards guarding the busy route from Astorga to Braga. Apart from this the oldest landmark is the keep, built by Dom Dinis 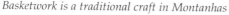 in the fourteenth century and acquired later by the first Duke of Bragança who is said to have spent some time there. It is not what one would call a very desirable residence by modern standards, the most obvious talking point being the openings provided for pouring boiling oil down on the heads of unwelcome visitors, but it makes an excellent setting for the military museum. The exhibits include ancient arms and armour, augmented by faithful reproductions wherever necessary, as well as items from World War I. There is also a section devoted to Portugal's overseas

Basketwork is a traditional craft in Montanhas

territories with examples of the various types of weapons used by the local inhabitants in the vain attempts to defend their homelands.

The Museu de Regiào Flaviense, adjoining the keep, includes both archaeology and ethnology to good effect. Relics from prehistoric times include a stone figure said to be some 4,000 years old, surrounded by other discoveries that have proved to be even more ancient. The Romans are represented by stonework removed from the bridge, altars and suchlike, contrasting sharply with a section devoted to the everyday life of the community, which has changed very little down the years. Admittedly the oxcart is gradually being replaced by the tractor, but basketwork is still a popular local craft and the straw cape remains an essential part of a shepherd's protective clothing when he is caught out in the mountains in bitter winds and drenching rain.

Chaves has its full quota of churches, although none of them are either large or imposing. The Misericord has a gilded altarpiece, a painted ceiling and a great many tiles, whereas the Igreja Matriz next door relies for attention on its decorative organ-front, leaving the Igreja da Madalena out on a limb beyond the bridge with nothing of interest to offer. The town is well known for its black pottery, which is unusual and can be quite attractive, and also for delectable smoked ham called *presunto*, cut in wafer thin slices and eaten raw like *prosciutto*. The Parque de Campismo Municipal de São Roque has most of the basic requirements for those camping or caravanning and also tries to make life a little easier for handicapped travellers. The local hotels and pensions are quite adequate for an overnight stop, but it is possible to do rather better by driving on to Vidago, about 17km (10 miles) down the road to Vila Real.

Vidago is another but more up-market spa with the large, slightly old-fashioned Palace Hotel complete with a pump room, a swimming pool and a night club. Visitors with internal complaints or allergies can take the waters while others play tennis or golf, go riding, shooting or fishing, sunbathe beside the river or inspect the surrounding countryside.

A small, occasionally suspect road links Vidago with Boticas, an elderly village hidden away behind the pine trees, beyond which is the Alto Rabagão reservoir. Driving from Chaves it is easy to take the wrong turning at Sapiãos on the N103, skim through Boticas, and continue on westwards along a road which appears to have escaped the notice of cartographers, local or otherwise, thereby missing the lakes altogether. However there is no need to worry because it has a good surface and eventually rejoins the N103 near Venda Nova. By making a sharp right-hand turn there is a pleasing drive back along the northern shores of the dam with a side trip to Montalegre some 8km (5 miles) away. This is a typical blending of ancient castle ruins surrounded by little world-weary houses and more modern buildings in various shades of white, depending on how recently they have been painted. From here it is possible to explore a couple of other lakes on the Rio Cávado to the west or head back to Chaves or Vidago on the way to Vila Real.

As the largest town in Trás-os-Montes with a long and varied history behind it **Vila Real** has surprisingly little in the way of tourist attractions. The cathedral is all that is left of a fifteenth-century monastery while the church of St Peter is being enthusiastically restored. Among its fifteenth-century houses is one where Diogo Cão is thought to have been born. He followed in the wake of Henry the Navigator's team of explorers and discovered the mouth of the Congo River in 1482, ahead of Bartolomeu Dias who rounded the Cape of Good Hope six years later. There is no doubt that Vila Real's most outstanding attraction is the view over the gorges of the Rio Corgo and the ravine away to the left.

Chestnut trees, vineyards and orchards line the N322 on its way to Mateus, some 3.5km (2 miles) outside the town. Its famous manor, belonging to the Counts of Vila Real, appears on the label of every bottle of Mateus Rosé. The palace, as it is frequently called, dates from the early eighteenth century but does not look quite so spic and span as the photographs suggest. None-the-less it is a good example of Portuguese Baroque, set in formal gardens with a large forecourt, a decorative if rather too obtrusive chapel and a beautiful double stairway behind the stone balustrade. The interior of the mansion fulfils its early promise. It still has its original heavy draperies, splendidly carved wooden ceilings and a library of old books. A small area has been set aside as a museum and contains, among other things, some exquisite porcelain, rich vestments, a collection of lovely fans and copperplate engravings by Fragonard and Gerard for a special edition of *The Lusiads*.

The area between Vila Real and Lamego to the south of the Rio Douro, and eastwards to the Spanish frontier, is almost entirely preoccupied with grapes and the production of electricity. The vines, planted in shallow soil on slate terraces stepped up the hillsides on either bank of the river, first took root there about 2,000 years ago. In former times the harvest was carried downstream in flat bottomed, square rigged boats that took the rapids in their stride but the arrival of the railway and the creation of barrages for the country's hydro-electric system have put an end to that. However the countryside has remained virtually unchanged. Little villages like Barrô, Sabrosa — the birthplace of Fernão de Magalhães, better known to posterity as Megallan of circumnavigation fame — and São João da Pesqueira are still encased in a network of dry-stone walls with golden eagles, Egyptian vultures and peregrine falcons circling overhead.

The area is also peppered with the remains of medieval religious centres. The Santa Maria de Cárquere Priory, between Resende and Cinfães, has been considerably restored and is worth seeing for its stone carvings, Romanesque window and decorative sarcophagi. The São Pedro de Balsemão chapel is even older. It was built by the Visigoths in the seventh century, added to and embellished by Afonso Pires, the bishop of Oporto, 700 years later and provided with a painted ceiling and altarpieces some 300 or more years ago.

The town of **Lamego**, a thriving textile centre in days gone by, has been well known for its wines since the sixteenth century. It is surrounded by orchards and terraced vineyards, nicely balanced on the Rio Balsemão which meanders northwards through a wooded valley to join the Rio Douro. The local hotels are neat without being gaudy and charge realistic prices. Keep-fit enthusiasts might well gravitate towards the Villa Hostilina, a converted farmhouse on a hill outside the town, which has facilities for tennis, swimming and fishing as well as the Instituto Kosmos with its gymnasium and resident karate black belt.

The municipal museum, in the stylish episcopal palace next to the cathedral, is full of interest with some fine sixteenth-century Flemish tapestries and paintings on silk in the Chinese salon. Delicate porcelain and a collection of glazed tiles jockey for position with some rather pleasing furniture, statues, and gold and silver religious relics. The paintings on display include five by Vasco Fernandes, known as Grão-Vasco, that were commissioned for the cathedral in the early sixteenth century but were moved across when the building was up-dated a little over 200 years ago. One panel shows the blessing of the animals, among them an unmistakable unicorn. Also on view are a clutch of little reconstructed chapels, appropriately carved and gilded, that were rescued from an ancient convent and taken to the museum for safekeeping.

Although the cathedral started life as a Romanesque church in the twelfth century, repeated attempts to improve and modernise it have left practically nothing of the original fabric. Nevertheless it has a richly ornamented doorway, a painted ceiling and beautifully carved choir stalls. The silverwork in the Capela do Sacramento is particularly arresting, after which even the cloister comes as a slight anticlimax. The Igreja do Desterro, or Chapel of the Exile, dates from 1640 and is worth seeing for its gilded wood carving, seventeenth-century tiles and coffered ceiling painted with scenes from the New Testament.

Lamego is dominated by two hills, one of them crowned with an ancient castle that has seen far better days. However the site has been cleaned up considerably in recent years and still commands a worthwhile view. The other is home to the far more entrancing Santuario Nossa Senhora dos Remédios (Sanctuary of Our Lady of the Remedies). Visitors with enough energy and enthusiasm can climb up the ornamental stairway from the Avenida Dr Alfredo de Sousa to the Court of the Kings with its central fountain, pillars, arches and elegantly dressed statues. The church at the top is not particularly ancient and contains very little except for a few portraits. It is also possible to drive up the wooded hillside to the sanctuary, passing the Raposeira Wine Factory on the way where conducted tours are laid on during working hours. The company produces sparkling wines using a process similar to the one employed by the famous champagne houses of France. This includes the method of allowing the sediment to collect on a temporary cork fitted to each bottle which is then drawn out with all the dregs attached. It is worth while finding enough time to visit São João de Tarouca, even though it means negotiating a sometimes doubtful little road off the N226 roughly 10km (6^1/$_4$ miles) south of Lamego. This was where the first Cistercian monastery in Portugal was founded in 1124. There are some interesting paintings, a tomb which recalls a wild boar hunt, apparently the favourite pastime of the Count of Barcelos who is buried inside, and a sacristy festooned with more than 4,000 different tiles. The idea is carried through into the chancel in order to provide a pictorial history of the monastery from the moment when a thunderbolt was sent down to locate the exact site.

From Lamego the N2 continues on its merry way to Viseu, accompanied by vineyards and by-passing a number of small hamlets that have little of interest for most visitors. The only place where a motorist might take the wrong turning is below Castro Daire, but even that does not matter because there is a pleasant secondary route available across country from **São Pedro do Sul**. This is a thriving spa frequented by people with skin complaints, rheumatism or who are suffering from gout. Those on the way to recovery can fish, swim, play tennis or take a gentle stroll along the river bank. The Romans were there some two thousand years ago, when

The cathedral at Viseu

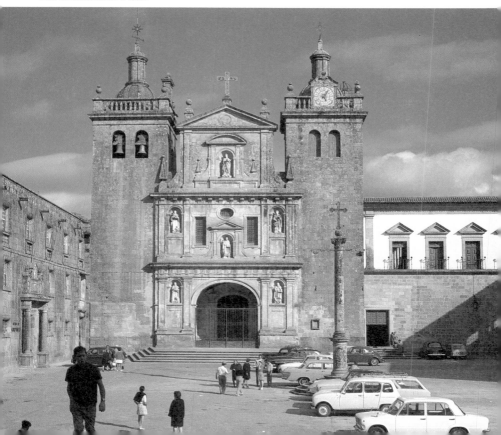

they stayed long enough to build their customary baths, but nothing remains today except a few ruins. They also established a military camp at **Viseu**, now the capital of Beira Alta and an important wine centre.

The old quarter of Viseu has changed very little down the years and still has its cobbled streets and narrow alleyways, antiquated houses with wrought iron balconies and the attractive Adro da Sé infront of the cathedral. They are all clustered together behind a gateway known as the Porta do Soar, built by Afonso V in the fifteenth century to safeguard the inhabitants. It is barely a stone's throw from the cathedral which, like so many other ancient churches, has been constantly modernised. This has not always been in the best interests of the original buildings and often results in a strange mixture of architectural styles, as here at Viseu. The façade was completely reconstructed in the seventeenth century and is presided over by St Theotonius, the patron saint of the town, attended by other ecclesiastical figures and flanked by businesslike towers that have sprouted somewhat incongruous minarets.

Nor is the interior able to decide exactly what century it is meant to represent. There is impressive vaulting whose cross-ribs are lightly knotted together, while cherubs and unlikely looking birds vie for attention in the sacristy. The massive Baroque altarpiece, glazed with gold, was fitted in the eighteenth century whereas the lectern is carved from wood brought over from Brazil about 500 years ago. The cathedral museum in the chapterhouse has some very viewable exhibits, among them two reliquary caskets decorated with enamel by craftsmen in Limoges during the thirteenth century. Also on show are a number of valuable crosses, a white satin cloak embroidered in gold and a twelfth-century Gospel that needed rebinding after four hundred years. The Renaissance cloister was given a fresh set of tiles in the eighteenth century but the Chapel of Our Lady of Mercy still has its carved *Descent from the Cross* thought to be the work of the Coimbra school, founded by French sculptors in the early sixteenth century.

The Grão-Vasco Museum adjoining the cathedral is certainly not blinkered in its choice of subjects although many of them have a distinctly religious flavour. It is named in honour of Vasco Fernandes, one of Portugal's leading medieval painters who spent much of his adult life in Viseu and died there in the mid sixteenth century. The most outstanding example of his work is *St Peter on His Throne* but there are also a number of panels designed for the cathedral that were replaced by the present altarpiece. He and his pupils obviously believed in adapting history to suit current events and, because Brazil had only recently been discovered, *The Adoration of the Maji* depicts Balthazar as an Indian chief from the New World instead of an African king. African art makes a brief appearance in the form of carved ivory while some of the tiles on display were obviously influenced by the Moors. Also facing on to the cathedral square the Igreja da Misericórdia is elegantly Baroque with matching towers, balustrades and a flight of shallow steps leading up to the main door.

The Praça de República is, to all intents and purposes, the centre of modern Viseu. It is pleasantly shady and unassuming with two of the towns leading hotels quite close by, the Hotel Grão Vasco and the Hotel Moinho de Vento, both of which are moderately priced. Alternative accommodation is available at the Casa de Rebordinho in a small village of the same name a few kilometres to the south. There are two campsites — the rather basic Parque de Campismo de Serrazes at São Pedro do Sul and the Parque de Campismo do Fontelo/Orbitur which has slightly more to offer besides being nearer at hand. Things to buy in Viseu include lace, carpets, brassware and black pottery as well as baskets which come in assorted shapes and sizes. St John the Baptist's Day is celebrated on 24 June with a parade through the streets with floats and drums accompanied by a large escort of men on horseback.

Mangualde, just off the N16 to Guarda, is a typical medieval town with modern aspirations. Its most important building is the Palácio des Condes de Anadia, still a private home but open to the public in the afternoons when the family is in residence. Otherwise it is possible to look round in the mornings as well. There is a monumental staircase decorated with tiles covered in hunting scenes, a great hall and a salon with equally fascinating tiles and old family portraits as well as some lovely porcelain and objects d'art.

The Igreja de Misericórdia is also decorated with tiles, most of them illustrating scenes from the New Testament in the nave, while the gilded ceiling in the chancel once glittered in the light of lamps suspended from expertly carved wooden brackets attached to the walls. It is in keeping with the old town, full of tiny winding streets lined with unexceptional but nevertheless atmospheric little granite houses. The Casa da Insua in Penalva do Castelo, 12km ($7^1/_2$ miles) to the northeast, is fitted out with battlements and has its own seventeenth-century chapel. The manor house is not open to the public although visitors can wander round the gardens, full of beautiful old trees, flowering shrubs and exotic plants.

There is more than one way of getting from Mangualde to Seia, a pleasant enough little town on the edge of the Serra da Estrela, but none of them is straightforward. The N232 wriggles through to join the N17 about 13km (8km) to the northeast whereas the N231 from Viseu makes the connection with slightly less effort and a better sense of direction. Either way it is as well to bear in mind that the Pousada de Santa Bárbara in Povoa das Quartas is only a dozen or so kilometres further down the main road. This is as good a place as any to start exploring the Serra da Estrêla, the highest mountain range in Portugal, sandwiched in between the valleys of the Mondego and the Zêzere. Some of the ravines were eaten away by glaciers during the Ice Age and even now the road across from Seia to Covilhã is often snowbound in bad weather although plans are afoot to turn Penhas da Saúde into a winter sports resort.

Until quite recently the whole area was ignored by everyone except the hill farmers who divided their attention between flocks of sheep and goats, planting rye and a few vegetables and making a delectable cheese called *queijo da serra*. Life is still by no means easy for people living in the little isolated hamlets where even the dogs wear collars spiked with nails to protect them if they get into conflict with a wolf. The minor roads can range from poor to quite dangerous in places if the surface water freezes, or if the hairpin bends are obscured by mist or driving rain. On the other hand the distances are not excessive and motorists who are prepared to drive slowly and carefully are rewarded with splendid views, an occasional lake or waterfall, strangely shaped rock formations and a bewildering array of spring flowers to compensate for any disadvantages.

Given good weather the choicest route is through Gouveia, in the Mondego valley, to **Manteigas**, a picturesque little spa of white houses with wooden balconies, at one end of the Vale Glaciário do Zêzere. The Pousada de São Lourenço, overlooking the town from its vantage point about 13km to the north, is small and somewhat Alpine in appearance. It is only a shortish walk from a mountain lake at Vale do Rossims, near Penhas Douradas, with its basic café-bar, clear often quite warm water and a little beach for sunbathing and impromptu barbeques.

At the opposite end of the Vale Glaciário do Zêzere is the Torre, at 1,993m (6,537ft) the most lofty peak in Portugal. Near at hand the carved stone image of Nossa Senhora da Boa Estrêla is the focal point of a religious festival held there every year on the second Sunday in August. The N339 passes close by on its way from Seia to **Covilhã**. This is an enterprising town with a few unenterprising hotels but a thriving textile industry. It makes *queijo da serra* from a mixture of goat and ewe's milk, spins enough yarn from the local wool to meet more than half the nation's total requirements, provides accommodation for skiers in the winter and is determined to become a centre for excursions into the mountains. The only tourist attraction is a map, etched in granite outside the town hall, tracing the route taken by Pêro de Covilhã in the fifteenth century. He set out ostensibly to find the domain of an African king known as Prester John, diverted to India after the death of his travelling companion but returned to Cairo to continue his original journey. In what is now known as Ethiopia he located a Christian kingdom where he spent the rest of his life on an estate thoughtfully provided by the ruler, who also found him a wife.

Pedro Álvares Cabral, who officially discovered Brazil in 1500, was born in the castle at **Belmonte** on the road to Guarda, although most of it has now disappeared apart from the keep and a trace of the protecting walls. The Igreja de São Tiago, which was old when Cabral was a boy, is a delightful little church opposite the castle which still has the remains of its ancient frescoes, baptismal fonts and some of the family tombs. The statue of Nossa Senhora da Esperança which also went on the voyage of discovery to Brazil, is housed in the modern Igreja Matriz on the other side of town. Some 2km further up the road the Centum Cellas is an odd sort of ruin with doors or windows on three different levels which has been described variously as a Roman temple, a governor's residence or a second-century inn but so far has provided no clues to its real identity.

Anyone with enough time to explore the Serra de Estrêla thoroughly will find plenty of other places of interest such as Alvoco da Serra and

Belmonte

Loriga, clinging like limpets to their respective hillsides, the waterfall at Poço do Inferno (Hell's Well) and the Cabeça da Velha, or Old Woman's Head. Sculptured by the elements this is a good fifteen minutes' walk from Senhora do Desterro, just off the return route to Seia on the western side. If the weather closes in, making mountain driving, climbing or walking pointless and uncomfortable, an obvious solution is to head for Guarda, regardless of the fact that it is the highest town in Portugal.

Not even its most ardent admirer would describe **Guarda** as appealing, quaint or picturesque. It is, in fact, rather grim and purposeful as befits its name and its role as an important fortress. There was an ancient settlement on the site when the Romans chose it for a military base. The Visigoths approved and added a stronghold of their own which the Moors captured and held until they were driven out by Afonso Henriques, the first king of Portugal. It was enlarged and strengthened by Sancho I, given the seal of royal approval by King Dinis and eventually pressed into service by Wellington during the Peninsular War.

The cathedral reflects the whole character of the town, solid and somewhat dour with very few redeeming features apart from a Gothic doorway and two sixteenth-century altarpieces which are over-elaborate but somehow lacking in atmosphere. The town has one of its old gates — the Torre dos Ferreiros — and a fairly run-of-the-mill museum in the seventeenth-century seminary. However there are some perfectly adequate hotels and a two-star campsite which offers visitors all the usual amenities apart from boating and fishing.

In its heyday Guarda spawned a whole bevy of attendant fortresses and even now it is difficult to drive any distance from the town without coming up against one or more of them. Determined seekers after ancient warlike villages can take their pick from about a dozen examples within a range of 72km (45 miles). For instance, the N16 leads directly to Celorico de Beira where the old castle keep has an excellent view over some rather uninspiring countryside. Slightly to the south Linhares, along a questionable little road off the N17, is better placed with a pillory in the main square, some elderly houses and a circlet of defensive walls built by King Dinis on a spur above the Mondego valley.

From Celorico de Beira it would probably be easier to turn in the opposite direction and spend more time in **Trancoso** where the castle is larger and much more imposing. The town has never quite got over the fact that it was a present from King Dinis to his bride, Isabel of Aragon, when the couple were married there in 1282. It recalls being dressed overall for the occasion and laying down a carpet of rose petals for the young queen. The antiquated houses still jostle each other along narrow, winding streets interspersed with mansions flaunting their wrought iron balconies and original coats-of-arms. The defending walls date back to the ninth century but have been renewed and strengthened a good many times since then, whereas the keep was an afterthought a mere seven hundred years ago.

From Trancoso there are two options open to motorists. The first is to carry on along the N102 past Marialva, where the ruined fortress contains all that is left of a deserted village including a sixteenth-century church, and then turn off to the right along the N222 just short of Vila Nova de Foz Côa, which has an interesting little church of its own. This route takes in Castelo Melhor, whose tiny medieval hamlet clambers up a rocky peak to the remains of a fortress at the top, before pausing at Figueira de Castelo Rodrigo just long enough to inspect the gilded altars in its eighteenth-century church. The companion village of Castelo Rodrigo is older and much more battered with a castle that has been in ruins for the past four hundred years. It has a direct road link with Almeida which is pleasantly undemanding and an infinitely more scenic connection, once known as the 'Accursed Road' because of its tortuous path across the bleak Serra de Marofa, levelling out in the fertile area round Pinhel.

The second option from Trancoso is the N226 that winds its way across the countryside with nothing much to see apart from vineyards and olive trees until it also reaches **Pinhel**. This is an attractive little place, hemmed in by two small rivers with a couple of towers left over from the days when it was fortified. There are some decorative old houses, a fourteenth-century church and a municipal museum in the Praça de Sacadura Cabral. The last of these dabbles in all manner of different subjects ranging from prehistoric artifacts to pottery, handicrafts and sacred art. It is possible to find a bed in Pinhel for the night or carry on to the Pousada da Senhora das Neves in Almeida less than 30km (18 miles) away. **Almeida** is another ancient frontier town, amply protected by its double line of fortifications in the shape of a six-pointed star. Apart from the old gateways, some typical houses and the old barracks that were converted into a prison during the Civil War, there is nothing of any particular interest hidden away inside the walls.

Much the same can be said for Castelo Bom which has only managed to hang on to part of a medieval tower, an elderly gateway and a sixteenth-century house. On the other hand Castilo Mendo has been more fortunate or, perhaps, more diligent. Two towers keep watch over the gateway in what still remains of the Gothic walls beyond which are a variety of ancient buildings, a seventeenth-century church and the tallest pillory for miles around. A ruined keep, attended by a chapel of comparable vintage, has a commanding view over the Côa valley and the main road linking Spain with Guarda, roughly 40km (25 miles) to the west.

The easiest and quickest route to the south is the N18 through Fundão, although there are also secondary roads that take a bit longer but have more to offer in the way of tourist attractions. For instance, the N324 calls at **Sabugal** in the valley of the Rio Côa. The town was founded by the Spanish ruler of Léon in the early thirteenth century and formed part of the dowry of Isabel of Aragon when she married King Dinis. It was a useful gift that may have prompted him to give her Trancoso in exchange, especially as it still remained in the safekeeping of the Portuguese crown.

Sabugal is another pleasing fortress town whose castle has been partly restored and can be inspected by simply enquiring at the town hall.

Sortelha, a short drive to the west along a minor road, is just as attractive. Its jumble of granite houses overlooking the Zêzere valley are reached through a gateway in the fortified walls, strong enough to deter an invading medieval army but now protecting a handful of residents from the more modern village outside. There are two very businesslike towers with their own forbidding entrances and a watchpath that has commanding views over the valley, although the wind can be somewhat daunting.

At Penamacor, a left-hand fork takes leave of the N233 in order to visit **Monsanto**, without any doubt one of the most enchanting hill villages of all. The houses seem to grow out of the rock, some of them with decorative doorways and matching windows, rabbits and chickens are housed on the premises and the steep, ankle-twisting alleys stumble up the hillside to the castle ruins. The views from the top are magnificent and may account for the fact that everyone from the Lusitanians onwards regarded it as a very important outpost. The only drawback is that Monsanto is in grave danger of becoming a popular tourist attraction and it would not take many souvenir shops and commercial cafés to destroy the atmosphere completely. Already the place is crowded for the Festival of the Castle, held on the first Sunday after 3 May. The event recalls one of the many occasions on which the fortress was besieged but this time, instead of waiting to be starved into submission, the defenders decided to see if they could hoodwink the enemy. They took the carcass of their last remaining calf and tossed it nonchalantly over the battlements as though there was plenty more food where that came from. It was by no means a unique ploy but it worked, demoralising the attacking forces who decided that the venture was a waste of time and left to find an easier target. Nowadays the carcass is made of flowers but it causes nearly as much local rejoicing.

Idanha-a-Velha, just to the southwest of Monsanto, was originally the Roman city of *Igaeditânia*, most of which has either disappeared or is waiting to be excavated. The Visigoths did some rebuilding during their occupation, which of course the Moors knocked down again. As a result the much restored sixth-century cathedral and the ancient graveyard are about the only things to be seen at the moment. A medieval tower was built on the foundations of a Roman temple in the thirteenth century, but that has also fallen down.

Castelo Branco, the capital of Beira Baixa, is the last town of any size between Guarda and the Rio Tejo. The town has been battered about by so many people and at such frequent intervals that it is surprising to find anything of historic interest there at all. However the episcopal palace has managed to survive and is now home to the Tavares Proença Regional Museum with its comprehensive collection of prehistoric discoveries, Roman relics, ancient weapons and pieces of pottery. There are several Flemish tapestries, one or two rather good paintings and interesting items of furniture. Also on display are embroidered bed covers which have been an essential part of every young girl's trousseau for about three hundred years. The designs are traditional with birds representing lovers, fruit, trees, flowers and symbolic vegetables. In addition to a display of tools, including a loom, there is an embroidery workshop that will accept orders for coverlets, but because of the amount of work involved they are quite expensive.

The formal gardens surrounding the museum have a little bit of everything, from box hedges to ornamental pools and a Crown Lake to balus-
trades whose statues represent the Apostles and the Evangelists on one side and the kings of Portugal on the other. It is said that the reason why some of the monarchs are smaller than the others was so that everybody could see at a glance which had been dominated by Spain. The best overall view of the town is from the Miradouro de São Gens at the far end of the Rua do Mercado, a few minutes' walk from the museum. The site is shared by the church of Santa Maria do Castelo and the exceedingly sparse remains of a fort that once belonged to the Knights Templar.

Present-day Castelo Branco is an affluent town with wide streets, a few small gardens, very ordinary houses, and makes its living from cork, cheese, honey and olive oil. The hotels are definitely on the modest side for a provincial capital and so, to avoid any difficulties with parking, quite a few motorists opt for the Motel da Represa, about 8km (5 miles) south of the town. It provides individual bungalows, a predictable restaurant and a swimming pool. There is a local municipal camp site and one at Fundão, a tidy drive away up the N18.

Anyone looking for souvenirs in Montanhas may feel a trifle restricted because there is not a great deal on offer apart from basket work, wrought iron, brass and pottery. However embroidered bed covers can be ordered from the workshop in the Tavares Proença Museum but seldom if ever bought off the shelf. Nor are there a great many local specialities with the exception of a thick soup made from tripe and chestnut purée, trout or eel served with smoked ham and memorable cheeses from the Serra da Estrela and Beira Baixa.

Possibly because tourists, as opposed to travellers, are somewhat of a rarity in this area the back roads can be unappealing or quite horrible in places, more suited to flocks of sheep than motor vehicles. There are bus services between the outlying villages but apparently no timetables, which makes moving about decidedly awkward, while the little trains are operated entirely for the convenience of their passengers, stopping when they see a red flag or a friend waiting hopefully at an almost non-existent station. However the main routes are usually in good condition and anyone lacking the necessary spirit of adventure has really no need to deviate from them.

Additional Information

Places of Interest

Belmonte
Centum Cellas
Strange ruined tower on the outskirts,
near the road to Guarda.

Matriz Church
With statue of Nossa Senhora da
Esperançe.

São Tiago Church
Opposite the castle with flaking frescoes
and tombs of the Cabral family.

Bragança
Castle
In good state of repair containing a
military museum.

Cathedral
With a sacristy recalling episodes in the
life of St Ignatius.

Domus Municipalis
Beside the cathedral
To view apply at No 40, Rua Dom
Fernão o Bravo da Cidadela Bragança.
Thought to be oldest town hall in Portugal.

Museu do Abade de Baçal
Rua do Conselheiro Abilio Beça
Open: 10am-12.30pm, 2-5pm. Closed
Mondays and holidays.
Exhibits include archaeological finds
and sacred art.

Castelo Branco
Museu de Francisco Tavares Proença Júnior
Rua de Frei Bartolomeu da Costa
Open: 9.30am-12noon, 2-5.30pm. Closed
holidays.
Excellent and varied collection in the old
Episcopal palace.

Museum Gardens
Formal style with pools, statues, trees
and flowers.

Chaves
Castle
Open: 9.30am-12.30pm, 2-5pm. Closed
Saturday and Sunday mornings, Mon-
days and holidays.

Matriz Church
Praça de Camões
Mainly worth seeing for its very decora-
tive organ.

Misericord Church
Praça de Camões
A gilded altarpiece and tiles depicting
scenes from the New Testament.

Museu de Região Flaviense
Adjoining castle keep
Open: 9.30am-12.30pm, 2-5pm. Closed
Saturday and Sunday mornings, Mon-
days and holidays.
Interesting exhibits of archaeology and
ethnology.

Guarda
Cathedral
Not very impressive with carved
altarpiece and choir stalls. Gothic tomb
in the Pinas Chapel.

Regional Museum
In seminary near the Misericórdia
Open: daily except Mondays.
Not particularly absorbing but some
items have curiosity value.

Idanha-a-Velha
Site of Roman town still to be excavated
with a much restored Visigoth cathedral
and an ancient graveyard.

Lamego
Cathedral
With a decorative façade, carved choir
stalls and an attractive cloister.

Chapel of the Exile (Igreja do Desterro)
To view enquire at No 126 Rua da
Calçada or No 9 Rua Cardoso Avelino.
Seventeenth-century chapel with
colourful tiles and ceiling.

Church of Our Lady of the Remedies
    (Santuário Nossa Senhora dos Remédios)
On a hilltop above the town reached by
ornamental stairs.

Regional Museum
In episcopal palace, next to cathedral.
Open: 10am-12.30pm, 2-5pm. Closed
Mondays and holidays.
Exceptionally good museum with
tapestries, pictures and reconstructed
chapels.

Raposeira Wine Company
On the road to the sanctuary
Conducted tours 10am-12noon, 2-5pm.
Closed to the public at weekends.

Mangualde
Southeast of Viseu

Palácio des Condes de Anadia
Open: 3-6pm and also in the mornings
when the family is away.
A country mansion in the grand style
with decorative tiles, furniture and
porcelain.

The Misericord Church
Next to the local school
An attractive little church with statues,
tiles and decorative altars.

Mateus
East of Vila Real
Guided tours 9am-1pm, 2-6pm in the
summer. Occasionally open in winter on
request.
Home of the famous Mateus Rosé wine.
An elegant château with appropriate
furniture and a small museum.

Miranda do Douro
Former Cathedral
Open: 8.30am-6pm in summer. 9am-
5pm in winter. Closed Mondays and
holidays.
Baroque altarpiece, tiles and endearing
statue of the Child Jesus in a top hat.

Terre de Miranda Museum
In the main square
Open daily.
Interesting collection of exhibits, mainly
local twentieth-century items.

Pinhel
Northeast of Guarda

Municipal Museum
Praça de Sacadura Cabral
Open: 10am-12noon and 2-6pm. Closed

Saturdays, Sundays and holidays.
Small collection of prehistoric and
Roman remains, sacred art and local
crafts.

São João de Tarouca
Southeast of Lamego
Former monastery with a great many
tiles, interesting pictures and a granite
tomb.

Sao Pedro de Balsemão
East of Lamego
A much restored Visigoth chapel.

Viseu
Cathedral
Interesting ceilings, a small museum in
the chapter-house and eighteenth-
century tiles.

Grão-Vasco Museum
In bishops' palace beside cathedral
Open: 9.30am-12.30pm, 2-5pm. Closed
Mondays.
Mainly works by Vasco Fernandes and
Gaspar Vaz, also African art.

Tourist Information Offices

Bragança
Avenida 25 de Abril
☎ 073 22271 or 22273

Castelo Branco
Alameda da Liberdade
☎ 072 21002

Chaves
Rua de Santo António
☎ 076 21029

Covilhã
Praça do Municipio
☎ 075 22170

Guarda
Praça Lúis de Camões
☎ 071 22251

Manteigas
Rua 1 de Maio
☎ 075 47129

São Pedro do Sul
Estrada N16
☎ 032 71320

Vila Real
Avenida Carvalho Araujo
☎ 059 22819

Accommodation

Almeida
Pousada da Senhora das Neves
☎ 071 54283

Bragança
Pousada de São Bartolomeu
Estrada de Tourismo
☎ 073 22493

Hotel Bragança
Rua Dr Francisco Sá Carneiro
☎ 073 22579

Castelo Branco
Motel da Represa
(8km south of town)
☎ 072 52327

Lamego
Villa Hostilina
☎ 054 62394

Manteigas
Pousada de São Lourenço
☎ 075 47150 or 98150

Miranda do Douro
Pousada de Santa Catarina
☎ 073 42255

Oliveira do Hospital
Pousada de Santa Bárbara
Póvoa das Quartas
☎ 038 52252

Vidago
Palace Hotel
☎ 076 97356

Viseu
Hotel Grão Vasco
Rua Gaspar Barreiros
☎ 032 23511

Hotel Moinho de Vento
Rua Paulo Emilio
☎ 032 24116

Casa de Rebordinho
☎ 032 284 4464

6

Planicies

The Planicies region corresponds more or less to the province of Alentejo. It is by far the largest in Portugal, stretching from the Tagus southwards to the line of hills separating it from the Algarve and from the Atlantic Ocean across to the Spanish frontier. Much of it is rolling country blanketed with cereals which has earned it the title of the Granary of Portugal. This mainly consists of sizeable estates with appropriately large, functional houses, their outbuildings full of modern machinery. Water is a constant problem, and so is the weather — blazing hot during the summer months but bleak and unfriendly in the winter.

In addition to wheat a considerable proportion of the countryside is planted with olive trees and cork oaks. The latter differ in almost every respect from their more familiar relatives, with contorted branches, comparatively slender leaves and outsize acorns, much appreciated by the pigs that snuffle around making short work of them. Portugal is the world's largest supplier of cork, which is stripped off the trunks and lower branches at appropriate intervals and piled up nearby waiting to be collected for delivery to the nearest factory. There are some vineyards, particularly in the north, and a modicum of rice in the salt marshes of Alcácer do Sal, while several industries have taken root along the coast among the sand dunes and ever-present pine trees.

Touring in the region presents very few problems. The main roads are, for the most part, reasonably straight, only slightly undulating and generally quite well maintained, although some of the interlocking minor roads could do with attention. Alternatively it is possible to take a train from Lisbon to Portalegre, Elvas or Beja, catch a fast bus from Beja to Évora or use one of the local services.

There are one or two rivers such as the Guadiana, the Sado and the Mira and a few man-made reservoirs, but in only a very few cases have attempts been made to provide them with anything that could be remotely described as tourist facilities. Even the campsites are few and far between — one outside each of the three major towns, another on the Tagus and half a dozen more within nodding distance of the sea.

Portalegre, Santarém, Évora and Beja all have districts of their own and a good way of getting to know them would be to select an acceptable hotel or two and travel each morning in a different direction. However the distances involved are not too great, so it would be quite possible to visit most of the main places of interest in a reasonably short time and leave the rest for some future occasion. The longest drive would be between Beja and Santarém, and even that is less than 200km (125 miles).

Three main routes cross into the Planicies region from Spain. The most southerly runs from just north of Sevilla to Beja, the E90 connects Badajoz with Elvas and Estremoz while anyone travelling from the north through Cáceres has a choice between Marvão and Portalegre, 22km (14 miles) to the south. Marvão might be a marginally better choice, especially after a long, wearisome drive, because it has the delightful Pousada de Santa Maria, and a great deal of atmosphere, besides being on the major route.

Marvão is essentially a walled village left over from the Middle Ages whose narrow cobbled streets and small white houses are huddled together inside the ramparts. The fortress was built on the orders of Dom Dinis at the close of the thirteenth century and is poised at the end of a granite spur with a commanding view over Spain's Sierra de Torrico and the hills and valleys of Portugal. The first of its two most important tourist assets is the Monastery of Nossa Senhora da Estrêla, so called because a star is believed to have led a group of shepherds to the place where the statue of the Virgin was hidden. Much of the building was up-dated a little over 200 years ago and is now the local hospital. However the church has been preserved and has a marble altarpiece that is well worth inspecting. This also applies to the Municipal Museum in the church of Santa Maria which concerns itself with dozens of different subjects including prehistoric remains, traditional costumes, pills and potions and the town's original charter. Apart from the *pousada* and the Pensão Dom Dinis it is possible to rent furnished accommodation in the village, some of which is very basic, and then explore the Serra de São Mamede on horseback. All the relevant addresses are available from the Tourist Office in the Rua Dr Matos Magalhães.

Slightly to the northwest of Marvão on the N246 is **Castelo de Vide**, a little spa whose waters are said to be particularly beneficial for diabetics and anyone suffering from kidney problems. It clings tenaciously to the hillside below its 700-year-old castle, containing hardly anything of interest apart from an old brick tower and a small tiled chapel dating from the seventeenth century. The ancient Jewish quarter has been left almost intact — a jigsaw puzzle of twisting alleys, whitewashed houses, flower-filled balconies and laundry lines — with the oldest synagogue in Portugal. It is a very plain building, both inside and out, but is easily identified by the tabernacle with its customary indentations and a shelf for the sacred scrolls. The Praça Dom Pedro V, hemmed in by a number of elderly houses, is more extrovert with a seventeenth-century town hall, the Torre Palace and the Church of Santa Maria da Sevesa. The village boasts a handful of modest hotels which are quite acceptable but little in the way of taverns or restaurants.

A couple of small roads, the more scenic of the two currently being better suited to four-wheel drive vehicles than family cars, turn sharply off the N246 beyond Castelo de Vide and head south for **Portalegre**, the capital of Alto Alentejo. It is an old town, complete with a ruined castle, that made its name and fortune out of tapestries and still keeps very busy producing them. The workshops are installed in a former Jesuit monastery near the Parque Bombarda and are open to visitors on weekdays. Among the things to be seen are the hand-operated looms in the weaving room, the drawing section where all the different designs are prepared and an exhibition hall. Neither the cathedral, the Convent of Santa Clara nor the former church of São Francisco have anything very spectacular to offer, the castle is almost non existent and the church and convent of São Bernardo have been taken over by the army. On the other hand the Municipal Museum next to the cathedral springs any number of surprises, dividing its attention between sacred art and fripperies like snuff boxes and fans, twentieth-century paintings of no particular moment and even an old car. The José Régio Museum is nearly as unpredictable with elderly furniture and household appliances, folk art and unusual crucifixes acquired by the poet over nearly half a century. There are also some pleasing old houses in the Rua 19 de Junho leading from the cathedral to the city walls. The hotels are nothing special nor is the local one-star campsite.

Anyone with time to spare and a liking for out-of-the-way places might easily decide to ignore the N18, which heads due south through Monforte to Estremoz, in favour of a more tortuous, less frequented parallel route via Crato. This would provide an ideal opportunity to visit **Flor da Rosa** which keeps itself occupied making pottery in the shadow of an ancient monastery. The group of fortified buildings encased in their original walls once belonged to the Order of the Knights of Malta and was built in the fourteenth century by Álvaro Gonçalves Pereira whose son defeated the Spanish at the battle of Aljubarrota in 1385. The small chapel is delightfully simple with an attractive cloister, watched over by a caretaker who can usually be found in the farmyard round the back of the monastery.

Some 13km (8 miles) to the south the castle at **Alter do Chao** is about the same vintage with an extensive view from the top of the keep and a courtyard full of greenery and orange trees. Nearby is a sixteenth-century marble fountain which does not appear to have been cleaned since the day it was installed but still manages to look attractive. Somewhat further down the road, beyond Fronteira, the N243 links Montforte to the east with **Avis** about the same distance away to the west, surrounded by cork oaks and olive groves. It is an ancient town where the first king of Portugal founded the oldest order of chivalry in Europe, known eventually as the Order of St Benedict of Avis. It still has a clutch of medieval towers and the monastery church of St Benedict, rebuilt in the seventeenth century but somewhat overshadowed these days by an elongated reservoir serving the power station at Maranhão a few kilometres downstream. Meanwhile the N245 presses on resolutely to Estremoz.

There are quite a few excellent reasons for stopping in **Estremoz**, one of the most persuasive being the Pousada de Santa Rainha Isabel. It occupies the thirteenth-century palace built by King Dinis, was named after his queen, Saint Isabel of Aragon, and is furnished throughout in an appropriately regal style with antique furniture, silk tapestries and damask curtains as well as beautiful pictures and objects d'art. Many of the beds are canopied four-posters, pale green marble is used for the bathrooms while the dining hall, lit by chandeliers, has a baronial atmosphere well-suited to delicious dishes like braised quail, venison and wild boar followed by peaches flamed in brandy that not so long ago were peeled with an antique dagger and impaled on the point of a sword.

View over Marvão and its fortress

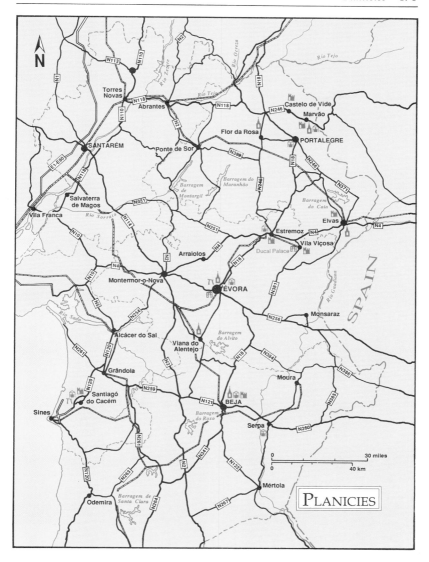

Quite apart from the *pousada* the castle contains an antichamber where Queen Isabel died in 1336. It was turned into a chapel about three hundred years later and decorated with tiles recalling various episodes in her life. One of the most charming, and probably the best known, is the legend of the roses. Apparently the king objected to his wife giving food and money to beggars and on one occasion he demanded to see what she was hiding in her skirts. When she dutifully obliged there was nothing concealed in the folds but roses. Other relics from the past include the Church of Santa Maria, the original keep and an old almshouse which has been converted into a small but interesting museum.

Estremoz is actually built on two levels, the upper fortified section concentrated round the castle with the more modern town spreading out beyond the walls. This contains two diminutive museums — the Museu Rural on the Praça Rossio, with a whole variety of items that were once part of the everyday life of the community, and the Agricultural Museum on the Rua Serpa Pinto full of implements and equipment used on the local farms. The church of São Francisco is marginally interesting, although the adjoining monastery is now an army barracks, while a nearby convent has been taken over by the town hall.

Every Saturday morning the Praça Rossio is turned into an open-air market, full of local produce and distinctive pottery. Typical examples include *moringues* which have one handle and two spouts and are usually decorated with a leaf pattern to which blobs inlaid with marble chips are added, rather like barbola work, to give the impression of buds or flowers. The potteries also turn out all kinds of little figurines which may be saints, the three kings and assorted shepherds for Nativity scenes or typical peasants going about their daily tasks.

Elvas, less than 30km (18 miles) to the west on the main road to Spain, and only 12km (7 miles) from the frontier, is a typical border town in more ways than one. The castle and the severe, entirely functional ramparts with their gateways, moats and curtain walls underline the fact that it has been an important stronghold since Moorish times. The Arabs built their *alcázar* on foundations laid down by the Romans but this was modernised in the fourteenth century and reinforced quite substantially two hundred years later. In 1801 Elvas was besieged by the Spaniards in what became known as the War of the Oranges. Forced by Napoleon to declare war on Portugal a Spanish army under Godoy was dispatched across the frontier and had just started to attack Elvas when news reached him that the town of Olivença had capitulated. To celebrate this unexpected victory he sent Queen Maria-Luisa two branches cut from local orange trees which fired the imagination of his countrymen. It was left to Wellington to redress the balance when he used the fortress as a base for his assault on Badajoz a decade or so later.

Visitors whose time is limited would probably do well to miss the cathedral, facing the Praça da República, in favour of the slightly younger but much more unusual Church of Nossa Senhora da Consolação just behind it. The marble pillory outside in the triangular Largo Santa Clara is worth a second glance because it still has its four iron hooks attached to the capital and an oddly decorated column which has a rash of unidentified little lumps. Beyond the walls the main attractions are the Aqueduct of Amoreira, which has been supplying the town with water for more than three hundred years, and an unexpectedly large museum of ex-votos in the Church of Senhor Jesus da Piedade. There are several rooms full of totally unrelated articles, anything from paintings and photographs to locks of hair and crutches, left by people hoping for a miracle or expressing their thanks for a prayer that had been granted. Among several places to stay in Elvas are the Pousada de Santa Luzia and the Hotel Sancho II.

On the way back to Estremoz the little town of **Borba** consists almost entirely of marble from the nearby quarries of Montes Claros. It has been used on every possible occasion, providing altars, fonts and suchlike for the Church of São Bartolomeu, steps for private houses and bits and pieces for the pavements, creating an overall effect which becomes a trifle monotonous.

Some 6km away **Vila Viçosa** is larger and considerably more historic, having been the family seat of the Dukes of Bragança and patronised by royalty for well over 600 years. The castle, surrounded by a deep moat, was built by King Dinis in the late thirteenth century and used as a not particularly desirable residence by the Dukes of Bragança until they moved into their own palace on the other side of town. There is not much to see apart from a few pleasing little houses and a small fifteenth-century church that has been considerably altered on more than one occasion.

The Ducal Palace, on the other hand, has a good many things to offer, spread out over the salons and state apartments behind its long, bland marble façade overlooking the Terreiro do Paço. There are some imaginatively painted ceilings in the main wing, complimented by fine French and Flemish tapestries, Arraiolos carpets and a varied selection of porcelain, but the furniture is mostly rather nondescript. The best pieces are said to have found their way to Lisbon, only to be lost in the earthquake, although a few choice items turned up in Brazil when the royal family went into exile there during the Peninsular War. Carlos I, who was assassinated in 1908, was the last of the royal residents. Both he and the queen left behind quite a few of their personal possessions, which have now been put on display in what is, in reality, a large somewhat draughty museum. This also includes an armoury in the former cloister and an array of totally innocuous coaches lined up in the stables nearby. The only remaining places of interest in Vila Viçosa are conveniently grouped around the palace square. The Convento das Chagas on the south side was chosen as a mausoleum for the duchesses of Bragança while the white marble tombs of their husbands can be seen in the church belonging to the Mosteiro dos Agostinhos directly opposite their former home.

From Via Viçosa a secondary road — the N254 — picks its way carefully through fields of wheat, scattered vineyards and interminable olive groves to **Évora**, one of the most unforgettable towns in Portugal. Admittedly it has expanded in recent years in keeping with its status as the capital of Alentejo and developed industrial interests ranging from cork and ceramics to agriculture, furniture and carpets. Nevertheless it has managed to preserve its ancient heart inside an almost continuous circle of fortified walls and towers, punctured by less than a dozen access roads and the Aqueduto da Água da Prata.

There are hotels to suit all pockets from the luxury Pousada dos Lóios, through more modern establishments like the Albergaria Vitória just outside the walls with a restaurant next door, to atmospheric little places such as the Pensão Policarpo near the cathedral. Visitors who prefer riding horses to inspecting ancient buildings would feel very much at home in the Estalagem Monte das Flores just outside the town on the road to Alcáçovas whereas the Parque de Campismo de Évora/Orbitur provides all the basic necessities for camping and caravanning. The local restaurants may be either expensive and interesting or quite plain and unexceptional with menus to match.

In order to appreciate Évora thoroughly it is useful to know a little of its past history, going back to the days when it was an important Roman centre established by Julius Caesar in about 61BC. As usual the Visigoths were next on the scene, followed by the Moors who held on to it until 1165 when they were outwitted by a Christian adventurer nicknamed Gerald the Fearless. The early kings of Portugal became extremely fond of the city which consequently attracted writers and artists, artchitects and men of learning, leading in turn to the foundation of a Jesuit university in 1559. However, when Philip II of Spain invaded Portugal some twenty years

The Aqueduct of Amoreira at Elvas

The Temple of Diana,
Évora

Évora

later Évora went into a decline from which it has never really recovered. The university was closed by the Marquês de Pombal in the mid-eighteenth century and it was only comparatively recently that the town re-emerged as a busy provincial capital with great potential as a leading tourist centre.

The first place to visit is the Roman temple standing in solitary splendour in the Largo Conde de Vila-Flor, a stone's throw from the cathedral. It is an impressive ruin, consisting of more than a dozen tall granite columns with marble capitals, dedicated to either Diana or Jupiter in its heyday but pressed into service as a fortress during the Middle Ages. It looks out over a flower-filled garden adorned with modern sculptures, but behind the façade are heaps of rubble that rather spoil the overall impression.

The temple's nearest neighbour is the Igreja de São João Evangelista built in the fifteenth century on the site of a Moorish castle. Beyond its over-protected Gothic doorway the nave is lined with tombs belonging to members of the de Melo family but they are far less viewable than the profusion of beautiful tiles added less than three hundred years ago. Its former monastery — the Convento dos Lóios next door — has been converted into a *pousada* where tables are arranged round the central courtyard with its obligatory fountain which was part of the original cloister. The cells once occupied by monks have been transformed into bedrooms, each with its own bathroom attached. They are obviously quite small, described variously as cosy or cramped, depending on one's point of view.

On the same side of the road, a little further down the hill, is the former palace of the Dukes of Cadaval whose northern tower formed part of the city's medieval defences. It was a present from João I to Martim Afonso de Melo in the late fourteenth century and played host to at least two other kings before it was renovated and provided with a small museum in the gallery. With the exception of an occasional painting the exhibits are unlikely to hold the attention of anyone apart from members of the Cadaval fraternity. The Municipal Museum at the opposite end of the Roman temple is a rather different matter. It is housed in the sixteenth-century episcopal palace which was given a facelift about two hundred years ago and later adapted to form a background for an admirable collection of sculptures including two rather splendid tombs. Also on show are some Roman fragments and examples of twentieth-century art which may not appeal to the majority of visitors. Upstairs among the paintings is an altarpiece, originally designed for the cathedral, which covers several panels with events in the life of the Virgin Mary.

Yet more items of sacred art are kept in the cathedral museum, leading off a terrace above the west door. The embroidered vestments, church plate and reliquaries are all worthy of attention but, for sheer novelty value, pride of place must go to an ivory statue of the Virgin which opens up to reveal various episodes from her life. The cathedral itself is a splendidly schizophrenic hangover from the twelfth century, apparently unable to decide whether to praise the Almighty or gird its loins for war. The main door is guarded by statues of the Apostles while the Evangelists have their allotted places in the huge Gothic cloister which has a faintly Moorish air about it. In addition to all this there are decorative choir stalls in the gallery and a staircase up to the roof with its panoramic views across the city.

Another church with something out of the ordinary to offer is the Igreja de São Francisco off the Rua da República. It is surprisingly spacious inside with contrasting galleries in the chancel — one Renaissance and the other Baroque — ebony columns and decorative tiles in the chapterhouse and a most unpleasant Ossuary Chapel. The walls are intricately patterned with more than five thousand human bones of all descriptions, including skulls, which the monk who designed it imagined would give his fellow creatures something to think about. He probably did not anticipate the day when young girls thinking of getting married would bring along plaits of hair to hang in the entrance as ex-votos.

The old heart of Évora is a tangled maze of narrow interlocking alleys, picturesque archways, white houses and tiled patios, enlivened here and there by a self-styled mansion, an elderly church or an unusual fountain. The Largo das Portas de Moura is a case in point. It is separated from the cathedral precincts by two medieval towers, originally part of the defences, and overlooked at the far end by the sixteenth-century Cordovil mansion with its horseshoe arches and matching arcades. The Renaissance fountain in the middle consists of a large basin, a central column and a surprisingly modern-looking marble sphere. An equally aged fountain makes its presence felt in the Praça do Giraldo. This is linked to the cathedral by the Rua 5 de Outubro which is the best place to go in search of souvenirs. Other local attractions include the university, the public gardens with just a trace of King Manuel's palace and the Monastery of São Bento de Castris, outside the city limits beyond the aqueduct.

The road past the monastery joins the N4 at **Arraiolos**, famous since the seventeenth century for its highly original and brilliantly coloured wollen carpets. They are still made in the traditional manner and sold by showrooms attached to the various workshops at somewhat lower prices than one would pay elsewhere. However, this is the only reason for pausing in Arraiolos because there is nothing left of the ancient castle apart from the outer walls. Nor has **Montemor-o-Nova**, 25km to the west along the N4, a great deal more to offer. It is an unobtrusive little village in the shadow of some ancient ruins where St John of God was born at the close of the fifteenth century. He founded the Order of Hospitallers and, in the absence of any clues to his actual birthplace, the connection is emphasised by a statue of him carrying a beggar in need of medical care.

From Montemor-o-Nova there are two alternative routes back to Évora. The N114 is the shortest and quickest, partly because there is nothing of any consequence along the way, whereas the N2 heads due south with a turning off from Alcáçovas to **Viana do Alentejo**. Although this little out-of-the-way town seldom receives any visitors it is nevertheless both attractive and interesting, mainly on account of its stylish fortified church. The building is all of a piece with the castle walls, flanked on one side by a courtyard colourfully dressed with flowers, orange trees and palms. The cross of the Order of Christ and the Portuguese coat-of-arms both appear over the doorway and, as usual, the lower walls inside are decorated with tiles.

There is plenty evidence to prove that the area to the southeast of Évora, within easy reach of the Guadiana River, was quite densely populated in prehistoric times. The inhabitants apparently had an insatiable desire to surround themselves with dolmens, menhirs, mystical stones of various

A picturesque whitewashed village in the Planicies

descriptions and even an occasional magic circle. These are concentrated to a certain extent round Monsaraz and Reguengos de Monsaraz and by exploring thereabouts several good examples may be discovered. San Pedro do Corval, just off the road, has its Lovers Rock while Monsaraz lays claim to the Cromlech do Xerez, within sight of a shortcut that connects it with the N256 west of Mourão. The village also offers its visitors an elderly castle, a parish church with a decorative marble tomb and a passable hotel in the Largo de São Bartolomeu.

Mourão, on the opposite side of the Guadiana, has nothing whatever to recommend it and much the same goes for Moura, although the latter can provide a faded hotel in an emergency, a couple of restaurants and a typical legend associated with its ruined castle. It also has a back way into **Serpa** on the major road from Spain to Beja. Here the main reason for stopping is the Pousada de Sao Gens, a modern building on the outskirts with both a reasonable restaurant and a swimming pool. The local attractions are somewhat limited although some prehistoric artifacts are on view in the castle museum while more modern aids to country life are displayed in the Ethnological Museum off the Largo do Corro.

Beja, the capital of its own small province, was an important centre in

In Portuguese bullfights the bulls are not killed

Roman times, christened *Pax Julia* in honour of the peace treaty signed by Julius Caesar and the Lusitanians. It also carried a lot of weight during the Moorish occupation, after which little of any importance happened until part of the French army was stationed there in the early days of the Peninsular War. In 1808 the townspeople and a group of French soldiers indulged in some street fighting of their own and in the reprisals that followed more than a thousand citizens were killed and much of the town was looted and burned. Today it is busy and prosperous, the old wounds have been obliterated but it is predictably short of really worthwhile tourist attractions.

The thirteenth-century castle has definitely seen better days, having lost all its fortified towers to make way for some relatively modern urban developments. Either luck, or perhaps superior management, stopped the demolition of the rest of the fortress. The only things that remain for the tourist are the keep, looking out over interminable fields of grain, a military museum of sorts and a small church nearby, supposedly founded by the Visigoths. The former Convento de Nossa Senhora de Conceiçao dates from the mid-fifteenth century and has been pressed into service as a regional museum. The chapel is Baroque but not particularly beautiful and proves to be less fascinating than the chapterhouse with its profusion of tiles and painted ceiling. Among the museum's rather muted treasures are one or two excellent paintings, a Roman tomb, some local costumes and a grille through which Sister Mariana Alcoforado is supposed to have carried on a passionate affaire with a French officer, Count Chamilly, who was stationed in the area. *The Love Letters of a Portuguese Nun*, published in the seventeenth century, were attributed to her but some critics maintain that they were a flight of fancy on the part of an imaginative writer at the court of Louis XIV.

Beja has nothing very attractive to offer in the way of hotels or restaurants and nor has **Mértola**, a sleepy little hamlet on the banks of the Guadiana some 50km (31 miles) away. Despite its ruined castle the village would be most unlikely to appeal to anyone except birdwatchers and open-air enthusiasts intent on exploring the lower reaches of the river down to the Spanish frontier. In fact the whole region south of Beja as far as the Algarve should be regarded as a no-go area by visitors in search of comfortable hotels, spectacular churches, good restaurants or well-equipped museums.

The nearest thing to a genuine tourist attraction in this part of the world is the ruined city of *Miróbriga*, due west of Beja, near **Santiago do Cacém** and fractionally inland from the industrial port of Sines. The site may well have been a Celtic settlement before the Romans took it over, built a couple of temples, the inevitable baths and a market place, all of which have been excavated, and a number of unexcavated villas. Anything of interest that was unearthed found its way into the museum at Santiago do Cacém in the Praça do Municipio, an efficiently organised establishment occupying the former prison. One or two cells have been left as they were, others have been turned into replicas of more congenial living quarters while the larger sections are laid out in the conventional manner and include a traditional kitchen. The castle seems to be in an admirable state of repair from the outside, but there is nothing inside the walls apart from a cemetery.

The Pousada de São Tiago on the outskirts of the town is the best place to stay for anyone who wants to explore the coast on either side. For campers there are about half a dozen different sites in the vicinity, the best of them being the Parque de Campismo de Melides and the Parque de Campismo da Lagoa de Santo André to the north. However the municipal campsite at Sines and the Parque de Campismo de Milfontes at Vila Nova de Mil Fontes further south are both reasonably well equipped, the latter making special provisions for handicapped visitors.

The whole Atlantic seaboard from the Algarve northwards to the Rio Sado is a mixture of rocky cliffs and little sandy bays that give minimal protection from the wind and weather. The sea tends to be on the cold side and there are some strong undercurrents that should be treated with extreme caution. There is little urban development, with the result that the many miniscule resorts are only popular with local holidaymakers.

Alcácer do Sal, tucked away in the salt marshes and rice fields of the Rio Sado, was founded by the Phoenicians and exploited by the Moors for its fine saline deposits. Although still moderately active the town is much more accustomed to the clatter of storks that build their nests on the rooftops than the presence of sightseers inspecting its ruined Arab castle, small churches and modest archaeological museum.

From Alcácer do Sol the N5 heads northwards to Marateca where it takes on a dual role and becomes the N10. The left-hand fork makes straight for Setúbal while the right-hand section continues on its way north before turning to the west to cross the Tagus at **Vila Franca de Xira**. This is the last place where it is possible to drive over the lower section of river, with the exception of the Ponte 25 de Abril in Lisbon. It is an uncomplicated industrial town with two self-effacing little hotels and a reputation for staging some extremely picturesque festivities and bull-fights. The best known of these is the Festival of the Colete Encarnado, usually referred to as the Red Waistcoat Festival from the scarlet jerkins worn by the *campinos*, or cattlemen, whose job it is to herd the fighting bulls. It is held on the first Saturday and Sunday in July when there is bullrunning and folk dancing in the streets, sardines are grilled and eaten in the open air, boat races are organised on the Tagus and *touradas* are staged in the arenas on the southern outskirts of the town. Everyone enjoys the event so much that a repeat performance takes place on the first Sunday in October. Examples of the cattlemen's distinctive costumes as well as other types of traditional dress are displayed in the Ethnographic Museum of the Arenas, along with exhibits connected with bullfighting in the Portuguese manner which has banned the killing of bulls for more than two hundred years.

Visitors looking for souvenirs in the region have an attractively wide choice ranging from Arraiolos carpets and sheepskin mats, glazed earthenware and copper goods to a variety of articles made from cork as well as cow bells and even hand-painted furniture. Then there are crystallized plums from Elvas, olives and marzipan. Alentejo is famous for its cheeses, smoked sausages and hams but other local dishes to try are the traditional stews made from lamb or kid, roasted eels and pork cooked with clams. The wines from Cartaxo, Reguengos and Vidigueira may not be world class but they usually blend in well with the local recipes.

Motorists who prefer to drive from one large centre to another, ignoring any possible attractions on either side, need never deviate from the main through roads. There is a direct route from Albufeira, in the Algarve, via Alcácer do Sal and Setúbal to Lisbon, another from Faro which is almost parallel but provides an option at Castro Verde for anyone travelling to Beja, Évora, Estremoz and Portalegre, while traffic from Spain can head straight for the capital or weave from one major highway to the other. Visitors who are dependent on public transport have a choice of trains, express coaches and bus services. Nearly every town of any size has its train and bus stations but journeys to outlying areas may well entail one or more changes and a certain amount of hanging about waiting for connections which can be ill-timed and often quite infrequent.

Additional Information

Places of Interest

Arraiolos
Carpet workshops and showrooms.
Carpets for sale at reasonable prices.

Avis
The remains of a castle and a restored monastery near a reservoir.

Beja
Castle
Walls and keep with small military museum
Open: 10am-1pm, 2-6pm in summer.
9am-12noon and 1-4pm in winter.
Closed on holidays.

Municipal Museum
Convento de Nossa Senhora da
    Conceição
Open: 10am-1pm, 2.30-5pm. Closed
Sundays and holidays.
Decorative chapterhouse, tombs and
paintings.

Elvas
Cathedral
Praça da República
Closed Tuesdays.

Church of Our Lady of Consolation
Behind the cathedral
Beautiful interior with marble pillars
and very colourful tiles.

Church of Senhor Jesus da Piedada
Museum of ex-votos. Just outside the
walls
Open: 10am-12noon, 2.30-6.30pm.
Miscellaneous collection of offerings.

Fortress
Includes the governor's residence
Open: 9am-12.30pm, 2-7pm. Closed
Thursdays.

Estremoz
Castle
Houses the *pousada* and the Queen
Isabel of Aragon Chapel lined with tiles.
Closed on Mondays.

Church of São Francisco
Near the Praça Rossio

Museum of Agriculture
Rua Serpa Pinto
Full of implements mainly of interest to
farmers.

Museu de Cristo
10km east of the town at Villa-Lôbos
Open: 9am-9pm.
Literally hundreds of crucifixes covering
twelve hundred years.

Museu Rural
Praça Rossio
Open: 10am-1pm and 3-6pm. Closed
Mondays.
Typical folk museum with some inter-
esting exhibits.

Municipal Museum
Facing the castle square
Open: 10am-1pm, 3-6pm.
Pottery, some furniture and a selection
of pictures.

Évora
Cathedral and cathedral museum
Behind the Roman temple
Open: 8.30am-1pm, 2.30-6pm.
A severe fortress-church with large
cloister, rich treasures and staircase up
to the roof.

Church of St Francis (São Francisco)
Rua da República
Open: 8.30am-1pm, 2.30-6pm.
Spacious, decorative interior and
macabre Casa dos Ossos lined with
thousands of human bones.

Church of St John the Evangelist
To one side of the Roman temple
Privately owned and often locked. For
guided tours 10am-12.30pm, 2-5pm
enquire at door No 9 in the Cadaval
palace down the road. Guide unlikely to
be available on Mondays.
Part mausoleum with very eyecatching
tiles.

Museum of Ancient Art
In episcopal palace near cathedral
Open: 10am-12.30pm, 2-5pm.
Roman fragments, medieval tombs,
modern sculptures and a wide range of
paintings.

Palace of the Dukes of Cadaval
Slightly down hill from the Roman
temple
Open: 10am-12noon, 2.30-5.30pm.
Renovated fourteenth-century palace
with small museum in the gallery.

Roman Theatre
Somewhat sparse but impressive
remains overlooking a garden in the
Largo Conde de Vila-Flor.

University
Inner courtyard open to the public on
request 9am-12.30pm, 3-5pm. Closed
Saturday afternoons and Sundays.

Flor da Rosa
Pottery orientated village with ancient
monastery. To view enquire at the
adjacent farmyard.

Marvão
Monastery of Nossa Senhora da Estrêla
Now a hospital but the chapel is open to
the public. Key is kept opposite the
door.

Municipal Museum
Church of Santa Maria
A miscellaneous collection of exhibits. If
closed enquire at the tourist office.

Mértola
Ruined castle and former mosque,
slightly converted into a church. If
closed enquire at the house next door.

Portalegre
José Régio Museum
Off the Praça da República
Open: 9.30am-12.30pm, 2-6pm.
Personalised collection accumulated by
the poet and displayed in the house
where he lived.

Municipal Museum
Next to cathedral
Open: 9.30am-12.30pm, 2-6pm; Saturday
8.30-11.30am, 3-6.30pm. Closed Tuesdays and holidays.
Large selection of sacred art, carpets,
furniture, porcelain and miscellaneous
items.

Tapestry Workshops
In former Jesuit monastery near the
Parque Bombarda
Open to visitors 10am-4pm weekdays
only, sometimes closed for lunch.

Santiago do Cacém
Miróbriga
Open: 9am-12noon, 1.30-5pm. Closed
Sundays, Mondays and holidays.
The remains of a Roman city about 1km
from the town. Partly excavated tem-
ples, baths and market.

Municipal Museum
Praça do Municipio
Open: 9am-12noon, 1.30-5pm. Closed
Sundays, Mondays and holidays.
Typical folk museum with additional
Roman relics from *Miróbriga*.

Viana do Alentejo
Castle
With attractive courtyard
Open: 10am-12.30pm and 2-5pm. Closed
Mondays and holidays. Possibly also in
August.
Church attached to the castle, remark-
able for its size.

Vila Franca de Xira
Ethnological Museum of the Arenas
Open: 10am-12.30pm, 2-6pm. Closed
Mondays and holidays.
Traditional costumes, some art work
and exhibits connected with bullfight-
ing.

Vila Viçosa
Castle
With a drawbridge, some small houses
and a fifteenth-century church.

Paço Ducal
Terreiro do Paço
Open: 9.30am-1pm, 2-6pm. Closes 5pm
in winter and on Sundays, Mondays
and holidays.
A large, rather soulless palace with
paintings, tapestries, carpets and items
left by the last king and queen of
Portugal. Also armoury and coach
museum.

Tombs of the duchesses of Bragança in
the Convento das Chagas and of the
dukes of Bragança in the Mosteiro dos
Agostinhos, both facing the palace
square.

Tourist Information Offices

Beja
Rua do Capitão João Francisco de Sousa
☎ 084 23693

Castelo de Vide
Rua de Bartolomeu Alvares da Santa
☎ 045 91361

Elvas
Praça da República
☎ 068 62236
Open: 9am-7pm on weekdays. 9am-1pm
weekends.

Estremoz
Largo da República
☎ 068 22538
Open: 9.30am-1pm, 2-5pm.

Évora
Praça do Giraldo
☎ 066 22671
Open: 9am-12.30pm, 2-7pm.

Marvão
Rua 19 de Junho
☎ 045 93226

Portalegre
Rua 19 de Junho
☎ 045 21815

Vila Viçosa
Praça da República
☎ 068 42140

Accommodation

Elvas
Pousade de Santa Luzia
Avenida de Badajoz
☎ 068 62194

Hotel Sancho II
Praça da República
☎ 068 62684

Estremoz
Pousada de Santa Rainha Isabel
☎ 068 22618

Évora
Pousada dos Lóios
Largo Conde de Vila-Flor
☎ 066 24051

Albergaria Vitória
Rua Diana de Lis
☎ 066 27174

Pensão Policarpo
Rua da Freiria de Baixo
☎ 066 22424

Estalagem Monte das Flores
☎ 066 25490

Marvão
Pousada d Santa Maria
Rua 24 de Janeiro
☎ 045 93201

Pensão Dom Dinis
Rua Dr Matos Magalhões
☎ 045 93236

Santiago do Cácem
Pousada de São Tiago
Estrada National
☎ 069 22459

Serpa
Pousada de São Gens
☎ 084 90327

7

THE ALGARVE

The Algarve is to Portugal what the Riviera is to France or the Costa Blanca and the Costa del Sol are to Spain. At the moment, however, it is less built over than the Cote D'Azur, less bumptious than Benidorm and far less brazen than Torremolinos. At the same time it is neither chic nor sophisticated. The beaches are pleasantly sandy, much of the scenery is attractive without being particularly memorable and the architecture tends to be characteristic rather than historically interesting. Conversely it makes an ideal holiday playground. The temperature seldom drops below about 10°C (50°F) in winter or climbs higher than 30°C (86°F) in summer, which compares very favourably with Mallorca or California, and it claims to have more than 3,000 hours of sunshine every year with a moderate amount of rain, mostly during the winter months.

Like other popular holiday areas the Algarve has its fair share of highrise buildings, both hotels and apartment blocks, as well as sprawling modern seaside developments where most of the white villas stand in their own gardens filled with brilliantly coloured flowers and shrubs like hibiscus, bougainvillaea and geraniums, interspersed with greenery. At the same time there are stretches of coastline that are virtually untouched whose little bays, folded in between high cliffs, occasionally have a small fishing community attached. Further inland there are orchards and mar-ket gardens, hillsides misted with almond blossom in January and Febru-ary, orange groves, cotton fields, rice paddies, figs and sugar cane. Water seeps down from the hills behind, forming streams and a river or two that keep the area fertile and come in useful for doing the laundry in places that do not yet have modern domestic appliances. Fishing is the main local industry with agriculture and tourism running it a close second.

Until quite recently the Algarve was a small, isolated region, cut off to a certain extent from the rest of the world. The Caldeirao and Monchique mountains form a natural boundary with Planicies to the north, the Guadiana river effectively separates it from Spain while the Atlantic Ocean forms the whole coastline, creating sandbanks at the eastern ex-tremity while pounding furiously against the cliffs round Cape St Vin-cent, the most south-westerly point in Europe. Its first inhabitants were the Cynetes who were joined in due course by the Phoenicians, the Carthaginians and the ancient Greeks. They all set up trading posts but

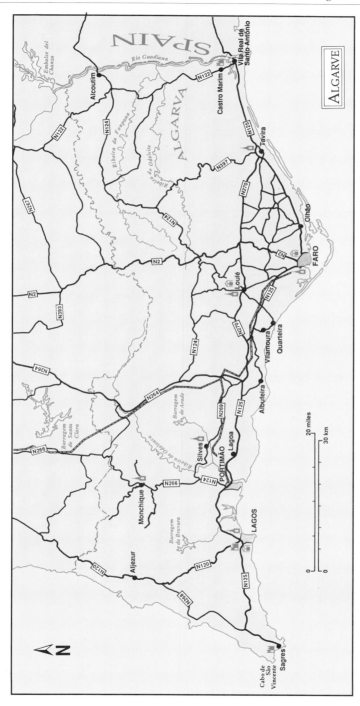

showed no inclination to take over the country, whereas the Romans saw it as a useful addition to their rapidly expanding empire. They just had time to establish one or two towns and introduce a successful irrigation system before making way for the Visigoths who were succeeded in their turn by the Moors.

The Moorish occupation lasted for more than five hundred years and left an indelible mark on both the region and its people. They called it *el gharb* which meant simply 'the west country' and created their capital at *Chelb*, now known as Silves. At that time it was a thriving inland port on the Rio Arade but its influence gradually diminished as the river silted up. In 1189 the town was captured by Sancho I with the help of a party of Crusaders on their way to the Holy Land, Faro was retaken by Afonso III sixty years later and thereafter the Algarve was left very much to its own devices for the best part of two hundred years. Henry the Navigator was largely instrumental in drawing attention to the province when he established his school of navigation at Sagres which paved the way for men like da Gama, Magellan, Columbus, Cabral and Dias to explore the far flung corners of the world.

Today the picture is quite different. International airlines operate scheduled services to Faro from London and other Continental cities, charter companies fly in thousands of tourists every year and there are daily flights to and from Lisbon that take less than three quarters of an hour. Trains and coaches shuttle backwards and forwards between Faro and the capital every day while motorists have several alternative points of entry. The three major routes are the N120 down the west coast to Lagos, the N2 to Faro and the E1 from Lisbon that nods at Albufeira, calls at Faro and continues along the southern shoreline to Vila Real de Santo António. At the moment anyone crossing over into Spain is obliged to use one of the ferries across the Rio Guadiana but it will not be long before a new bridge is opened quite close by, which will save a great deal of time but deprive those travellers who are in no hurry of a very pleasant interlude.

It would be a fairly simple matter to divide the Algarve up into two unequal sections, namely the comparatively small area to the east of Faro the provincial capital, and the larger and in some ways more attractive part of the country down to Sagres, in the far western corner. The only drawback is that there are so many different popular resorts along the coast, each offering its own particular brand of holiday attractions, that it would be difficult to decide which one to pick as an ideal base for touring the whole region.

One alternative would be to opt for the N120 down from Odeceixe, on the border with Planicies. Unfortunately there is not a great deal to explore along the first part of the route. The coast is somewhat desolate and under-populated and hotels, with the exception of one at Vale da Telha, 5km from Aljezur, are non-existent at the moment, although backpackers maintain that rooms can be found by asking in the larger villages. Aljezur itself has a castle of sorts but nothing else worth mentioning. However the beaches are blissfully empty apart from an occasional swimmer and perhaps a few bird watchers who may have left a tent or caravan at either Aljezur or Espiche although, because of the lack of facilities, these can hardly be described as official campsites.

At Alfambra, which has changed very little since the Arabs chose its name roughly one thousand years ago, the N120 takes a shortcut across the Serra do Espinhaço de Cão to Lagos. This leaves the more scenic N268 to find its own way through Bordeira to Carrapateira where the fishing is described as some of the best to be found anywhere in Portugal. From here it is only about 23km (14^1/$_2$ miles) to **Sagres**, the most westerly of all the Algarve's up-and-coming tourist resorts. It is now complete with the Pousada do Infante, hotels — one of which has a tennis court and a private sea water swimming pool — and a motel which claims to be open throughout the year but can on occasions look rather deserted. The bars and restaurants are rather nondescript but there is a small fishing and pleasure boat harbour where it is possible to hire a vessel equipped with bait and fishing tackle for four people.

A little to one side of the village, poised on the arid, windswept heights above the ocean within sight of Cape St Vincent, are the remains of a fortress built by Henry the Navigator but completely rejuvinated at the end of the eighteenth century. Beyond a handful of flimsy souvenir stalls that do nothing for the atmosphere, a functional gateway leads into a vast open square overlooked by the 600-year-old chapel of Nossa Senhora da Graça. Away to the left is the old navigation school and, in front of it, a huge, rock-strewn compass protected by a circle of low chains. Provided there are no other tourists about it is not difficult to imagine the early explorers standing round planning their epic voyages against the background of a turbulent, seemingly boundless ocean. In order to venture across the Atlantic and to explore the west coast of Africa it was also necessary to design a new type of vessel and this gave birth to the caravel. It was long, fairly beamy, was able to hoist mobile triangular sails not unlike those of a dhow, and was fitted with a stern rudder to make it easier to handle. The ships were perfected by Prince Henry's team of experts at Sagres and were so successful that they continued to be used well into the sixteenth century.

A minor road continues along the top of the cliffs to Cape St Vincent, known in the olden days as O Fim do Mundo — the End of the World. A strange rock formation off the point, called simply The Throne, was where seamen believed that the saint waited to bless them as they passed by and for a great many years it was customary to dip the ensign in salute, both as an acknowledgement and as a mark of respect. According to legend the body of St Vincent, who was martyred in Valencia, arrived off the promontory in an otherwise empty boat guided by ravens and was buried on the site in 304AD. Both the craft and its winged pilots must have been extremely durable because more than eight hundred years later the voy-

The marina on the outskirts of Sagres

The clear blue water, as here at Praia do Dona Ana, near Lagos, makes the Algarve a popular holiday destination

Praia de Rocha, near Portimão is developing as a popular resort

Portimão is a busy fishing port

age was resumed up the coast to Lisbon, arriving there in 1173. The city immediately adopted him as its patron saint, although he was replaced later by St Anthony.

Henry the Navigator died at Cape St Vincent in 1460, possibly in the monastery which once stood on the site now occupied by the lighthouse. It is one of the most powerful in Europe, with a beam that is visible sixty miles out to sea, and can be visited with the permission of the keepers. More than a hundred years after Henry's death his entire library was destroyed when Drake attacked the Spanish garrison at Sagres before going on to deal Philip II another blow when he met the Armada off the English coast. Thereafter Britain won a series of naval engagements in the vicinity of Cape St Vincent, especially in the late eighteenth century, culminating in Nelson's victory in 1797. The whole area is wild and desolate with some extraordinary sunsets. The fishing fleet, operating out of Sagres, brings back some of the best lobsters in the country.

From Sagres it is necessary to backtrack as far as Vila do Bispo, where the Parque de Campismo da Quinta dos Carricos has two stars to its credit, and continue in the direction of Lagos. Along the way a number of small roads make for the coast, providing a link with a succession of little beaches, just occasionally with cottages attached. One of the bigger and more progressive examples is Salema which now has a rash of holiday villas on the hillside overlooking a sheltered bay. There is nothing much to recommend it at the moment but in due course it will probably blossom into a typical seaside resort. Burgau, Luz and Porto de Mós are all very similar with furnished accommodation to let and, as far as Luz is concerned, a sports centre that will hire out windsurfing boards and aqualungs and provide some tuition if necessary.

Lagos, at the western end of a large and lovely bay, is by far the most important holiday resort on this stretch of the coast. It was originally occupied by the Lusitanians who lost the greater part of their settlement during an earthquake before the Carthaginians decided to rebuild it in about 350BC. It played host to the Romans and to the Moors, dabbled in both the slave trade and the crusades and was designated as the capital of the Algarve in the sixteenth century, but lost its title after less than two hundred years. Nowadays it concentrates mainly on fishing and tourism and makes a good job of both of them. It is an important yachting centre with a clutch of quite acceptable hotels and restaurants and has motorcycles, bicycles and mopeds for hire in the Rua São José.

The Mercado de Escravos, in the Praça da República, was the first slave market to be established in Europe, close to the former royal palace which is now a hospital. Other historic attractions include the remains of some ancient walls, an imposing fortress overlooking the harbour and the little chapel of São António a short walk away on the Rua Henrique Correira Silva. It is an extremely extrovert example of Portuguese Baroque with so much art work and gilded wood carving that it is known locally as the Golden Chapel. Its nearest neighbour is the Regional Museum next door, full of all sorts of unrelated items including some church vestments and an embroidered altar front.

Open-air enthusiasts have plenty to occupy them in and around Lagos. There are boats for hire, facilities for tennis and playing golf, swimming pools and sea bathing and even a special beach where sardines are grilled on the sands and served with local wine. It also boasts a sailing school, a bullring and boat trips to the grottos and caves in the vicinity of Ponta da Piedade during the season. As a change from sea and sand a minor road follows a river valley up to the Bravura Dam, 15km (9 miles) away in the foothills of the Serra de Monchique, through smallholdings planted with melons, figs, tomatoes and maize.

Alvor, which also had Roman and Moorish associations, stands on a shallow estuary mid-way between Lagos and Portimão with all the facilities required to attract holidaymakers. It offers large hotels and small sandy beaches, a golf course and riding stables in the surrounding area, swimming pools and tennis courts attached to the larger establishments as well as entertainments for visitors in the evenings. There are even more hotels at Praia da Rocha that fall into much the same categories, set in among expensive villas and watched over by the old fortress of Santa Catarina. The coast hereabouts is well equipped with campsites, the best of them being the Parque de Campismo do Valverde at Praia da Luz and the Parque de Campismo de Lagos at Porto de Mós, but there are others which have nearly as many facilities.

For all practical purposes Praia da Rocha can be regarded as a suburb of **Portimão**, the largest town in the Algarva after Faro and a busy fishing port and canning centre. It has been in existence for two thousand years or more but has nothing to prove it. The main attractions are the fish quays within sight of a bridge that spans the estuary, a wide variety of shops in and around the Rua do Comércio and the Rua Santa Isabel selling everything from souvenirs to clothes and furniture, and any number of small restaurants. Another point in its favour is that it has a direct link with Monchique, some 25km (16^1/$_2$ miles) away up in the mountains.

The Serra de Monchique is one of only two or three volcanic areas in Portugal, thrown up in the days when the world was young. It has weathered very pleasantly since then and is now coated with pines, peonies, eucalyptus, mimosa and wild rhododendrons, to which generations of farmers have added cultivated terraces and orange groves. The highest point is Mount Foia, surmounted by an obelisk, a relay station and a modest restaurant. The area is ideal for walking, especially in the spring when the flowers are out and in the autumn through woods daubed with every colour from dark green to the russet shades marking the clumps of chestnut trees. Little streams tumble down between the shale ridges while springs bubble up in the undergrowth, many of them with medicinal qualities. At Caldas de Monchique the waters have been harnessed to a modest spa that was well patronised in the nineteenth century and still plays host to people suffering from internal problems or who have trouble with their breathing. The old casino now sells handicrafts and the nearby bottling factory supplies drinking water to shops, hotels and restaurants all along the coast.

The village of **Monchique**, 7km ($4^1/_2$ miles) to the north on the slopes of Mount Foia, could almost be described as quaint if it were not for the relatively modern houses that tend to suffocate the older buildings. Foremost among these is the Igreja Matriz with its unusual Manueline doorway flanked by twisted columns that meet at the top, rather like ship's cables, and equally spaced carved knots, each with its own small stone extension. Slightly above and beyond the town are the ruins of Nossa Senhora do Destêrro, a Franciscan monastery founded in the seventeenth century by Pêro da Silva who went on to become viceroy of the Portuguese territories in India.

On the return drive to Portimão a secondary road doubles back just north of Porto do Lagos, which is currently being developed as a very upmarket housing estate, and threads its way through orange orchards and almond trees to **Silves**, the ancient Moorish capital of *el gharb*. In those far off times it was a magnificent city, more beautiful and prosperous than Lisbon with a busy port and an enviable reputation. However constant trouble among the Arabs themselves and between the Moors and the Christians destroyed the greater part of it, assisted by earthquakes and the silting up of the Rio Arade. All that remains is the *alcázar*, built on Roman foundations and much restored in the early nineteenth century. The view from the castle walls is festooned in spring with almond blossom and therein lies another legend.

It is said that one of the Arab rulers married a Scandinavian princess and installed her in the palace where she grew more and more unhappy, yearning among other things for a glimpse of snow. To pacify her the Emir planted almond trees for miles around and when they all came into flower she was so enchanted that they apparently lived happily ever afterwards. It is doubtful if she would have appreciated the addition of orange groves and cork factories but that is another story.

The cathedral of Santa Maria started life in the thirteenth century, replacing an ancient mosque parts of which have been preserved behind the altar. It was up-dated after the reconquest and several of the existing tombs are said to belong to Crusaders who were killed during the battle for the city in 1242. In 1495 João II was given a temporary resting place in the cathedral but when the coffin was recovered four years later much of it had disintegrated although his body was perfectly preserved. This was considered to be a miracle so slithers of wood were distributed as holy relics while the king was hastily reburied in the monastery church at Batalha. It was little short of a miracle that the cathedral survived the earthquake that destroyed Lisbon, Faro, a large proportion of Silves and many other places in 1755. However it was badly damaged and had to be extensively repaired whereas most of the old houses were simply pulled down and then replaced. Another survivor was the large, ornate lime-

There is alays a ready market for dried fish and other seafood

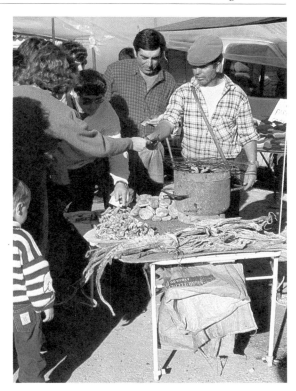

Mending the nets at Armação de Pêra

stone cross known as the Cruz de Portugal on the road to Messines.

A small secondary road connects Silves with Lagoa, an important wine town on the highway to the east of Portimão. It is possible to visit the local winery or stop for a traditional meal at a small restaurant that also specialises in Moroccan cookery, but there are no hotels or campsites and the most attractive furnished accommodation is at Carvoeiro on the coast 5km (3 miles) away. Motorists in search of an hotel should drive on to Alcantarilha and take the right-hand turning to **Armação de Pêra**, a fairly typical resort/fishing village with what is claimed to be the largest, sandiest beach in the Algarve. It is very much geared to tourists but, with the exception of the small chapel of São António and the Romanesque chapel of Nossa Senhora da Rocha, there is not much to see apart from some nearby caves and grottos. The owners of fishing boats can usually be persuaded to take holidaymakers on a tour of inspection after the morning's catch has been auctioned off on the beach.

The next place of any size along the foreshore is **Albufeira**, a former Arab stronghold that has progressed from being a small fishing centre to probably the most controversial of all Algarve's many holiday playgrounds. It is a resort which some visitors dislike while others love it and return regularly. If a main square lined with souvenir shops and supermarkets, a hotel room overlooking a crowded beach, or a campsite with tennis and swimming as well as nearly every other facility, allied to a wide variety of cafés, bars, restaurants and discotheques are what are required then there is no need to look any further. On the other hand, what you will not find are peace and solitude and even the beaches on either side are filled to capacity at the height of the season.

A tunnel through a large outcrop of rock links the main shopping street with the foreshore where fishermen pull their brightly painted boats up on to the sand and keep the nearby market well supplied with many different species. White houses, some of them quite elderly and separated by cobbled streets and alleys covered here and there with Moorish arches, straggle up the hillsides in company with more modern urban developments. There is nothing left of the fortress that held out against Afonso III until 1250 and a likely-looking belfry turns out on closer inspection to be part of the old town hall. Anyone in search of atmospheric churches or interesting museums will be disappointed but this is counteracted by some good views from the footpaths that run along the top of the cliffs.

Holiday villages, leisure complexes, swimming pools, magnificent golf courses, residential parks and other similar attractions are being created all around Albufeira. The Hotel Montechoro 3.5km (2 miles) northeast of the town, is one example with several tennis and squash courts, swimming pools, a gymnasium and a night club with both a dance band and traditional entertainments. Visitors with more modest means can find villas and apartments in the Montechoro Holiday Village or rent a chalet, a mobile home or a caravan at the Parque de Campismo de Albufeira.

Just down the main road to the east there is a turning off to **Vilamoura**, so far one of the largest tourist developments in Portugal. Once again this is an acquired taste, an anathema to some and a Mecca to others. For yachtsmen the focal point is a large marina, well maintained and somewhat aggressively guarded on the sheltered Bay of Quarteira, surrounded by small shops and pleasant restaurants. No option is overlooked in an effort to keep visiting holidaymakers happy. Three different day cruises are available, the longest and most expensive is down to Portimão, leaving at 9.30am with time for lunch and sightseeing ashore before returning at 5pm. A barbeque lunch of sardines and salad is provided at no extra charge on the beach at Benagil, with plenty of time for swimming and sunbathing before heading back to Vilamoura, for those who opt for the second alternative. Finally there are short morning and afternoon trips to Ponta da Galé, each one taking about three hours. For deep-sea fishermen a fully equipped motor yacht leaves every morning on a trip of about seven to eight hours. There are two big game fishing chairs and plenty of room in the cabin and the cockpit for other members of the party. Everyone can order drinks from the bar but must either take a packed lunch or ask in advance for a light meal to be provided.

Golfers have a choice of two different courses, both of which provide buggies if required. Playing time is necessarily limited to four hours, handicap limits are imposed and it is as well to book one or two days in advance. Several of the hotels have their own tennis courts and swimming pools, while the Casino de Valamoura provides dancing and floor shows as well as gaming tables and ample space for parking. The Clube de Tiro Vilamoura claims to be one of the largest gun clubs in Europe and has a comprehensive range of facilities including four hunting trails.

Although the town with its highrise blocks and attractive villas is something of an innovation the site was once occupied by the Roman city of *Cerro da Vial*. The excavations carried out so far have unearthed traces of several buildings and mosaic floors as well as discarded lamps and pieces of jewellery, and other items left behind by the Visigoths and later by the Arabs.

The whole coast from Vilamoura down to Faro is punctuated by very similar seaside resorts, among them Quarteira, Vale de Lobo and Quinta do Lago, offering golf and tennis, riding, swimming, windsurfing, manmade lakes and long sandy beaches. Roger Taylor's Tennis Centre and the golf course designed by Henry Cotton have been largely instrumental in drawing attention to the area but over-enthusiastic property development is threatening to swamp them completely.

Almansil, on the main road north of Vale do Lobo, is a small village without much to recommend it but 2km further east the church of São Lourenço is certainly worth visiting. The original building was considerably altered in the eighteenth century and drenched with tiles tracing the life and work of St Lawrence. He is shown curing the blind, distributing money to the poor, conferring with the pope, languishing in prison and being prepared for martyrdom.

The beach at Albufeira, reached by way of a tunnel through the rock

A cruise ship waiting in the harbour at Vilamura

It is only a matter of 8km (5 miles) or so to **Faro** which has been the provincial capital since the mid-eighteenth century. Very little is left of the old town that was recaptured from the Moors in 1249, burned to a cinder by the English under Lord Howard of Effingham when Elizabeth I and Philip II were at loggerheads, and subsequently flattened by earthquakes in 1722 and 1755. On each occasion it managed to rise from the devastation, with widened streets, re-planted trees, repaired walls and rebuilt houses.

As a result there is a small historical oasis enclosed in ancient walls on the far side of the harbour. The way in is through the Arco da Vila, an eighteenth-century gateway presided over by a white marble statue of St Thomas Aquinas. From here a short cobbled street leads in to a large open square, all set about with orange trees and dominated by the cathedral, most of which is only about 250 years old. It is mildly viewable inside, having been decorated in the accepted manner with a great many tiles.

Just behind the cathedral the Museu Arqueológico Lapidar do Infante Dom Henrique is housed in the expertly restored cloister that belonged to the Convento de Nossa Senhora da Assunção, founded in the sixteenth century. Some of the contents were discovered in the Roman town of *Milréu*, including the busts of the Emperor Hadrian and Agripina, the wife of Claudius. Also on display are fragmentary Roman mosaics, Moorish pottery, old weapons, coins and everything else that was unearthed each time Faro had to be rebuilt. The former chapel is home to the Ferreira do Almeida Collection, consisting mainly of items of sacred art, some not very memorable pictures and various pieces of furniture. Apart from the town hall there are small, unexceptional old houses facing the square whose occupants stand about in the doorways inspecting each new batch of sightseers while their assorted dogs make straight for the nearest orange trees.

The Museu Marítimo in the harbour master's office on the opposite side of the marina is filled with model ships, each one identified in English and faithfully copied down to the last detail. The Museu de Etnografia Régional, a shortish walk away in the Jardim da Alagoa down the Rua de Santo António, draws attention to every aspect of life in the Algarve from a grocer's shop to a farm kitchen, traditional costumes and local arts and crafts. These are augmented with photographs and paintings, everyday implements and utensils and models of different kinds, especially where the articles in question are too large to be included.

Faro has also managed to preserve one or two old churches. The Igreja do Carmo in the Largo do Carmo has an attractive Baroque façade, a gilded altarpiece and an Ossuary Chapel lined throughout with hundreds of bones and skulls retrieved from the adjoining graveyard nearly three hundred years ago. The Church of Pé da Cruz in the street of the same name has some interesting frescoes and a small chapel dedicated to Nossa Senhor dos Aflitos, whereas St Anthony has a minute chapel museum all to himself on the Praça do Infante with a panoramic view across the city.

The main places to shop in Faro are the Rua Santo António and round the Largo do Terreiro de Bispo, just inland from the harbour behind the Praça Dom Francisco Gomes where traffic streams past the central obelisk. To one side are the Manuel Bivar gardens beyond a restaurant whose tables are usually crowded with visitors watching the world go by. There are one or two hotels in the vicinity led by the Eva whose roof-top restaurant and swimming pool have an uninterrupted view of the pleasure boats moored outside. Less expensive establishments range from the Hotel Albacor and the Residencial Madalena to a scattering of typical pensions. They all tend to fill up fairly quickly because one advantage of being in the city centre is that everything is close to hand, ranging from the bus and railway stations to car hire firms and tour companies who cover the whole country with overnight stops where necessary along the way.

Faro is separated from the sea by an uninhabitable area, described variously as mud flats or broken sands. This is enclosed by a series of long sand spits that continue up the shoreline to a point not far from the mouth of the Guadiana, peppered with little beaches that will no doubt emerge eventually as popular sun spots with coloured umbrellas, ramshackle cafés and even a palm tree or two. The most westerly of them is already connected to the mainland by a bridge and a causeway, as well as by boat from the harbour, and is almost invariably littered during the season with partly clad bodies, sand castles and assorted debris.

Under the circumstances it is far better to head for the beaches off **Olhão**, 9km ($5^1/_2$ miles) along the main road in the opposite direction, where the island of Armona is a good place for swimming, angling, underwater fishing and scuba diving. Parts of Olhão have a distinctly North African flavour with houses that would not look out of place in Tunisia or Libya, possibly because of its long-established trading links with them. It is a sadly rundown little fishing port with a brace of totally forgettable churches and more or less regular ferry services to the off-shore islands of Armona and Culatra. In both cases tickets are available at a kiosk on the quay near the tourist office.

Some 11km (7 miles) north of Faro on the N2 the Roman ruins at **Milréu** are small, intensely world-weary and, in some places, hardly visible above the ground. Very little has been done to preserve them since they were discovered in 1876 and in fact everything that could be moved without too much trouble was either begged, borrowed or stolen within a remarkably short time. However there are the remains of some rather nice mosaics, broken columns that were once part of a temple and the interlocked foundations of baths and living quarters. Some people are inclined to think one building was a third-century Christian church which, if they are correct, would make it one of the earliest so far discovered anywhere. Some of the statues and mosaics from Milréu, known in its youth as *Ossonoba*, are reputed to have found their way into the gardens of the Estói Palace only a short walk away. The eighteenth-century mansion is not open to the public but the grounds are worth seeing for their terraces and balustrades, pools, decorative tiles and a pleasing view across the countryside to Faro in the middle distance.

Slightly further to the north the N270 cuts across the N2 near São Brás de Alportel, within striking distance of the Pousada de São Brás. It is not everybody's idea of a good place to stop. The outside needs painting and a good deal of the furniture has seen better days but the atmosphere is warm and friendly, the service is above reproach and the menus, although rather restricted, include tasty local dishes like *ameijoas na cataplana*, a mixture of sausage, ham and clams cooked with onions, peppers and tomatoes. **Loulé** makes no attempt to provide a suitable alternative, possibly because it is within easy reach of Faro, Santa Bárbara de Dexe and seaside resorts like Vilamoura. Nevertheless it is an interesting market town with the remains of a medieval castle containing a small local museum. The parish church dates from the twelfth century but has been revamped on more than one occasion since then and provided with the obligatory tiles, a somewhat unusual wrought iron pulpit and a 400-year-old statue of St Brás. However, most of Loule's visitors are there in search of souvenirs. Its craftsmen are well known all over the Algarve for pottery, leather harnesses and saddles and metalwork of varying descriptions. Coppersmiths can be seen in action along the narrow streets round the Praça Dom Afonso III, especially in the Rua 9 de Abril where the show-rooms are filled with attractive and useful articles, not all of which are highly priced.

Back on the coast, east of Faro, **Tavira** has frequently been described as the loveliest town in the Algarve, and not without good cause. No-one is quite certain when the site was first occupied but it undoubtedly goes back to the Greeks and the Romans who built a bridge over the Rio Gilão that, with a good deal of help at regular intervals, is still in place today. The town is well supplied with churches, the best of them being the Misericórdia with its fine Renaissance doorway and the Church of Santa Maria do Costrelo in which Dom Paio Peres Correia is buried. He was the man who attacked and recaptured the town in 1242 after the Moors had ambushed and killed a party of the Knights of Santiago who were out hunting during a temporary truce.

In its heyday Tavira was an important tunny and sardine fishing centre but when the river silted up and the port was hit by the earthquake of 1755 these activities were considerably curtailed. The Ilha de Tavira, an off-shore sandspit reached by ferry, has some pleasant beaches, although these can be very crowded during the holiday season. The best-equipped local hotel is the Eurotel Tavira on the outskirts which has a swimming pool, tennis courts, mini golf, table tennis and a children's playground but is often overflowing with families on package tours. The Quinta do Caracol is an old farmhouse that has apartments to let but the facilities could be described as rather hit-and-miss and it is fairly close to the railway line. São Pedro Santa Luzia, 3km west of Tavira, and Cabanas, about the same distance away to the east, both have purpose-built holiday

Enjoy a meal of the local food and wine

A wide range of typical pottery for sale in the Algarve

villages with furnished villas, lawns and swimming pools, restaurants and supermarkets, telephones and postal facilities and are conveniently close to the delightful, and as yet unspoiled beaches. The three-star campsite has all the ingredients necessary for an enjoyable holiday, although dogs are not allowed. Alternatively, the Parque de Campismo O Caliço at Vila Nova de Cacela accepts pets and can provide a limited amount of furnished accommodation.

The Parque de Campismo Municipal at Monte Gordo is large, quite shady and popular with foreign visitors, some of whom spend the winter there year after year. The village, only a few minutes walk away, is entirely predictable with moderately highrise hotels and apartment blocks, run-of-the-mill shops, snack bars and a large discotheque where the noise can be almost unbearable. Its one saving grace is the long sandy beach with pine trees set well back from the water's edge. From here it is only a short step to Vila Real de Santo António, the most easterly town in the Algarve and the embarkation point for ferries across the Rio Guadiana to Ayamonte on the Spanish side.

Very few people seem to approve of **Vila Real de Santo António**, with the possible exception of the permanent residents, regardless of the fact that there are undoubtedly one or two points in its favour. This may be because it was only built in 1774 on the orders of the Marquês de Pombal as the hub of the local fishing industry and was completed in less than six months. Its streets are arranged in a grid system with a shopping street in the middle, a bullring on the outskirts, fish canning factories and a take-it-or-leave-it attitude which is strangely out of character with the rest of Portugal. However the sea at Monte Gordo is within easy reach for a variety of water sports, with the addition of tennis courts and a casino.

A secondary road heads north across the marshes to the ancient village of **Castro Marim**. The history of this small town goes back to the thirteenth century when Afonso III decided that the hill needed a fortress to make the Spaniards think twice about launching an invasion across the river. Dom Dinis went a step further and when the Order of Templars was dissolved in Portugal he transferred the castle to his newly-formed Knights of Christ who remained in occupation until their headquarters were moved to Tomar in 1334. Three centuries later João IV up-dated the existing strong-hold and added the São Sebastião fortress on the hill opposite as a second line of defence. This was probably just as well because the red sandstone castle came to grief during the Lisbon earthquake and has not been rebuilt.

Castro Marim's only other attraction is the nearby Reserva do Sapal, a modest and decidedly marshy nature reserve with a 7km (4^1/$_2$ mile) walk mapped out by its guardians whose offices are in the fort. It is visited by many sea birds and a few determined ornithologists but has a limited appeal for tourists planning an idle stroll. They would be better advised to concentrate on the area round **Alcoutim**, roughly 40km (25 miles) further up the river. It is a typical little border town with the remains of a castle, a small church and a road designed for walking but now considerably improved for the motorist, which keeps company with the river down as far as Foz de Odeleite and then swerves inland to join the N122 back to Vila Real de Santo António.

In due course the main highway into Spain will bypass the marshlands south of Castro Marim and use a new bridge over the Rio Guadiana. Meanwhile it is necessary to drive back into Vila Real de Santo António, buy a ticket for the ferry at the entrance to the quay, change any surplus escudos in the building opposite and join the queue of cars and lorries waiting patiently to go on board. The boats run at half hourly intervals, so the whole operation will only last up to an hour.

Shopping in Portugal is not a very expensive pastime as a general rule. The main items to look for in the Algarve are pottery including all sorts of glazed tiles, copperware, handbags, shoes and articles made from cork or woven out of palm leaves or esparto grass, all of which are useful as well as being decorative. In addition there are the inevitable souvenirs, not forgetting the cockrel, or *gallo*, which comes in assorted sizes.

Anyone who is anxious to try traditional dishes should sample the fish in one of its many different guises. Sardines grilled on the beach and served with or without a salad and glasses of red wine are delicious and very popular. Dried octopus, cuttlefish and squid are also grilled while swordfish thinly sliced with onions and tomatoes makes tasty sandwiches with bread still warm from the wood-burning ovens. The meat is not particularly good but fish soup and Caldo Verde, a potato soup laced with shredded cabbage, are specialities worth trying and so are sweets made from figs and almonds that were probably inspired by recipes inherited from the Moors. The local wines are drinkable and *aguardente de medronho*, distilled from the ripe berries of the arbutus trees, although not strictly a brandy is nevertheless very palatable.

The region celebrates frequently and with considerable enthusiasm, almost invariably accompanied by folk music and traditional dances in the streets and squares overlaid with flowers and feasting. Loulé anticipates Shrove Tuesday with its Carnival and Almond Gatherers Fair marked by processions that take on a more religious aspect during the pilgrimage of Our Lady of Pity on Easter Sunday. Thereafter the events include music festivals, golf and tennis tournaments, bullfights, competitions and other celebrations culminating in an International Car Rally and Portimão's Great November Fair.

Once in the Algarve several options are open to visitors who wish to explore the area. Apart from the main highways a host of small roads, some in urgent need of attention, set off across the countryside to make contact with isolated villages where they may well decide not to proceed any further. There are bus services, some of them quite infrequent outside the major resorts, as well as car hire firms and bicycles for hire in Monte Gordo. A little local train runs from Vila Real de Santo António to Sagres, stopping more than a dozen times en route for the benefit of passengers loaded down with heavy shopping baskets. It may not be the most comfortable means of travelling but it is an excellent way of experiencing the atmosphere of the country.

Additional Information

Places of Interest

Almansil
Church of São Lourenço, 2km to the east
Full of decorative tiles.

Cape St Vincent
Rugged, rocky scenery and a lighthouse which may be visited on request.

Estói
Small palace not open to the public, but visitors are allowed in the attractive gardens.

Faro
Cathedral
Open: 10am-12noon, 3-5pm.
Rebuilt after the earthquake and liberally decorated with tiles.

Carmo Church
Largo do Carmo
Attractive façade, gilded altar and Ossuary Chapel lined with skulls and human bones.

Church of Pé da Cruz
Rua do Pé da Cruz
If closed knock on the door.
Old frescoes, paintings and Chapel of Our Lord of the Afflicted.

Maritime Museum
Facing the harbour
Open: 9.30am-12.30pm, 2-5.30pm on weekdays, 9.30am-1pm Saturdays.
Closed Sundays.
Mainly model ships and fishing vessels.

Municipal Museum
Behind the cathedral
Open: 9am-12noon, 2-5pm.
Contains Archaeological Museum with varied selection of exhibits and partly religious art collection including reproductions of well-known masterpieces.

Museum of Ethnology
Jardim da Alagoa
Open: 9.30am-12.30pm, 2-5pm. Closed Saturdays, Sundays and holidays.
Set pieces, traditional costumes and a whole range of everyday articles.

Santo António Belvedere
With small museum
Praça do Infante
Open: from sunrise to sunset.
Items related to the saint. Good views.

Lagos
Chapel of Santo António
Rua Henrique Correira Silva
Beautiful and decorative little church partly rebuilt after the earthquake.

Mercado de Escravos
Praça da República
The oldest slave market in Europe, beside the Customs House.

Regional Museum
Leading off the Chapel of Santo António
Open: 9.30am-12.30pm, 2.30-5.30pm.
Closed Mondays and holidays.
Miscellaneous collection, some amusing rather than informative.

Loulé
Castle
Remains include a small local museum of minimal interest.
Craft workshops in the vicinity of the Praça Dom Afonso III with showrooms attached.

Milréu
Ruins of the Roman *Ossonoba* with a few foundations, broken columns and a scattering of mosaics.

Sagres
Church of Nossa Senhora da Graça, the navigation school, the fortress and the large compass, slightly outside the village.

Silves
Cathedral
Contains tombs thought to belong to Crusaders who helped recapture the town.

Moorish fortress on Roman foundations with an ancient cistern and the remains of a disused mine. Now planted with trees and shrubs.

Vilamoura
A small museum installed in the warden's house
Enquire locally for opening times.

Tourist Information Offices

Alcoutim
Praça da República
☎ 081 46179

Albufeira
Rua 5 de Outubro
☎ 089 52144

Aljezur
Largo do Mercado
☎ 082 98229

Armação de Pêra
Avenida Marginal
☎ 082 32145

Faro
Rua da Misericórdia 8-12
☎ 089 25404

Lagos
Largo Marquês de Pombal
☎ 082 63031 or 57728

Loulé
Edificio do Castelo
☎ 089 63900

Monte Gordo
Avenida Marginal
☎ 081 44495

Olhão
Largo da Lagoa
☎ 089 73936

Portimão
Largo I de Dezembro
☎ 082 23695

Praia da Rocha
Rua Tomás Cabreira
☎ 082 22290

Quarteira
Avenida Infante Sagres
☎ 089 32217

São Brás de Alportel
Rua Dr Evaristo Gago
☎ 089 42211

Silves
Rua 25 de Abril
☎ 082 42255
Open: 9am-12.30pm, 2.30-5pm.

Tavira
Praça da República
☎ 081 22511

Vila Real de Santo António
Praça Marquês de Pombal
☎ 081 44495

Accommodation

Albufeira
Hotel Montechoro
☎ 089 85 94 23

Benfarras
Near Vilamoura
Parque das Lananjeiras
☎ 089 66368

Faro
Hotel Eva
Avenida da República
☎ 089 24054

Hotel Albacor
Rua Brites de Almeida
☎ 089 22093

Residencial Madalena
Rua Conselheiro Bivar
☎ 089 20806

Sagres
Pousade do Infante
☎ 082 64222

São Brás de Alportel
Pousada de São Brás
☎ 089 42305

Tavira
Eurotel Tavira
☎ 081 22041

Quinta do Caracol
☎ 081 22475

PORTUGAL FACT FILE

Accommodation

There is certainly no lack of accommodation in Portugal, ranging from luxury hotels to very basic pensions, augmented by a wide variety of guest houses, furnished cottages and apartments, a sprinkling of youth hostels and a reasonable selection of campsites.

Hotels

Hotels are rated from 1-star to 5-star and here, as anywhere else, visitors generally get exactly what they pay for. The luxury 5-star establishments are confined almost exclusively to the Lisbon area, while the majority of 4-star hotels are divided between the Costa de Lisboa and the Algarve. Every region has its compliment of comfortable 3-star hotels and an even greater number that only rate 2-star but are usually pleasant, quite well equipped and comfortable. At the bottom of the list some places are adequate but devoid of any frills.

Apartment-hotels are 2-star to 4-star, whereas the *estalagems* are either 4-star or 5-star in their own category, while the *albergarias* are only 4-star. There is hardly any difference between the last two and, by and large, they are very acceptable. *Residencials* often occupy part of another building and, although they are only 3-star, can be preferable to some smaller hotels and usually include breakfast in the price of the room. *Pensões* are predictably unpredictable and may be delightful or just the opposite.

Most tourist offices can provide a list of their local hotels, some lists may give only basic details, although a few have beautifully illustrated brochures. A large percentage of hotels have lifts, private bathrooms and their own restaurants, or one quite close by, and parking is seldom a problem except in city centres. At the lower end of the market bolsters are more usually supplied than pillows so anyone who is planning an inexpensive holiday and needs something larger and softer would be advised to take their own. There may not be hand soap but towels are usually plentiful and extra blankets are forthcoming on request.

Prices vary between high and low seasons, during festivals and sometimes from room to room: one with a balcony or a good view may cost slightly more than one that is tucked away or has some other disadvantage. All prices must be visible at the reception desk as well as in the rooms so it is easy to check before signing in, especially as nobody minds showing prospective guests the accommodation that is available. Single rooms can be expected to cost 60-75 per cent of the price of a double room, but one person occupying a double room will be charged the full rate, less the cost of one breakfast. An extra bed provided in a double room will add 30 per cent to the bill, but this figure is reduced if it is for a child under the age of 8. Guests who book in to hotels are not obliged to agree to either half-board or full-board terms, although this may be an advantage under some circumstances and is worth investigating. Generally speaking, it should be assumed that the Estoril coast and the Algarve are more expensive than other parts of the country.

In the unlikely event of any serious disagreement with the management a guest is entitled to ask for the *Livro Oficial de Reclamações* in which to make an official complaint. Should the occasion arise the initial request would almost invariably be sufficient to sort out any problem.

Pousadas

Pousadas are government-owned establishments, often referred to as State Inns which certainly does not do justice to the majority of them. Many are converted castles, palaces, convents or monasteries, beautifully furnished in keeping with their surroundings and with all the modern aids to gracious living. Occasionally the architecture can impose certain limitations — ancient cells do not make spacious bedrooms — and one or two may be slightly dilapidated, but this does not seem to spoil the atmosphere. The modern versions, added to fill in any gaps in the chain, are almost indistinguishable from comparable hotels and come in for similar amounts of praise and criticism.

Pousadas are divided into three categories — B are establishments which, although up to the required standards, are in no way exceptional, C indicates the middle category and are somewhat more expensive, while CH denotes luxury in one form or another and they charge accordingly. These grades are usually very accurate but one or two may be slightly overrated. All *pousadas* have their own restaurants and many of them include a few traditional dishes. They are also easy to locate because they are shown on the majority of road maps and are well signposted.

Detailed information can be obtained from ENATUR (Empresa Nacional de Turismo), Avenida Santa Joana a Princesa, 10A, 1700 Lisbon, ☎ 01 88 12 21 or 88 90 78 who will also make advance reservations for people who do not wish to do so personally. This is particularly necessary in cases where there is not a lot of accommodation available or where the pousada is exceptionally memorable as in the case of the Pousada da Rainha Santa Isabel in Estremoz, the Pousada dos Lóios in Évora, and the Pousada de Santa Marinha in Guimarães.

Turismo de Habitação

The more up-market accommodation listed under this heading is rather similar to the *pousada* but consists of stately homes or manor houses all of which are privately owned. Some are beautifully furnished and full of atmosphere while others are rather past their prime. Visitors may be treated as house guests, joining the family at breakfast, provided with dinner on request and invited to share a roaring fire if the evening is cold. On the other hand the guests may have their own sittingrooms and even kitchenettes, or may be faced with dimly-lit, over-furnished empty rooms and an all-too-obvious lack of heating. Farm houses sometimes turn their outbuildings into attractive cottages, but it is also possible to land up in an annex which is both bare and damp.

A publication issued by the Government Tourist Office called *Turismo no Espaço Rural* or 'Tourism in the Countryside', lists more than 120 of these establishments covering all the different regions. By far the greatest number are in the Costa Verde but only comparatively few in the Algarve. Each entry is accompanied by the address and telephone number as well as the name of the person who handles reservations, but unfortunately there is no indication of the amount or type of accommodation or the facilities provided. This is particularly unfortunate because most require three days' notice and will not accept bookings for less than three nights. The prices are charged on a bed-and-breakfast basis — any additional meals are obviously extra — and they expect a 50 per cent deposit in advance.

To give some idea of the variety on offer — the Paço de Calheiros, near Ponte de Lima is palatial and charming; the Paço da Ermida at Ilhavo is a pleasant well-equipped farm; the Casa da Rocheira at Estoril is purpose built and provides its guests with their own restaurant, tennis, swimming and a sauna while the Quinta do Caracol, at Tavira, in the Algarve is a farmhouse with apartments, a bar, tennis and an improvised swimming pool.

For those who do not wish to make their own reservations in the Costa Verde the TURIHAB (Associação do Turismo de Habitação), Praça de República, 4990 Ponte de Lima, ☎ 058 94 23 35 will make the necessary arrangements.

Furnished Accommodation

In addition to the apartments, cottages and other arrangements made for self-catering visitors approved by the Turismo de Habitação, there are apartments and villas to let in most of the major holiday resorts. Many of the local tourist offices can supply the necessary details or the names of agents who handle these properties.

Pousadas de Juventude

At the moment there are less than twenty youth hostels in Portugal but the majority of them are open throughout the year. Visitors must have valid Youth Hostel Association Membership Cards which, if necessary can be obtained from:

Associação Portuguesa de Pousadas de Juventude,
46 Rua Andrade Corvo,
1000 Lisbon
☎ 01 57 10 54.

Details of hostels are available in *The International Youth Hostels Guide to Budget Accommodation;* Volume 1, available from bookshops or National Youth Hostel Associations. Visitors must check in 9am-12.30pm or 6-9pm and stay for three consecutive nights. Many young travellers prefer to find rooms in private houses or inexpensive pensions.

Campsites

Most campsites in Portugal are located along the coasts or in the vicinity of historical inland towns. They are given 1-star to 3-star ratings which ensures that they can provide all the basic amenities. Some have facilities for swimming and other sports, restaurants or cafeterias, children's playgrounds, modest shops and are within reach of a bus route. Comprehensive lists, the *Roteiro Campista*, are available from bookshops while the tourist offices have a brochure *Portugal Camping* that also deals with the whole country. A few sites are able to provide additional, basic accommodation, either in bungalows or in local towns and villages. Unofficial camping is permissible in many outlying areas but this does not include the Algarve.

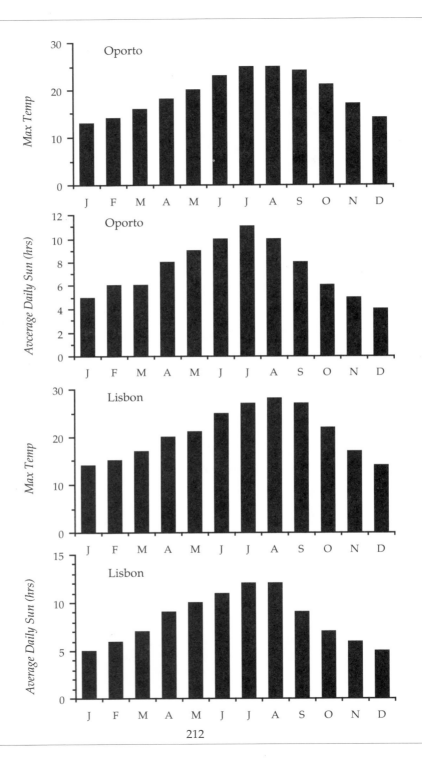

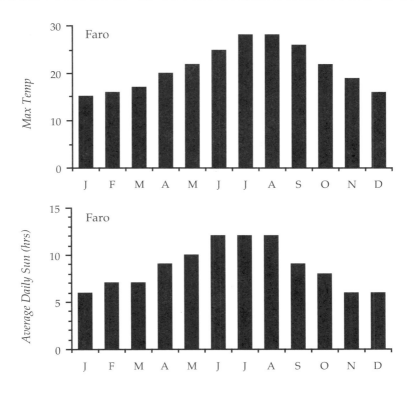

Climate

The climate varies quite considerably from one part of the country to another, and also from one season to the next. Generally speaking the winters in the north and up in the mountains are cold and frequently wet, whereas the Algarve is usually pleasantly mild. Conversely high summer in the south and the northeast can be hot with long hours of undiluted sunshine. The best times to visit Portugal are in the spring and the early autumn.

In the Lisbon area the average temperatures vary from 12°C (53°F) in January to 22°C (72°F) in August. The Costa de Prata is about 10°C (50°F) in January and 19°C (67°F) in August on the coast. The Costa Verde ranges from 9°C (49°F) in January to 20°C (68°F) in August roung Viana do Castelo, while the Algarve seldom drops below 12°C (54°F) but rises to 24°C (75°F) during July and August. Inland, Évora has temperatures of around 12°C (53°F) in January rising to 30°C in the height of summer. Castelo Branco also roasts in July while Bragança can drop down to 8°C (48°F) in the New Year.

213

Crime

Although there is obviously a certain amount of crime in Portugal it is not as much of a problem as elsewhere. The large towns and popular resorts suffer most and sightseers should be on their guard against pick-pockets and petty thieves. Nothing should be left on the seats of parked cars and visitors would be well advised to leave expensive jewellery, surplus money and important documents locked up in the hotel safe. There are some time-share touts and suspect property dealers about so it is very unwise to enter into any sort of arrangements without first getting expert advice. Children and women travelling alone are unlikely to be bothered on the streets, but it is asking for trouble to wander round unfrequented areas alone at night.

Currency and Credit Cards

The Portuguese monetary unit is the *escudo* made up of 100 *centavos*, and is written with a '$' sign where the decimal point usually is. For example $1^1/_2$ escudos would be 1$50. There are notes of 5,000$00, 1,000$00, 500$00 and 100$00 whereas the coins are 50$00, 25$00, 20$00, 10$00, 5$00, 2$50, 1$00 and $50. Obviously the exchange rate varies but for ease of operation it is safe to assume that a 1,000$00 note is currently worth about £4 or $6.50 (USA).

Major credit cards, such as American Express, Diner's Club, Mastercard and Visa, are accepted by many of the large hotels and restaurants, but not all of them, so it is essential to check in advance if the logo is not visible. Some garages also accept credit cards but the majority do not at the present moment. The further you travel off the beaten track the less likely you will be able to pay in anything other than cash.

Foreign currency and travellers cheques can be changed at most banks — Eurocheque cards are less generally acceptable — and some large hotels and travel agencies will oblige but their rates are considerably higher. Money can be transferred from abroad to the major banks in Lisbon and Oporto, a transaction which may take up to two weeks.

Customs Regulations

The customs regulations in Portugal are similar to those elsewhere in the EEC. However it is as well to check before leaving if you are thinking of bringing anything that is a little unusual. For example it is forbidden to take fresh meat into Portugal.

Disabled

So far not many places make provision for disabled visitors but there are a few hotels and campsites which provide basic facilities. Anyone with serious problems should ask for advice before setting out.

Dress

With the exception of large, expensive hotels and restaurants in Lisbon and in some of the leading resorts there are hardly any places where guests are expected to wear formal clothes. It is a good idea to take something to change into in the evening, or for special occasions, depending on the kind of holiday you have in mind. Warm clothes are necessary in the winter — a thick coat in the north and up in the mountains and a woollen sweater for cool evenings, even in the Algarve. Flat shoes are essential for walking along cobbled streets. Otherwise an ordinary holiday wardrobe is perfectly adequate. Nude and semi-nude bathing has not really caught on in Portugal so far but jeans and T-shirts are as much in evidence here as they are anywhere else. Particular care should be taken not to offend anyone when visiting churches and especially the basilica at Fatima where visitors are requested to cover their legs and shoulders and many pilgrims wear something on their heads as well. An umbrella comes in very useful and so does a waterproof of some description, particularly in the north during the rainy season.

Electricity

Generally speaking the electricity is 220 volts, 50 cycles. Adaptors will be needed for appliances not fitted with a 2-pin continental plug.

Emergencies

In an emergency the number to ring for the police or an ambulance is 115 from anywhere in Portugal.

Entertainments

Entertainments vary quite considerably between the different regions. Concerts are mainly confined to Lisbon and Oporto. Films are practically never dubbed and are usually new releases so it is possible to spend a pleasant evening at the cinema although, of course, not all of them are in English originally. Some hotel rooms have fitted radios, although they do not always work, and suites almost invariably have TV sets. In addition there are often TV sets in the public rooms and even in quite modest cafés and restaurants. For gamblers there are casinos in Estoril, Espinho, Póvoa de Varzim, Alvor, Vilamoura and Monte Gordo, some of which have restaurants and include floor shows as well.

Festivals

Festivals in Portugal are colourful, frequently exuberant and well attended although some may be solemn, religious celebrations such as the annual pilgrimages to Fátima in mid-May and mid-October. Nearly every town has its own particular events while others are held nationwide. Among the most outstanding are:

Carnival	Before Shrove Tuesday	Ovar, Loulé, Torres Vedras
Colourful Religious Processions	Holy Week & Easter	Braga, Loulé & elsewhere
Festival of Crosses	3 May	Barcelos
Festival of the Castle	1st Sunday after 3 May	Monsanto
Fishermens Festival	3-5 May	Sesimbra
Pilgrimage Procession	Last Sunday in May	Braga
São Gonçalo Festival	1st weekend in June	Amarante
International Folklore	1st Fortnight in June	Santarém
Festas dos Santas	During June	Lisbon
Festas de São João	23 June	Oporto
Tabuleiros Festival	1st fortnight in July (odd years)	Tomar
Festival of the Queen Saint	1st fortnight in July (even years)	Coimbra
Festival of the Red Waistcoats	1st weekend in July	Vila Franca de Xira
Gualterianas Festival	1st Sunday in August	Guimarães
Festival of the Green Hat	2nd weekend in Aug	Alcochete
Pilgrimage of Our Lady of Sorrow	3rd week in August	Viana do Castelo
Grape Harvest Festival	1st Sun in September	Palmela

Festival of Our Lady of the Cape (dating from thirteenth century)	Last Sun in September	Cape Espichel
Annual Fair	1st Sun in October	Vila Franca de Xira
Great Fair of Our Lady of Sorrow	2nd Sun in October	Santarém
National Horse Fair	1st Fortnight in Nov	Golegã
Great November Fair	11 November	Portimão
Festas dos Rapazes	Last week of Dec	Villages round Bragança

Health Care

English speaking visitors who need hospital treatment should go to the British Hospital, 49 Rua Saraiva de Carvalho, Lisbon, ☎ 01 60 20 20 in order to feel more at home. However a good many doctors elsewhere also speak English but some members of the staff may not. Large spas like Caldas da Rainha have some English speaking staff.

Pharmacies (*farmácias*) can help with minor ailments or suggest where to go for assistance.

Language

An unexpectedly large number of people in Portugal, especially the younger generations, understand and speak a modicum of English or French. However it is a mistake to think that Portuguese bears more than a slight passing resemblance to Spanish, except for the dialect of Galicia. Although it is seldom difficult to make oneself understood it is reassuring, polite and very rewarding to be able to recognise a few words, and even better to be able to pronounce one or two of them, despite the fact that this is more demanding than it seems. Nevertheless it gives a lot of pleasure to the people you are talking to, even if they cannot recognise a single word! Most visitors agree that a basic vocabulary makes a holiday much more enjoyable.

General

Mrs or Madam	*Senhora*
Mr or Sir	*Senhor*
Yes	*Sim*
No	*Não*
Please	*Por Favor*
Thank you	*Obrigado* when spoken by aman
	Obrigada when spoken by a woman

Good morning	*Bom dia*
Good afternoon/or evening	*Boa Tarde*
Goodnight	*Boa Noite*
Goodbye	*Adeus*
How are you?	*Como vai?*
See you later	*Até logo*
Do you speak English?	*Fala Inglês?*
I do not understand	*Não comprendo*
I am lost	*Estou perdido*
Please help me	*Ajude-me por avor*
Where?	*Onde?*
Why?	*Porquê?*
When?	*Quando?*
I am coming	*Venho*
Please tell me	*Informe-me por favor*
I am hungry	*Tenho fome*
I am thirsty	*Tenho sede*
I am sleepy	*Tenho sono*

Accommodation

A single room	*Um quarto simples*
A double room	*Um quarto de casal*
With a bathroom	*Com banho*
Blanket	*Cobertor*
Pillow	*Almofada*
Towel	*Toalha*
Soap	*Sabonete*
Toilet paper	*Papel higiénico*
Laundry	*Lavandaria*
Ironing	*Engomagem*
Luggage	*Bagagem*
Key	*Chave*
Writing paper	*Papel de carta*
Postcard	*Bilhete postal*
Stamps	*Selos*
Full board	*Pensão completa*
Bed and breakfast	*Quarto e pequeno almoço*
Please keep this for me	*Guarde-me isto por favor*

Medical

Doctor	*Médico*
Dentist	*Dentista*
I have a headache	*Tenho dores de cabeca*
I have stomachache	*Tenho dores de estomago*
I have toothache	*Tenho dores de dentes*
It hurts	*Doi-me*

Colds	Constipações
Bad sunburn	Queimaduras de sol
Painful feet	Pés doridos
Diarrhoea	Diarreia
Corns	Calos
Sore throat	Dor de garganta
Constipation	Prisão de ventre
Aspirin	Aspirina
Bandage	Ligadura
Cotton-wool	Algodão
Sticking plaster	Adesivos

Places

Bank	Banco
Chemist	Farmácia
Church	Igreja
Cinema	Cinema
Garage	Garagem
Hospital	Hospital
Library	Biblioteca
Museum	Museu
Police Station	O posto da policia
Post Office	Correios
Theatre	Teatro
Phone box	Cabine telefónica

Travel

Aircraft	Avião
Boat	Barco
Bus	Autocarro
Customs	Alfândega
Taxi	Táxi
Ticket	Bilhete
Train	Comboio
Tram	Eléctrico
Underground train	Metro
Passport	Passaporte
Nothing to declare	Nada a declarar
No smoking	Proibido fumar
Emergency exit	Saida de socorro

Time

What time is it?	Que horas são
Now	Agora
Later	Logo
Before	Antes

After	*Depois*
Quickly	*Depressa*
Slowly	*Devagar*
Today	*Hoje*
Tomorrow	*Amanhã*
Yesterday	*Ontem*
Morning	*Manhã*
Afternoon	*Tarde*
Evening	*Serão*
Monday	*Segunda-feira*
Tuesday	*Terça-feira*
Wednesday	*Quarta-feira*
Thursday	*Quinta-feira*
Friday	*Sexta-feira*
Saturday	*Sábado*
Sunday	*Domingo*
January	*Janeiro*
February	*Fevereiro*
March	*Março*
April	*Abril*
May	*Maio*
June	*Junho*
July	*Julho*
August	*Agosto*
September	*Setembro*
October	*Outubro*
November	*Novembro*
December	*Dezembro*

Colours

White	*Branco*
Black	*Preto*
Red	*Encarnado*
Blue	*Azul*
Green	*Verde*
Brown	*Castanho*
Yellow	*Amarelo*
Pink	*Cor de rosa*
Grey	*Cinzento*
Dark	*Escuro*
Light	*Claro*

Shopping

How much is it?	*Quanto custa?*
Expensive	*Caro*
Cheap	*Barato*

Newspapers	*Jornais*
Magazines	*Revistas*
Overcoat	*Sobretudo*
Raincoat	*Gabardina*
Suit	*Fato*
Shoes	*Sapatos*
Handbag	*Mala de mão*
Belt	*Cinto*
Dress	*Vestido*
Jacket	*Casaco*
Trousers	*Calças*
Blouse	*Blusa*
Skirt	*Saia*
Shirt	*Camisa*
Big	*Grande*
Bigger	*Maior*
Small	*Pequeno*
Smaller	*Mais pequeno*
Wide	*Largo*
Tight	*Apertado*
Long	*Comprido*
Short	*Curto*
Round	*Redondo*
Square	*Quadrado*
Thick	*Espesso*
Thin	*Fino*

Food and Drink

Eat	*Comer*
Drink	*Beber*
Breakfast	*Pequeno almoço*
Lunch	*Almoço*
Dinner	*Jantar*
The bill	*A conta*
The menu	*A ementa*
Tea	*Chá*
Coffee	*Café*
Small black coffee	*Bica*
Glass of white coffee	*Galão*
Cup of white coffee	*Garoto*
Large cup of white coffee	*Meia de Leite*
Small coffee diluted with hot water	*Carioca*
Milk	*Leite*
Juice	*Sumo*
Water	*Água*

221

Wine	*Vinho*
Beer	*Cerveja*
Bread	*Pão*
Butter	*Manteiga*
Toast	*Torrada*
Jam	*Compota*
Biscuits	*Bolachas*
Cakes	*Bolos*
Salt	*Sal*
Pepper	*Pimenta*
Olive oil	*Azeite*
Vinegar	*Vinagre*
Ice	*Gelo*
Eggs	*Ovos*
Boiled	*Quentes*
Fried	*Estrelados*
Poached	*Escalfados*
Scrambled	*Mexidos*
Hard boiled	*Cozidos*
Omelette	*Omoleta*
Fish	*Peixe*
Sole	*Linguado*
Bream	*Pargo*
Plaice	*Solha*
Skate	*Raia*
Mackerel	*Carapau*
Salmon	*Salmão*
Trout	*Truta*
Swordfish	*Espadarte*
Scabbard fish	*Peixe-espada*
Hake	*Pescada*
Sardines	*Sardinhas*
Shell fish	*Mariscos*
Clams	*Amêijoas*
Shrimps	*Camarões*
Prawns	*Gambas*
Crayfish	*Lagostins*
Lobster	*Lavagante*
Squid	*Lulas*
Mussels	*Mexilhões*
Oysters	*Ostras*
Octopus	*Polvo*
Crabs	*Caranguejos*
Scallops	*Vieras*
Meat	*Carne*
Lamb	*Anho*

Steak	*Bife*
Kid	*Cabrito*
Mutton	*Carneiro*
Ham	*Fiambre*
Liver	*Figado*
Suckling pig	*Leitão*
Tongue	*Lingua*
Fillet	*Lombo*
Pork	*Porco*
Kidneys	*Rins*
Bacon	*Bacon*
Veal	*Vitela*
Poultry and game	*Aves e Caca*
Rabbit	*Coelho*
Chicken	*Frango*
Duck	*Pato*
Partridge	*Perdiz*
Turkey	*Peru*
Quail	*Codorniz*
Vegetables	*Legumes*
Potatoes	*Batatas*
Onions	*Cebolas*
Carrots	*Cenouras*
Cabbage	*Couve*
Cauliflower	*Couve-flor*
Peas	*Ervilhas*
Spinach	*Espinafres*
Beans	*Feijão*
Turnips	*Nabos*
Fruit	*Frutas*
Apricots	*Alperces*
Plums	*Ameixas*
Pineapple	*Ananás*
Bananas	*Bananas*
Orange	*Laranja*
Lemon	*Limão*
Apple	*Maça*
Strawberries	*Morangos*
Raspberries	*Framboesas*
Pear	*Pêra*
Peach	*Pêssego*
Grape fruit	*Toranja*
Grapes	*Uvas*
Well done	*Bem passado*
Rare	*Mal passado*
Boiled	*Cozido*

Grilled	*Grelhado*
Fried	*Frito*

Numbers

1	um
2	dois
3	três
4	quatro
5	cinco
6	seis
7	sete
8	oito
9	nove
10	dez
11	onze
12	doze
13	treze
14	catorze
15	quinze
16	dezasseis
17	dezassete
18	dezoito
19	dezanove
20	vinte
21	vinte e um
30	trinta
40	quarenta
50	cinquenta
60	sessenta
70	setenta
80	oitenta
90	noventa
100	cem
101	cento e um
1000	mil
1001	mil e um

Maps and Brochures

Before leaving for Portugal motorists would be well advised to arm themselves with either Michelin or Lascelles maps of the country. Once there the best road maps are obtainable from the Automóvel Clube de Portugal. The tourist offices also have some very useful maps, among them one called simply *Portugal* which gives the location of a number of camp sites, spas, hotels, golf courses and casinos. Even more useful is the fact that it gives the position of a number of garages, indicating which ones are open 24 hours a day and which sell unleaded petrol. The Mapa da Região Centro, issued by the Central Region Tourist Board of the Costa de Prata, gives an artistic view of part of the region and useful maps of Figueira da Foz and Coimbra with some relevant information in five different languages.

The brochures which are obtainable from the tourist offices range from illustrated pamphlets with little or no information to small booklets complete with maps and suggestions for hotels and restaurants.

Markets

Nearly every town and village has a weekly market, designed to meet the needs of the local population. The most famous of these is the Thursday morning market in Barcelos which takes up nearly every square centimetre of the enormous Campo da República. In Lisbon the best-known open-air market can be found behind the church of São Vicente, to the east of the castle, on Tuesday and Saturday mornings. In Oporto the colourful Bolhao Market off the Avenida dos Aliados is open every day of the week and also on Saturday mornings.

Measurements

The metric system is used in Portugal. Conversions are: 1 kilogram (kg) = 2.2lb, 1 litre = $1^3/_4$ pints, 4.5 litres = 1 gallon, 8 kilometres (km) = 5 miles.

Newspapers and Magazines

Several leading British newspapers are flown into Lisbon every day and then distributed to other main towns and popular tourist resorts. American visitors can expect to find copies of the *International Herald Tribune* while the fortnightly *Anglo-Portuguese News* is available mainly in Lisbon and the Algarve. *Newsweek* and the European edition of *Time* appear shortly after publication. Other magazines take a little longer to reach the news stands, but there is often a reasonable selection in Lisbon and in the major holiday resorts. These are sometimes augmented by recent best sellers and other paperback books.

Opening Hours

Opening hours tend to vary to a certain extent so it is impossible to do more than generalise over the country as a whole.

Banks

These are usually open 8.30-11.45am and 1-2.45pm from Monday to Friday. In Lisbon some branches in the city centre do not close for lunch and may even reopen 6-11pm from Monday to Saturday. It is also possible to obtain money at the main airports and frontier posts.

Post Offices

The *correiros* open at 8am or 9am until 12.30pm and again 2.30-6pm on weekdays. The main offices are usually open at lunchtime and on Saturday mornings.

Museums and Monuments

These are generally open 10am-5pm on weekdays and often at weekends. Others open 10am-12.30pm and 2-5pm. Nearly all of them are closed on Mondays and holidays.

Churches

Some churches are not open to visitors during services. Those in the country are frequently kept locked and it is therefore necessary to find the caretaker who will either act as a guide or simply produce the key.

Shops

Shopping centres are open every day from 10am until midnight. Small, individual shops are a law unto themselves. They may open at any time between 9am and 10am, possibly close for lunch 1-3pm, and then remain open until 7pm. On Saturday the majority close at 1pm and do not open again until Monday morning.

Passports and Documents

Visitors holding valid British Passports, British Visitors' Passports or identity cards may spend up to 90 days in Portugal without a visa.

Holidaymakers from the United States and Canada with similar papers may spend up to 60 days in Portugal without a visa.

These limits may be extended by applying before the time expires to:

The Foreigners Registration Service,
22 Rua Conselheiro José Silvestre Ribeiro,
Lisbon 1600.

No medical certificates are required by British, American or Canadian citizens. However anyone travelling from a country with a smallpox or a cholera epidemic must produce an International Certificate of Vaccination regardless of their nationality.

British holidaymakers should apply to the DHSS for E111 forms which entitle them to free emergency medical treatment in Portugal, although these do not cover prescribed medicines. It is also advisable to enquire about some form of additional insurance.

American and Canadian visitors should make enquiries about similar types of insurance before leaving home.

Pets

Some hotels, restaurants and campsites will accept visitors with animals, others definitely will not. It is essential to enquire beforehand to avoid unnecessary trouble and to discover if there are any house rules or regulations. In any event visitors from overseas should be aware of any quarantine regulations when returning home (particularly the UK which are very strict).

Public Holidays

Nearly every town and village in Portugal has at least one annual holiday of its own in honour of its patron saint or to mark some special occasion. These are in addition to the following official National Holidays which are observed by almost everyone:

    1 January — New Year's Day
    Shrove Tuesday
    Good Friday
    25 April — Liberation Day
    1 May — May Day
    Corpus Christi — Late May or Early June
    10 June — Camões Day
    15 August — Assumption
    5 October — Republic Day
    1 November — All Saints Day
    1 December — Independence Day
    8 December — Immaculate Conception
    25 December — Christmas Day

Religion

Portugal is essentially a Catholic country and the services in many village churches are attented by a remarkably high percentage of the local population. Among the outward signs of religious devotion are the number of people who take part in the pilgrimages and the variety of votive offerings to be seen in the chapels. Other Portuguese citizens are not so rigid in their beliefs, particularly in urban areas, and although the subject is not taboo it is best avoided in casual conversation.

Restaurants, Cafés and Bars

Just as Portugal has a wide variety of accommodation for visitors, so it is amply supplied with restaurants, taverns, inns, cafeterias, cafés, bars and traditional open-air barbecues, the most popular of which are often on the beach.

Sophisticated restaurants provide international menus and imported wines and spirits, augmented on occasions by traditional dishes and the best of the local wines, followed, naturally, by port and a selection of liqueurs. Less exclusive establishments may well restrict the number and variety of items on offer and rely more heavily on seasonal produce and time-honoured recipes. Bottled water is always available and the coffee may be black or served with milk.

Generally speaking the breakfast provided is Continental, consisting of bread or rolls, butter, jam and tea or coffee. However in hotels with cafeterias it is possible to order something more substantial, such as boiled eggs, scrambled eggs or sausages. Lunch normally starts at about 12.30pm and runs through until 2pm or 2.30pm, whereas dinner may fluctuate slightly but is usually around 8pm.

There is no problem about taking children into restaurants; the Portuguese have a soft spot for them, particularly if they are well-behaved, and any complaints are liable to come from other visitors. Nor do you have to be very young to ask for a half portion. Many proprietors realise that holidaymakers do not always want the usual large helpings and will reduce them, charging about two thirds of the price.

The local dishes are not heavily spiced, full of garlic or swimming in oil, but oil and vinegar, and sometimes lemon juice, will be provided on request. Vegetables are conspicuous by their absence, but there are some tasty vegetable soups which are often served after the main course. It is a good idea to keep to fish stews on the coasts and meat stews in the inland areas. Pork is usually excellent and so is kid, particularly when it has been grazing on wild herbs. The sweets tend to be very sugary and based on recipes introduced by the Moors. The bread is heavy and delicious especially in outlying areas, and so are honey cakes known as *bolos de mel* and the *fatura* of the Algarve. These are substantial, sugar-coated doughnuts fried in deep fat and bought at little wayside stalls. *Vinho verde* is a delightful wine whereas the *vinho de casa*, or house wine, usually goes well with local dishes.

It is always a good idea to eat in restaurants full of local people and, if in doubt, order the *Prato do Dia*, or dish of the day, which is usually very palatable.

Shopping

The shops vary from large complexes and supermarkets to small private premises and craft workshops, some of which are open to the public. The open-air markets are colourful and functional rather than quaint and are usually more interesting for their atmosphere than for the articles on offer. Local arts and crafts are on sale almost everywhere but ideally it is best to buy them in their region of origin. A few examples are gold and silver filigree in Lisbon and Oporto, rugs in Arraiolos, crystal in Alcobaça, lace in Peniche, porcelain in Vista Alegre and embroidered covers in Castelo Branco.

Sports

Like any other European country Portugal spends a large percentage of its leisure time either watching sports or participating in them. A few, such as bullfighting, are traditional but they have been overtaken and all but overwhelmed by other popular activities, especially soccer. There is no lack of support for the country's three main teams: 'Porto' which naturally is from Oporto, and 'Benfica' and 'Sporting' from Lisbon. Sports facilities for visitors are mainly concentrated in the Algarve and in the major resorts along the Atlantic coast to the west and north of the capital, with additional opportunities for fishing, shooting and walking further inland. For full details holidaymakers should obtain copies of the *Sportugal* brochure from the tourist offices.

Bullfighting

Most of the fighting bulls are raised on the Ribatejo Plain near Santarém with the result that both Santarém and Vila Franca de Xira are major bullfighting centres. However *touradas* are also held in Caldas da Rainha, Cascais, Espinho, Évora, Lagos,

Nazaré, Praia da Rocha, Tomar, Viana do Castelo and Vila Real de Santo António as well as in a few other centres.

Climbing
So far there is not much emphasis on climbing anywhere in Portugal but there are possibilities in the mountains of Trás-os-Montes and the Serra da Estrela as well as in some places along the cliffs.

Fishing
It is necessary to have a licence to fish in the trout streams of northern Portugal and this can be obtained either from the Direcção-Geral dos Serviços Florestais e Aquícolas in Lisbon or from the local water authorities who will also provide details of the open and closed seasons.

No licence is required for either sea fishing or underwater fishing along the coasts.

There are angling clubs in Amarante, Caldas da Rainha, Castelo Branco, Chaves, Elvas, Leiria, Tomar, Vila Real and Viseu.

The best facilities for big game fishing are to be found in the Algarve when the ideal time is between October and mid-January. The Alvor Praia Hotel near Portimão, ☎ 082 24020, has open boats and cabin cruisers.

Cepemar Lda Praça da República, 24-A, 8500 Portimao, ☎ 082 25866 or 33933 operates out of Lagos, Portimão and Vilamoura and provides all the necessary equipment.

Golf

Golf is becoming increasingly popular in Portugal with some excellent courses, a number of them with hotels attached. The majority are sited on the Estoril coast and in the Algarve. Among the best known are:

The Estoril Golf Club
Avenida da República
☎ 01 268 0176
Also a swimming pool, caddies, a beginner's course and equipment for hire.

The Estoril Sol Golf Course
Linhó
☎ 01 923 2461
Squash courts as well as equipment for hire.

The Oporto Golf Club
Espinho
☎ 02 72 20 08
Clubhouse and bar. There are no green fees for guests at the
Praia Golf Hotel.

The Miramar Golf Club
On the road to Espinho
☎ 02 762 20 67
9-hole course with trolleys for hire.

The Quinta do Lago Golf Club
near Almansil
☎ 089 94529
Clubhouse, bar and restaurant.

The Vale do Lobo Golf Club
☎ 089 94444
Clubhouse, bar, restaurant, pro-shop and equipment for hire.

The Palmares Golf Club
near Lagos
☎ 082 62961
Caddies are available and there is equipment for hire.

The Vilamoura Golf Club
Two courses:
Course I ☎ 089 33652 and 32321
Course II ☎ 089 35562 and 32704
Course I has a golf museum; both have bars and restaurants,
pro-shops, practice grounds and equipment for hire.

Hunting and Shooting
Licences are required for shooting in Portugal in addition to
which permits must be obtained to import shotguns. Requests
for licences should be made to the Direcção-Geral dos Serviços
Florestais e Aquícolas in Lisbon. The game concerned are
mainly wild boar, deer, hares, quail and partridges.

Riding
Portugal's Lusitano horses need no introduction and are sometimes used to strengthen the blood-lines of the famous
Lipizzaners of the Spanish Riding School in Vienna. The stallions can be seen at the Portuguese School of Equestrian Art in
Lisbon when the riders wear the splendid traditional costumes
that are also an essential part of the atmospheric *touradas*.

Riding on a less impressive level is available both inland and
in some coastal regions. Pony trekking is arranged from Gerês
into the Peneda-Gerês National Park. Quinta da Marinha near

Cascais, ☎ 01 28 98 81, has extensive stables as well as a small racetrack, with additional facilities for golf and tennis. Horses are also available in Espinho, Ofir, São Martinho do Porto and Viana do Castelo. In the Algarve it is possible to ride all the year round with many stables that can provide anything from Anglo-Arab and Lusitano horses to children's ponies. Among the best known are the:

Horse Riding Centre at Valamoura, ☎ 089 66271,

the stables at Quinta do Lago, ☎ 089 94368,

the riding centre attached to the Paradise Inn at Almansil, ☎ 089 96804

and the Solear stables near Albufeira, ☎ 089 52444,

with others at Tavira and Meia Praia. Inland centres with opportunities for riding or pony trekking include Leiria, Evora, Tomar and Sintra.

Swimming

In addition to the wide, sandy beaches all along the coast most towns of any size, and the majority of the holiday resorts, also have their swimming pools and so do the majority of large modern hotels. This is particularly welcome along the western shores where the sea can be quite cold and occasionally much too rough.

Tennis

There are plenty of tennis courts open to visitors, many of them belonging to the various holiday hotels. In addition, the Cascais Country Club, Quinta da Bicuda, near Bairro da Torre, ☎ 01 28 93 01, has floodlit courts for its members and for long-term visitors. In the Algarve the Roger Taylor Tennis Centre at Vale do Lobo, ☎ 089 94145, has twelve all-weather courts — half of them floodlit — with a shop, equipment for hire and changing facilities. The same amenities are available at the David Lloyd Tennis and Squash Centre at the Carvoeiro Clube in Carvoeiro near Portimão, ☎ 082 57847, in addition to a swimming pool and a restaurant. On a less impressive scale the Hotel Montechoro Tennis Centre near Albufeira, ☎ 089 52653, has ten all-weather courts, the Vilamoura Tennis Centre has eight and the Luz Bay Club has three. Holidaymakers at Praia de Miramar, south of Oporto, will find six courts at the Tennis Club de Gandra with a clubhouse that provides all the various facilities.

Scuba Diving

There is so far very little organised snorkeling and scuba diving in Portugal. However it is very popular in the Algarve, especially in the Armação de Pêra, Luz Bay and Sagres areas. Some information is available from the Nautical Centre in the Alvor Complex and at Aldeia das Açoteias. Underwater swimming is also very popular round the Berlenga Islands off-shore from Peniche, at Aveiro, Cascais, Estoril and Póvoa de Varzim.

Walking

There are several places in Portugal where walking is extremely pleasant, among them the Parque Natural de Montezinho in the far northeast corner, the Parque Nacional da Peneda-Gerês, also in the north and partly in the Costa Verde, and the Serra da Estrêla, inland from Coimbra. Further south, the Parque Natural das Serras de Aire e Candeeiros, the Serra de Sintra west of Lisbon, and the Serra da Arrábida in the vicinity of Setúbal are all good areas to explore on foot and so is the Serra de Monchique, due north of Portimão in the Algarve. The only drawback is that there are no marked paths to speak of and hardly any maps that provide sufficient details. Those that do exist tend to be sketchy and out of date and should be treated with a certain amount of suspicion. One exception is the Buçaco Forest, which is very small by comparison, where the paths are clearly marked and maps are available.

Waterskiing and Windsurfing

There are facilities for waterskiing in Cascais, Estoril, Ofir and Praia de Guincho, the last of which is particularly good for windsurfing. Holidaymakers in the Algarve can hire windsurfing boards at more than ten different places along the coast, among them several hotels in addition to the Luz Bay Club, Meia Praia Beach, Quarteira Beach, Vale do Lobo Beach and the Nautical Centre in the Alvor Complex. Waterskiing facilities exist at the Luz Bay Club, ☎ 62640, Torralta, Vilamoura, ☎ 089 32321 and Vale de Lobo ☎ 089 94145, all of which, apart from Torralta, can also provide tuition if necessary.

Winter Sports

At the moment there are no winter sports centres, sophisticated or otherwise, in Portugal. However skiing is possible in the area round Penhas da Saúde in the Serra da Estrêla which has plans to develop its potential.

Yachting and Boating

There are at least twenty different places on the west coast of Portugal which have either sailing schools or boats for hire or charter, but only three so far that combine both services: Cascais, Estoril and Torreira. The south coast is slightly better placed — at Lagos, Praia da Rocha, Pedras d'El Rei, Vilamoura and Vila Real de Santo António. Enquiries should be made in each case at the pleasure boat harbour.

Telephone and Postal Services

The Portuguese telephone system is somewhat archaic at the moment. The best place to make a call is from a telephone booth in a post office where you pay at the counter afterwards. It is just as simple to telephone from an hotel but you must expect to add a large connection charge. There are plenty of telephone boxes but they tend to be out of order while the payphones in the *telefonaria* require constant feeding with 25$00 coins.

Nor does Portugal have any cheap rates for either local or long distance calls.

For Directory Enquiries ☎ 12 in Portugal. ☎ 155 from Britain.

When making calls to Britain dial 00 44 followed by the usual number, but drop the initial 0. The code for Canada and the United States is 0971.

When telephoning Portugal from Britain dial 010 351 followed by the number while Americans should prefix the number with 011 351.

Postage rates are now uniform throughout the EEC, but are higher to the United States and Canada. Stamps and local letter-cards are sold over the counter but there are no air letter cards available. People who want to use the *poste restante* services should mark their letters *Lista do Correios*, to be collected by the addressee who must also produce a passport and pay a small fee.

Tipping

Most hotels and restaurants add a service charge to the bill, but a small extra amount in recognition of attentive service, a pleasant atmosphere, or for any other reason is much appreciated. Other people who are in direct contact with the public such as taxi drivers, porters and cinema usherettes should also receive a tip. For example, 10 per cent of a taxi fare and 10$00 in the cinema.

Toilet Facilities

Apart from the facilities provided at train and bus stations there are very few public toilets. However, hotels and restaurants are quite used to requests from people who are not customers and so are garages which have the necessary amenities.

Tourist Boards

Britain
Portuguese National Tourist Office
22/25A Sackville Street
London W1X 1DE
☎ 071 4941441

USA
Portuguese National Tourist Office
590 Fifth Avenue
New York
NY 10036
☎ 212 354 4403

Canada
Portuguese National Tourist Office
500 Sherbrooke West
Suite 930
Montreal
 Quebec H3A 3C6
☎ 514 843 4623

Portuguese National Tourist Office
4120 Yonge Corporate Centre
Suite 414
Willowdale
Toronto
Ontario M2P 2B8
☎ 416 250 7575

For information or assistance not provided by Government
Tourist Offices application should be made to the Portuguese
Embassy, or consulate.

Travel to Portugal

There are many different ways of travelling to Portugal: by air,
rail, coach and car but only indirectly by ferry.

Air
TAP, the Portuguese National Airline, operates a number of
scheduled services to and from Britain, the United States and
Canada, namely:
In Britain: London (Heathrow) to Lisbon, Manchester to Lisbon,
Heathrow to Oporto and Heathrow to Faro.
In the USA: New York to Lisbon, Boston to Lisbon and Los
Angeles to Lisbon
In Canada: Toronto via Montreal to Lisbon.

British Airways services fly Heathrow to Lisbon, Gatwick to Lisbon, Heathrow to Oporto and Gatwick to Faro.

TWA flights operate between Lisbon and San Francisco.

Overseas offices of TAP are located:

Britain
19 Regent Street
London SW1 YLR
☎ 071 828 0262

Fountain House
Fountain Street
Manchester
☎ 061 499 1161

USA
521 Fifth Avenue
New York
NY 10017
☎ 212 944 2100

Canada
60 Bloor Street West
Suite 206
Toronto
Ontario M4W 3B8
☎416 364 7042

1010 Sherbrooke Street West
Montreal
Quebec H3A 2RT
☎ 514 849 6163

Tour operators offer a series of package holiday deals in Portugal, details of which can be obtained from travel agencies.

Caravala, a subsidiary of TAP, arranges bookings for *pousadas* and members of the Turismo de Habitação. Details are obtainable from their London office, ☎ 071 630 9223, and the Manchester Office, ☎ 061 437 7511.

Train
There is a daily train service from Victoria Station in London to Lisbon via Paris, where it is necessary to change trains. Anyone bound for Oporto must change again at Pampilhosa.

Reservations should be made with
British Rail,
Continental Section,
Victoria Station,
London SW1,
☎ 071 834 2345

who will also provide information. It is worthwhile enquiring about any possible concessions that may be available at certain times of the year and for various categories of passengers such as young people and senior citizens.

Coach

There are regular coach services to Portugal from the Victoria Coach Station in London, currently two a week to Lisbon, one to Coimbra, and two to the Algarve. Tickets can be obtained from the National Express agents or paid for by credit card by telephoning Eurolines, ☎ 071 730 0202. The only disadvantage is that passengers have to change in Paris.

Ferry

Currently there are no direct ferry services to Portugal — the nearest is the twice-weekly schedule operated by Brittany Ferries between Plymouth and Santander, in Northern Spain. However, until the Channel Tunnel is completed, motorists travelling with their own cars must opt for one of the ferry routes or for the hovercraft crossings to France. The shortest crossing is from Dover or Folkestone to Calais or Boulogne. It takes rather longer from Portsmouth and Poole to Caen, Cherbourg or St Marlo, in addition to which there is a night ferry from Plymouth to Roscoff and another from Portsmouth to the Normandy coast. Details of these and other sailings are available from travel agents but it is also possible to make reservations for the Plymouth-Santander run by telephoning 0705 827701 or 0752 221321.

Motorail

Motorists who are short of time, or who have no inclination to drive to Portugal through France and Spain, should consider using the Motorail service from Paris to Lisbon.

Details are available from:
French Railways,
179 Piccadilly,
London W1,
☎ 071 409 3518

French National Railroads,
Rockefeller Centre,
601 Fifth Avenue,
New York,
NY 10020.

Enquiries can also be made about motorail facilities at Aveiro, Coimbra, Figueira da Foz and Oporto.

Frontier Posts

Operational hours at the various frontier posts between Portugal and Spain vary somewhat. The border crossings at Tuy / Valença do Minho, Fuentes de Onõro / Vilar Formosa and Badajoz / Elvas are manned 24 hours a day, others open at 7am and close at 9pm in winter or 11pm in summer while the remainder are strictly seasonal.

Travel in Portugal

There are just as many ways of travelling in and around Portugal as there are methods of getting there. Some are simple and comfortable, others require a little forethought and a few are unpredictable and confusing but nevertheless are frequently worth the effort involved. Flights are straightforward and uncomplicated, rail journeys range from fast, luxury trains to antiquated steam trains, coaches are used between the major centres and for sightseeing tours, while country buses can be infrequent and have a healthy disregard for schedules. Boat trips are available on some rivers and in the Algarve, horsedrawn vehicles ply for hire in Sintra and Cascais while every town and large village has taxis of its own. Cars can be hired in the main cities and tourist resorts but it is necessary to search for mopeds and bicycles except in the Algarve.

Air

Visitors rarely find it necessary to take internal flights in Portugal, but should the occasion arise there are regular services several times a day between Lisbon and Oporto and Lisbon and Faro. Less frequent flights are available to and from Bragança, Chaves, Covilhã, Portimão, Vila Real and Viseu.

Train

The *rápido* trains are fast and comfortable with restaurant and refreshment facilities. They make very few stops between the main towns along their routes and are obviously priced accordingly. The *directo* stops somewhat more frequently, while the *tranvia* covers a shorter distance and keeps stopping all the time. Tours using little steam trains are arranged from Oporto and Livração.

It is very difficult to get hold of train timetables of any description, although the Thomas Cook Continental Timetable does include the main services in Portugal and is available in both Britain and the United States. Tickets must be bought before starting a journey; it is forbidden to try to buy them on the train and any attempt to do so might result in a fine.

Coach

A number of long distance coach services operate in Portugal with regular schedules between Oporto, Lisbon and the Algarve. The official Rodoviãria Nacional (RN) *expressos* leave from local coach stations — where tickets are available — and stop at infrequent intervals along the route. In this case some timetables are available.

Special sightseeing tours range from half a day to the best part of a week and are available in most of the main cities and major resorts. On the longer runs the coaches have air conditioning, toilet facilities, bars and even individual background music with multi-lingual hostesses who supply snacks and refreshments en route. Several of the companies involved operate with the approval of the Rodoviãria Nacional who can be contacted at their regional offices for full details:

Lisbon: 33 Avenida Fontes Pereira de Melo. ☎ 01 56 34 51
Oporto: 629 Rua Sá da Bandeira. ☎ 02 38 07 12
Faro: Avenida da República. ☎ 089 23025
Coimbra: 102 Rua da Sofia. ☎ 039 22944
Albufeira: 21 Avenida 25 de Abril. ☎ 089 55426
Portimão: 9 Rua Júdice Bicker. ☎ 082 25413
Evora: 133 Rua da República. ☎ 066 24254
Leiria: 3 Rua Teles Sampaio Rio. ☎ 044 22413

In Lisbon a variety of tours start from the Parque Eduardo VII, often at 8.30am, and offer an all-in price at selected hotels for both double and single rooms. It is possible to choose one that covers the whole country in ten days, choose either the north or south of Portugal taking about a week, or spend less time on the Portwine Route, visiting forests or beaches or concentrating on history. Details are obtainable from hotel reception desks. Children under 4 are carried free but their meals are extra, while those between 4 and 8 years of age pay 50 per cent of the adult price. Passengers who cancel 24 hours before departure are charged 10 per cent, but after that there is no refund at all.

Sightseeing tours from Oporto, Póvoa de Varzim, Ofir and Viana do Castelo include a Grand Tour of Minho lasting four days, stopping at *pousadas* and including the Peneda-Gerês National Park. At the other end of the time scale there is a half-day visit to the market at Barcelos or an evening of folkdancing, traditional dishes and local wines. Faro, Quarteria, Vilamoura, Albufeira and Armação de Pera have two-day tours to other regions and full days spent in the Algarve as well as barbecue evenings, shopping sprees in Portimão and a visit to the Sunday morning market in Estoi.

By Bus

There are services run by the Rodoviãria Nacional as well as private companies, tickets are bought at the bus stations, which seldom have anything remotely resembling schedules, and the number of changes involved are in direct relation to the length of the journey. In country areas the tickets are bought on the bus and the only way to find out where or when to catch them is to ask anyone who happens to be around. Municipal services in cities like Lisbon and Oporto are well organised and reliable, books of tickets are available in the capital for both the metro and the buses and timetables are frequently posted up at stops along the route.

Hire Cars

Hire car companies, such as Avis, Hertz, Europcar and Interrent have offices in many of the larger towns and cities such as Lisbon, Oporto, Ofir, Braga, Viana do Castelo, Faro, Vilamoura, Praia da Rocha, Lagos, and Vila Real de Santo António. Prospective drivers must have held a full driving licence for not less than one year and be at least 23 years old. Arrangements can often be made through hotel reception desks.

Taxis

Every city, town, coastal resort and large village has its own taxis. At the moment they are black with greenish-turquoise roofs, but it is rumoured that they are all to be resprayed yellow after 1992 on instructions from the EEC. Most of them have meters and charge extra for unsocial hours, quantities of luggage, waiting time and journeys outside the municipal boundaries. The price should always be agreed beforehand for longish trips and sightseeing tours, but as the charges are very reasonable at the moment they are well patronised by local people as well as visitors. Taxis can be hailed in the street, picked up at a taxi rank or ordered by telephone.

Boats

Boat trips are available in both Lisbon and Oporto as well as in several coastal resorts, especially in the Algarve. Among the most enjoyable is a mini-cruise up the Rio Douro from the Ribeir quay in Oporto to Régua with breakfast on board, lunch ashore at the Alpendurada Restaurant, sited in an ancient convent, returning the same evening or the following day. Details can be obtained from

Endouro, Praça da Ribeira, 20-D, ☎ 02 32 42 36.

In the Algarve there are mini-cruises of various durations from the marina at Vilamoura. These include morning and afternoon trips to Ponta da Galé, a day out to Benagil with a beach barbecue, and another to Pontimão with lunch ashore and time for shopping. They leave at 9.30am, getting back at 5pm, and reservations can be made at hotel reception desks or at the marina. Excursions leave the main dock at Portimão at 10am, returning at 4.30pm after a barbecue lunch on a deserted beach, Sagres organises day trips from Baleeira Beach, arranged through the Hotel Baleeira, the Pedras d'el Rei holiday resort near Tavira holds Saturday outings, while Vila Real de Santo António concentrates on cruises up the Guadiana River. The owners of fishing boats at Lagos and Armação de Pera are available to take holidaymakers out to see the nearby grottoes, while Albufeira has a variety of sea trips available in both fishing boats and launches.

For visiting yachtsmen there are moorings and harbour facilities in the Algarve at Faro, Lagos, Olhão, Portimão, Sagres, Vilamoura and Vila Real de Santo António. The calling channel is 16, transferring to 20 and 62, the Admiralty Chart 1972 NP 67, the *West Coast of Spain and Portugal Pilot* and the *Roteiro da Costa Algarvia* are all recommended. Further information can be obtained from

Marina Vilamoura, 8125 Quarteira. ☎ 089 32023.

By Car

Most people would agree that the best way of touring in Portugal is by car. Work is progressing on the new *auto-estrada*, sections of which are already in operation, and some of the main roads are excellent. Secondary roads vary from good to passable but the byways are frequently in need of attention. Cobbled stretches look good from a distance but can be decidedly bumpy and care should always be taken because of the number of potholes, livestock, slow farm carts, fast drivers and pedestrians. Journeys often take longer than expected in hilly country because of the profusion of hairpin bends, whereas there is very little to delay motorists on their way through Planicies.

Both British and International Driving Licences are valid in Portugal but anyone hiring a car must have held a full licence for at least a year.

Motorists may take their cars into Portugal for up to 6 months provided they have the registration documents and a green insurance card which is obtainable from the insurance company at home.

Membership cards from one of the accepted motoring organisations — such as the AA, the RAC or the AAA — entitle the holders to call for assistance from the Automóval Clube de Portugal. In the northern part of the country the ACP operates breakdown services from Oporto, ☎ 02 31 67 32 and in the south from Lisbon, ☎ 01 77 54 75, 77 54 02 or 77 54 91. The Head Office is at 24 Rua Rosa Araújo, Lisbon, ☎ 01 56 39 31.

The rules of the road are the same as those in other Continental countries: drive on the right, overtake on the left, and give way to cars approaching from the right who have priority unless there are signs to the contrary. In Portugal to turn infront of a policeman controlling traffic at an intersection. Seat belts are obligatory and drivers must be over 18 years of age. Speed limits for cars are 60kph (37mph) in built-up areas, 90kph (55mph) in rural areas and 120kph (75mph) on motorways. Traffic moves in an anti-clockwise direction at roundabouts, with traffic from the right having priority unless otherwise stated. The traffic signs mean exactly the same as they do elsewhere on the Continent but it is as well to remember one or two words that might crop up.

Atenção	Caution
Perigo	Danger
Gelo	Ice on the road
Obras	Road works
Estrada Interrompida	Road Closed
Estrada em mau Estado	Road in bad condition
Paragem Obrigatória	Compulsory Stop
Pronto Socorro	First Aid Station

Motorists are also obliged to carry a spare set of light bulbs, a red triangle to warn oncoming traffic in the case of an accident or a breakdown and a small first aid kit. A small fire extinguisher is obligatory. It is always as well to consult one of the motoring organisations before leaving home about such items as a kit to deflect headlight beams if taking a vehicle which usually drives on the left.

There are plenty of fuel stations on all the main routes but always set off on a tour of the outlying areas with a reasonably full tank. Apart from some familiar types of petrol, such as Mobil, the GALP fuel stations, owned by the government, have gasoline pumps which may be open 24 hours a day, and an increasingly large number provide unleaded fuel (*Gasolina sem Chumbo* or *Essence sans Plomb*). Several of these have small shops attached selling things like oil, sweets and soft drinks but few of them carry any spares, which means finding a repair garage in the vicinity.

Portuguese drivers are not among the best in the world. Quite a few have little compunction about drinking and driving and are not above ignoring the law if they think they can get away with it.

Useful Addresses

British Embassy
35-37 Rua São Domingos à Lapa
Lisbon
☎ 01 66 11 91

British Consulate
3072 Avenida da Boa Vista
Oporto
☎ 02 68 47 89

British Consulate
21 Rua de Santa Isabel
Portimão
☎ 082 23071

British Consulate
4 Rua General Humberto Delgardo
Vila Real de Santo António
☎ 081 43729

British Consulate
Quinta de Santa Maria
Estrada de Tavereve 3080
Figueira da Foz
☎ 033 22235

United States Embassy
Avenida das Forças Armadas
Lisbon
☎ 01 726 6600 or 01 726 8880

United States Consulate
826-3^0 Rua do Júlio Dinis
Oporto
☎ 02 63094

Canadian Embassy
2 Rua de Rosa Araújo
6th Floor
Lisbon
☎ 01 56 25 47 or 01 56 38 21

Automóval Clube de Portugal
24 Rua Rosa Araújo
Lisbon
☎ 01 56 39 31

Clube Naval de Lisboa
Pav Náutico
Doca de Belém
Lisboa
☎ 01 63 00 61
Contact for details of sailing events.

Direcção-Geral das Florestas
26-28 Avenida João Crisóstomo
Lisboa
☎ 01 53 61 32
Contact for licences for shooting or to fish for trout in the rivers.

The following can provide information about pony trekking and camping holidays in the Peneda-Gerês National Park:

CRT Verde Minho
Rua Justino Cruz
Edificio Atlântico 84/90 6^0
4700 Braga
☎ 053 76924

Turismo Juvenil
Rua Guedes de Azevedo 34/36 Loja C
4000 Oporto
☎ 02 38 27 63

Water

Tap water is quite safe to drink in Portugal except occasionally in the Algarve at the height of the season when supplies might be running a little short. However many spas produce excellent bottled water which is on sale everywhere.

Distances between the main towns and cities of Portugal

	Aveiro	Beja	Braga	Bragança	Caia	Castelo Branco	Coimbra	Évora	Faro	Fátima	Galegos	Guarda	Leiria	Lisbon	Portalegre	Oporto	Quintanilha	Santarém	Segura	Setúbal	Valença do Minho	Viana do Castelo	Vila Real	Vila Real de Santo António	Vila Verde de Ficalho	Vilar Formoso
Beja	380																									
Braga	120	500																								
Bragança	320	560	230																							
Caia	345	180	470	450																						
Castelo Branco	216	254	330	310	150																					
Coimbra	64	333	170	314	300	160																				
Évora	306	78	425	484	100	175	255																			
Faro	499	152	620	697	330	390	455	215																		
Fátima	136	256	261	402	206	156	90	178	360																	
Galegos	315	207	421	400	93	91	251	130	340	160																
Guarda	180	360	260	203	255	106	169	282	495	259	199															
Leiria	121	265	238	380	231	170	67	190	390	23	183	236														
Lisbon	242	193	361	510	237	250	196	150	300	136	253	365	128													
Portalegre	310	181	410	390	68	80	240	104	317	150	24	188	170	228												
Oporto	68	450	53	255	415	277	118	370	575	208	366	220	185	314	360											
Quintanilha	355	600	260	30	487	339	343	510	727	433	430	233	539	419	284											
Santarém	185	195	310	450	204	169	138	300	61	281	70	79	145	254	479	254										
Segura	285	315	388	370	207	59	218	234	450	215	150	165	226	304	136	335	396	225								
Setúbal	290	139	417	560	270	246	108	250	250	240	218	372	180	50	192	362	590	121	324							
Valença do Minho	194	580	91	323	538	407	250	502	702	338	497	348	314	443	484	123	350	384	467	492						
Viana do Castelo	140	524	49	280	480	355	194	448	648	283	444	295	261	390	434	71	310	331	409	440	53					
Vila Real	185	512	107	138	413	264	207	440	661	300	355	160	271	403	344	117	168	340	320	450	198	155				
Vila Real de Santo António	506	125	625	685	306	378	451	203	52	381	330	485	387	317	306	580	714	436	318	267	707	650	640			
Vila Verde de Ficalho	440	65	563	600	237	292	394	140	202	318	245	399	326	254	220	512	680	350	256	203	640	587	580	153		
Vilar Formoso	230	410	207	307	156	216	333	547	304	247	49	285	414	236	266	228	323	214	421	397	344	207	533	447		
Viseu	95	450	187	238	340	190	96	370	580	187	283	85	164	293	270	131	250	343	263	210	111			570	483	135

Index

MPC

A Note to the Reader

Thank you for buying this book, we hope it has helped you to enjoy your stay in Holland. We have worked hard to produce a guidebook which is as accurate and useful as possible. With this in mind, any comments, suggestions or useful information you may have would be appreciated. Those who send in the most helpful letters will be credited in future editions.

Please send your letters to:

The Editor
Moorland Publishing Co Ltd
Moor Farm Road West
Ashbourne
Derbyshire
DE6 1HD

MPC The Travel Specialists